EDINBURGH'S SUFFRAGETTES
The Fight for Votes for Women

NORMAN WATSON

2025

First published in 2025

ISBN 978-1-9999252-3-9

Percy Johnstone Publishing, 2025

CONTENTS

Arabella Scott - the Edinburgh teacher endured forcible feeding in prison for longer than any other British suffragette.

PREFACE

*T*he Edinburgh of the late 19th and early 20th centuries is the focus of this work. The city was Scotland's capital, second in size to Glasgow, with traditional trades such as printing, brewing and distilling boosted by a burgeoning service industry employing thousands of women. The Old and New Towns sat cheek by jowl, but stimulated by the railways, the city's boundaries had broken free from post-medieval shackles. Princes Street and George Street were its commercial heart, with newly affluent merchants and managers its incoming middle classes.

From the start to the end of this period of innovation and social upheaval, Edinburgh's population rose by 150,000 to 350,000 and it had become one of Britain's most prosperous towns.

The focus here on the Scottish capital offers the third work in a series charting the fight for women's parliamentary votes – the story of Edinburgh's Suffragettes.

LEFT: The fight for women's votes led to remarkable scenes in Edinburgh. (Courtesy of London Museum)

ACKNOWLEDGEMENTS

I am grateful to many people for help with the preparation of this work, among them family, friends and colleagues who have supported my writing activities over many years.

The National Records of Scotland, the British Library and the National Archives at Kew were extremely helpful and made research such a pleasure.

Nikki Braunton and Yiqing An of London Museum, which boasts an exceptional collection of suffrage ephemera and memorabilia, expertly answered my calls for help. Dr Gillian Murphy at the Women's Library, London School of Economics, Carol Campbell at the National Library of Scotland, Danielle Howarth of the University of Edinburgh and Jessica Barrie of Aberdeen City Archives, were all generous with their time and expertise.

Directors and staff at DC Thomson & Co were supportive, especially the late director Murray Thomson and his late sister, Julie Logan Thomson. I am also grateful to Jim Howie for permission to use one of his pictures and to my late friend Dr Frances Wheelhouse.

Journalist and writer Shirley Blair took great care and time reading the manuscript and correcting my many faults. Sara Cunningham's creative skills ensured *Edinburgh's Suffragettes* safely reached the publishing slipway. It could not have set sail without her artistic know-how. Sara and Shirley's helpful suggestions as the text and layout neared completion were invaluable, and I am lucky to count them friends as well as professional colleagues.

The unattributed images in this work are from the author's collection and have been exhibited previously at the Scottish Parliament and Museum of Edinburgh, the Women's Library, London and The McManus Galleries in Dundee. Sources of other photographs are noted in the text.

Numerous published works were consulted for this history. If I have omitted to mention the contribution of any author or publisher, I hope this note of gratitude will be acceptable.

4

One of the earliest images of a women's suffrage demonstration – a march to the House of Commons in 1906. (Courtesy of London Museum)

INTRODUCTION

The first published works in this series, *Dundee's Suffragettes* (2018) and *Glasgow's Suffragettes* (2023), showed that it is no longer necessary to accept that there was no women's suffrage movement in Scotland, to suppose that its story has vanished into obscurity, or to believe that the votes-for-women campaign was entirely London-centric.

But while Scotland's role and relevancy is today better understood, there has never been a comprehensive telling of the women's suffrage story that emerged from her great capital. Over five dramatic decades Edinburgh's sisters fought tooth and nail for the parliamentary vote, but their years of protests, if mentioned at all, are usually dismissed in a meagre quota of words.

Edinburgh's Suffragettes attempts to tell their story for the first time; from the creation of Scotland's first women's suffrage society in the capital in 1867, to the last Edinburgh suffragette jailing in 1914, when the city was central to the campaign of civil disobedience rocking Edwardian Britain as the 20th century began. Edinburgh women threw themselves into the struggle; marching and protesting with banners and flags flying, delivering speeches to vast crowds, and rushing to volunteer for the window-smashing, fighting with police and burnings and bombings that left the country shocked and bewildered.

A dozen were jailed and to the city's shame it was the scene of the first forcible feeding of a suffragette prisoner in Scotland. As the clamour for votes intensified, Edinburgh hosted nine major suffrage organisations, staged both of Scotland's national processions and, as this work reveals, formed its own 'Votes for Women Club' whose members wanted direct action and disruption.

This extraordinary outpouring of militancy was a defining period in Edinburgh's past, but it should be viewed also as the culmination of a much longer process towards gender equality. The headlines it brought overshadowed Edinburgh's role as the beating heart of the Victorian campaign. Much of the crucial first phase of the British women's suffrage movement took root in the city, and this is documented fully for the first time in the early chapters.

The Edinburgh National Society for Women's Suffrage, the second in Britain and first in Scotland, was founded in 1867 and grew to a membership of 1000 with a mission to challenge women's exclusion from government. It equalled in stature and influence the first London Society and orchestrated an effective, independent campaign to establish a network of branches and committees in Scotland. It interrogated politicians, bombarded the Press with letters and challenged in the courts women's exclusion from the polling booth. It staged the greatest gathering of suffrage leaders ever seen outside London, arranged Scotland's biggest demonstrations, marches and pageants, sent hundreds of Scottish petitions to Parliament and persuaded Edinburgh Town Council to become the first public body in Britain to support women's votes. As the Victorian campaign gathered pace, and new generations of reformers came along, no one was left in doubt as to Edinburgh's importance to the national movement.

Come the 20th century, however, it seemed that women were no further forward. Votes appeared as distant as ever. And by then the media and the public had lost interest in the slow-paced meetings and repetitive petitions to Parliament of the Victorian era. Newspapers in the new century rarely reported suffrage gatherings and often refused to publish articles and letters written by ageing franchise supporters trotting out familiar old arguments. They were tired of endless parliamentary debates, or Women's Suffrage Bills talked out at the behest of government Whips.

Instead, militancy offered women daring, stylish, highly-visible and exciting opportunities to fight with passion and in public for political rights. It gave many of them a new a sense of purpose, a chance to form lifelong friendships and to lead a fuller life without a thought of self-advancement. But as *Edinburgh's*

Suffragettes shows, for many it also proved a defining struggle that often led to ridicule, ostracism, hardship, sacrifice and pain.

Defiance of the law was also deemed necessary because women's lives had by then been transformed. They had joined school boards in 1870; voted in municipal elections from 1882; were admitted to Scottish universities in 1892; and by 1894 women could be elected to town councils. More had gone out to work, not only in mills and factories, but as typists, clerks and bookkeepers. There was a growing demand for nurses and for female staff in department stores and offices. Graduate women had become teachers and accountants, lawyers and doctors. And as women had grown independent in outlook and had made strides into hitherto closed professions, so their financial and social situation had improved. By the 1890s there was said to be an Edinburgh legal firm called 'McLaren & Daughter'. But the new economic independence that employment provided was not matched by political power. This was the glaring omission from the advance into public life. Women had gained a voice, but remained voteless. It was the only battle they were losing.

Veteran Edinburgh suffragist Jessie Methven saw the need for a change in tactics: "We had tried every conventional way of winning our cause. We were no nearer getting what we had started out to get, and I saw that militancy was the only way." [1].

Opponents, however, believed the demand for women's rights threatened to collapse the boundaries of social and domestic life. Scotland's newspapers were also sceptical of, and often hostile to, women's emancipation. Above all, suffragists faced a government content to brush aside demands for the vote. Time after time, women's suffrage legislation was voted down or talked out amid jeers and mockery on the floor of the House. While female suffrage seemed to loom more conspicuously above the political horizon, there were just as many voices claiming that the majority of women had no desire to participate in parliamentary elections and in any case were unsuited to do so.

Adding to the complexities, the escalating militancy of the new century widened the ideological gap to the brave suffragists who had patiently and

Edwardian Edinburgh - Princes Street in 1908.

hopefully worked on the uphill fight for 30 years. Where, hitherto, workers for the cause had met with good-natured tolerance, soon they would face frightening hostility and ever-harsher punishment – not least in Edinburgh where several suffragists sustained violent attacks.

In this comprehensive study of the city's campaign, the energy and enthusiasm of this female rebellion is explored. The special women that shaped the struggle are brought to life as they fought with passion and persistence against the fear, ridicule and ignorance that had kept Victorian women in their place – and for the real change that could be effected only by the parliamentary vote.

In telling their story, *Edinburgh's Suffragettes* shows unequivocally that the city filled a role in suffrage activism more visible and more important than hitherto recorded.

Norman Watson,
March 2025.

References
1. Miss J. C. Methven, 'Women's Suffrage in the Past, A Record of Betrayal' in The Suffragette, 17 January 1913.

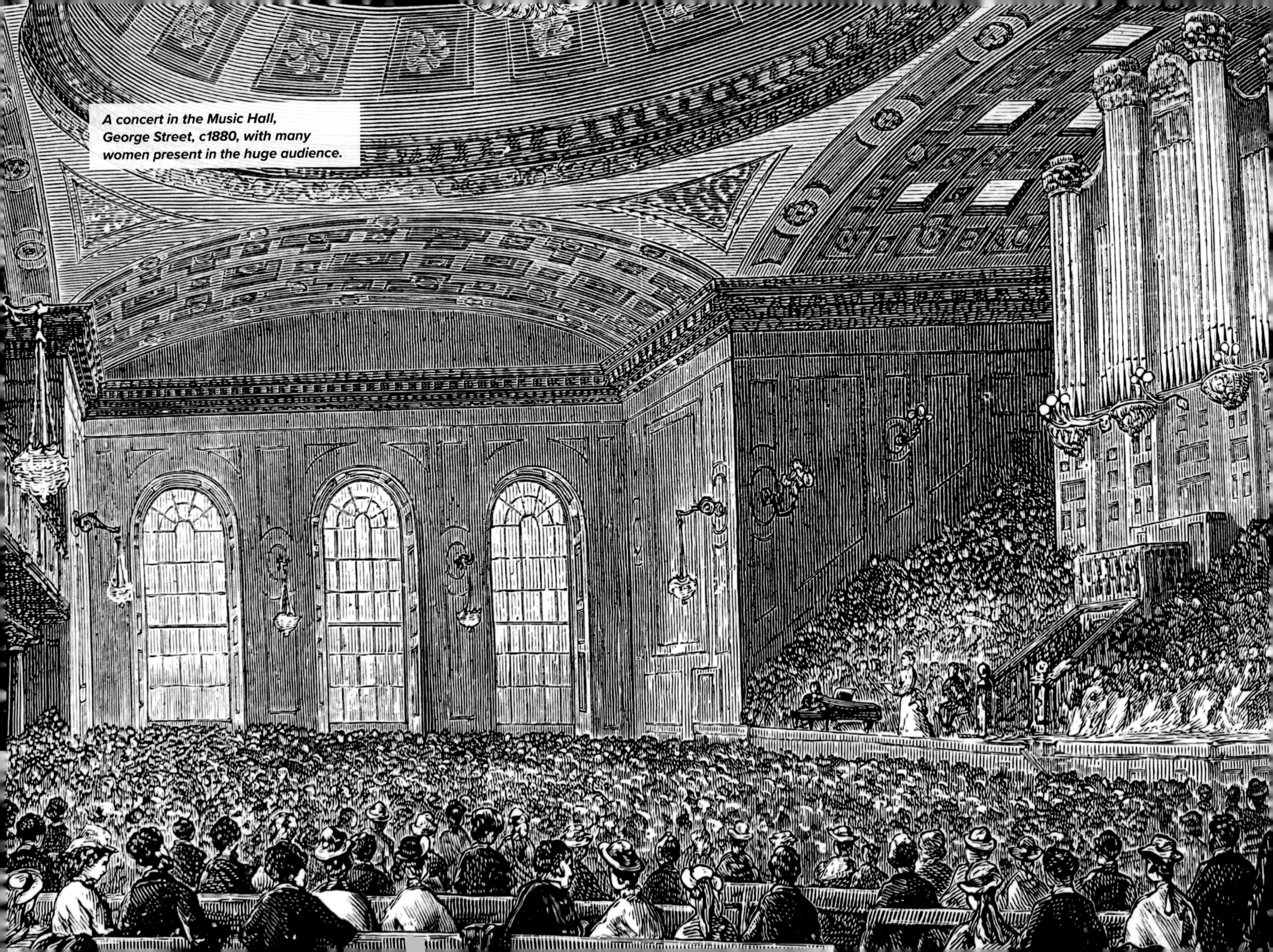

A concert in the Music Hall, George Street, c1880, with many women present in the huge audience.

ONE:
RISE UP, WOMEN! 1867-1879

"All we ask is that you get out of our way, that you raise those barriers which impede our progress and the nation's welfare and unseal the fountains of knowledge that all may drink who thirst. Let not our daughters lower their flag till they possess that what is justly and truly their right…"

Anonymous suffragist in *The Edinburgh Daily Review*, 21 February 1867.

The opening of the 20th century overlapped with a dramatic and at times violent push for women's votes, resulting in those now-familiar images of suffragettes parading and protesting, delivering speeches to vast crowds, chaining themselves to railings, breaking windows, fighting with police and languishing in jail after rushed convictions by all-male judiciary and juries.

Edinburgh figured prominently at this time as its militants became increasingly combative with breathtaking deeds which caused widespread outrage and alarm. The city's suffragettes were harangued, condemned, attacked, arrested and imprisoned. It was a decade of escalating action in which Edinburgh Prison was the first in Scotland to forcibly feed a woman, and in which the death of an Edinburgh militant was attributed to a brutal beating she had endured at a protest meeting for votes.

Yet women's limited role in society and the inequalities they faced in everyday life had been debated in the Scottish capital throughout the Victorian era. It took time for patience and optimism to give way to anger and confrontation. As this work will show, the so-called 'shrieking sisterhood' – the time of the Pankhursts and the suffragette window-smashers – formed only one phase of the struggle, and the city's remarkable story.

For much of the 1800s politics was deemed unsuitable for women. Participation in the parliamentary process was seen as improper, unseemly and alien to what was perceived as the "woman's sphere." As four-times Prime Minister William Gladstone put it, to foist a political role on females would "trespass on their delicacy, their purity, their refinement…" And if any woman had the temerity to assert herself, she was derided as 'masculine'. [1]

Despite overwhelming barriers, women of the mid-1800s steadily became involved in education, housing and health, as well as with campaigns dealing with contagious diseases, temperance and slavery. Such causes were viewed by them as outlets for unused talents and an opportunity to deploy skills hitherto unseen. [2]

John and Jane Wigham of Edinburgh were important figures in the British anti-slavery movement. They were founders of the Edinburgh Emancipation Society in 1833 (known from the 1840s as the Edinburgh Ladies' Emancipation Society). Their daughter, Eliza Wigham, corresponded with many of the leading anti-slavery activists and, in 1846, organised a petition against slavery with the names of 10,337 "women of Edinburgh." Twenty years later, Eliza Wigham became the founding secretary of the Edinburgh National Society for Women's Suffrage (ENSWS), a position she held for 20 years. Primarily an

Duncan McLaren.

abolitionist group, the Edinburgh Ladies' Emancipation Society mostly avoided politics and is remembered today for its graffiti on Salisbury Crags – 'Send Back The Money' – a giant message gouged out of the turf and aimed at the Free Church of Scotland, which had accepted funding from slave-owning families in America. 3.

The twice widowed Duncan McLaren was another heavily involved in the abolitionist movement. As the leader of the New Edinburgh Anti-Slavery Association and later the city's Lord Provost and MP, he also became increasingly vocal and influential in the long years of the Victorian women's suffrage campaign, primarily as its champion in the House of Commons. His third wife, Priscilla Bright McLaren, a member of the Edinburgh Ladies' Emancipation Society, was a signatory of John Stuart Mill's 1866 women's suffrage petition, the instigator of the nine Grand Suffrage Demonstrations in the 1880s, and led the Edinburgh National Society for Women's Suffrage – Scotland's first – from its start in 1867 until her death 39 years later. Agnes McLaren, Duncan McLaren's daughter from his second marriage, became the first secretary of ENSWS and one of the earliest female doctors. 4.

In 1840, Marion Reid of Edinburgh attended the World Anti-Slavery Convention in London, where women delegates were allowed only to listen to the debates from behind a curtain and were not permitted to speak. It is likely that this extraordinary affront, brought about by male delegates voting to exclude females, motivated *A Plea for Women*, which Reid published in 1843, and which is now regarded as one of the world's earliest and most influential texts on women's political emancipation. With its strong advocacy of women's economic and political independence, it has been described as the first book "to give importance to gaining both civil and political rights for women." *A Plea for Women* was a window to women's potential and proved influential in the early years of the campaign for female emancipation.

The founding in 1865 of the Edinburgh Essay Society, which became the Edinburgh Debating Society four years later, was another important development in the city's suffrage story. The society met on the first Saturday of each month and drew its membership, as with other 'improvement' groups, from the wealthier classes in the city. Votes would be taken on the issues discussed, including women's suffrage from 1866. Indeed, the body changed its name to the Ladies' Debating Society in 1880, "and for the first time it offered women a forum to discuss public affairs without fear of male scorn." The society's 19-year-old founding secretary, Sarah Elizabeth Siddons Mair, devoted her entire adult life to the pursuit of the parliamentary vote for women, and succeeded Priscilla McLaren as ENSWS president. 5.

Sarah Mair, with the Leith campaigner Mary Crudelius, also launched the Edinburgh Ladies' Educational Association in 1867 to demand higher education opportunities for women. Among participants were Louisa and Flora Stevenson, who joined its first academic course. The same year the Stevenson sisters joined the Edinburgh National Society for Women's Suffrage. In 1871 they were founder members of the London-based Central Committee of the National Society for Women's Suffrage. 6.

Thus, by mid-century, a number of organisations involved in reforming campaigns on temperance, slavery, educational improvement, employment opportunities, married women's rights – even anti-lynching – began to see the sense of having political influence. And, asserting themselves as feminist groups evolved, were those whose impact upon the women's suffrage campaign was key to progress and improvement in these other areas. Millicent Fawcett later called these Edinburgh pioneers "a brilliant group of men and women." 7.

The McLaren family, Eliza Wigham, Marion Reid, the Stevenson sisters and Sarah Mair worked tirelessly, and in different ways, to improve the lot of their sex, and the time was coming when "more and more women came to believe that the parliamentary franchise was a necessary corollary to every other women's right." 8.

The objective – a law allowing women's votes – depended on the alignment of parliamentary time, the support of MPs and the government's blessing. None of them appeared likely until John Stuart Mill, the son of the Scottish

MRS. HUGO REID'S PLEA FOR WOMAN.*

"A PLEA FOR WOMAN"; not by errant knight with lance in rest, vowed to high devoirs to "the peacock and the ladies;" not by courteous minstrel, singing rare ditties to their bright eyes and dove-like gentleness; not by modern bard insulting while he flatters the sex, is this stout plea maintained, but by a cultivated and independently-thinking woman for her sex, which she considers either positively wronged by Man, or in a false social position.

Burns rhymes—

"A'e night at tea began a *plea*;
About America, man,"

and we all know how that ominous plea terminated; though the wisest among us cannot yet foresee the whole of its mighty results to the human race. That Plea which Mrs. Reid opens, is hardly less pregnant with mighty consequences; for what immediately concerns the one half of mankind—the women—must have a vast influence upon the whole species, whether for good or ill.

The Plea which Mrs. Reid urges, is far from being novel in England. It has been maintained, chiefly by women, though eminent men also, philosophers and wits, to take antipodes, Jeremy Bentham and the Rev. Mr. Sydney Smith, have taken it up. Mrs. Macaulay flung her female gauntlet into the arena sixty years since. Mary Wolstoncraft followed as the eloquent and fearless champion of "The Rights of Women." In the earlier period of the French Revolution—now half a century ago—she addressed Talleyrand, the ex-bishop of Autun, as the determined and uncompromising advocate of her sex: contending that, in the general emancipation of society from the civil bondage of ages, women should participate; and that the mass of Frenchmen, who then for the first time claimed to be free, and to think and act for themselves, should, in common justice, approve of the same liberty being extended to that half of the rational creation, hitherto held in civil and political thraldom. Miss Martineau has said something precisely similar of the assertors of American Independence, the framers of the original American Constitution; the fundamental principles of which are contained in the famous Declaration of Rights. If it be seriously asked how such monstrous exceptions are practically made as the whole of the women and the people of colour of Free Republican America, a reply would be somewhat difficult to find by a Republican statesman.

Modern female advocates for the rights of the sex, though contending for the principles of Mary Wolstoncraft, are either ignorant that they are hers, or else are afraid to use a name which prejudice has covered with unmerited obloquy. Women dread something they know not what in her writings; whereas, the fact is, that the philosophy of Mary Wolstoncraft, in her apology for her sex and the Rights of Women, is severe and even stoical. No

* Edinburgh: Tait, Foolscap octavo, pp. 227.

stoic can more sternly repudiate the fleeting empire of personal beauty, or the fickle, short-lived, disturbing passion of youthful love. Her work would seem to have been written after she had bitterly experienced the miseries too often, in the most powerful minds, attendant on that fatal passion; at a time when hope was crushed, or during the collapse of an agonized heart.

"Who,"—to come to the heart of her theory, she demands,—"who made *man* the exclusive judge, if woman partake with him the gift of reason?" Man, however, according to Mrs. Reid, still claims, whether rightly or not, to be the exclusive judge on nearly every point of interest to the species; yet, the women—though silently and indirectly—borne quietly on, as it were, with the stream of social improvement, have come to have much more to say on topics of high and vital interest than they ever had before; and the world, we imagine, is none the worse for it. The last twenty years have been remarkable for the mental development, and social progress, of all the "inferior orders of society:" that is, of the slaves in the British colonies, the working-classes of manufacturing England; and the women, at least those of the middle rank, in France, England, and America:—we may add, of the whole North of Europe. The great, if silent, change in the attainments and knowledge, and consequently in the social, if not civil, position of women which has already taken place, portends still greater changes; while it indicates the progress already made. The working-classes have obtained no actual extension of political privileges, or but a trifling section of them have been so fortunate; and the women have made no apparent approximation to results which Mrs. Reid regards as not more desirable than just. But we think that she labours under an error, when she asserts that women, whether individually or collectively, have not influence, nay, a great and increasing influence, even on public affairs. So now have the working-classes, though neither have they a direct voice; and if it is asked, why either class—that is all the women, and a great body of the men—should be longer deprived of political rights, the same answer must, we presume, suffice for both: they are not yet sufficiently instructed to exercise such rights either for their own, or the general good. But, admitting the preponderance of influence, this can never, we confess, counterbalance the want of positive rights; and influence, often tainted by the means of its acquisition, must also be tainted in its action. The alleged natural mental inferiority of women, their "inaptitude," is an argument, or a fallacy, very generally abandoned in these days, so we shall not enter upon it.

Some fertile seeds of truth regarding women were long since scattered abroad: reason has not slept; and opinion, on this as on other questions, advances slowly but steadily, gathering impetus as it moves on. A very great point has been gained for the sex, when it is acknowledged that female ignorance is neither virtue nor the safeguard of the

A contemporary review of Marion Reid's A Plea for Women, 1843.

philosopher James Mill, agreed in 1866 to put forward a women's suffrage amendment to a new Reform Bill if the names of 100 supporters could be added to it. Over 1400 women answered the call.

Mill's signatories were published in pamphlet form and laid before Parliament on 7 June 1866. That 57 of the 60 Scottish names were from Edinburgh reflected a focused mobilisation among the city's reforming societies and network of influential families. Among those who signed were Priscilla McLaren, her stepdaughter Agnes, Mary Crudelius and Flora Stevenson. Another was the abolitionist Elizabeth Pease Nichol, who would shortly move to the Scottish capital to become treasurer of the Edinburgh National Society for Women's Suffrage. Emily Rosaline Orme was another. She would marry Professor David Masson of Edinburgh University, a founder and leading speaker of the ENSWS. Emily would act as its secretary for a time, and in due course introduce their daughters Rosaline and Flora to the membership.

In the earliest phase of the suffrage campaign, then, many Edinburgh women recognised the significance of the developments taking place in Parliament and were prepared to put their names to them. 9.

John Stuart Mill's amendment to the 1867 Reform Bill would have extended the franchise to females on the same terms as males in England (and in Scotland the following year), but it was voted down in Parliament by 194 votes to 73. Its defeat meant the Act extended the franchise only to more men – the parliamentary vote now going to around 2.5 million male householders, a half-million more than before.

The irony was that the amendment's failure did not stall the women's progress. In response to a measure seen by some as shocking, and by others timely, and treated with scorn by the Press, the idea of women's votes gathered momentum. The political campaign was galvanised and the surge of interest led to the co-ordinated formation of the first modern women's suffrage societies in London, Manchester and Edinburgh, following negotiations in London in the spring of 1867 attended by Priscilla and Agnes

McLaren. The three societies, although 'united' in a loose alliance, remained independent.

In May 1867, Sarah Ann Jackson condensed the women's situation into a dozen lines:

I wonder, Mr Editor,
Why I can't have the vote;
And I will not be contented
Till I've found the reason out
I am a working woman,
My voting-half is dead,
I hold a house, and want to know
Why I can't vote instead
I pay my rates in person,
Under protest tho' 'tis true;
But I pay them, and am qualified
To vote as well as you. 10.

The Edinburgh National Society for Women's Suffrage (ENSWS) staged its first formal meeting in November 1867. Its founding members were active earlier, however. Jessie Methven recalled joining the society in 1866 and there is a record of "a few women" meeting in the drawing room of Priscilla McLaren's home that year "for the purpose." As early as February 1867 Edinburgh campaigners organised the city's first petition to Parliament, which argued for the extension of parliamentary votes to unmarried women and widows. Volunteers canvassed the city for names, and one wrote to the Press claiming it was disingenuous to be shut out among the disenfranchised when they had been "the teachers of politics to their children, dependants and sometimes their husbands." The contributor signed herself 'A Female Citizen' and went further, claiming that women had been "swindled" by men out of their "own identity." Her letter posed the question women around the

Priscilla Bright McLaren, founding president of the Edinburgh National Society for Women's Suffrage.

unworthy of the franchise." Given the times, this is one of the most remarkable letters of the entire campaign for women's votes. 11.

The Edinburgh National Society for Women's Suffrage remained Scotland's only women's suffrage organisation for three years. From its first formal meeting on 6 November 1867 (the Manchester Society was formed the same day) it was led by Priscilla Bright McLaren, the "most represented" woman in the country – her brother was the free trade campaigner Jacob Bright, her husband was the radical Liberal MP Duncan McLaren, another brother John Bright was a prominent Liberal MP, and two sons and a nephew were all Members of Parliament. This made Mrs McLaren more determined that every woman should have a say in electing the men who made the laws she was asked to obey and imposed the taxes she had to pay.

The new society's joint secretaries were Eliza Wigham and Priscilla McLaren's stepdaughter Agnes McLaren (soon to be replaced by Eliza Scott Kirkland when McLaren left Scotland to study medicine in France). Elizabeth Pease Nichol, who had moved to Merchiston after her husband's death, became treasurer. It was decided at the society's first formal meeting that the ENSWS would welcome all who approved of its object "to obtain for women the ancient right of voting for Members of Parliament, and who also subscribed to its funds." It was also resolved that another Edinburgh petition would be "speedily prepared," and to organise committees, societies and petitions in other Scottish towns. 12.

Meanwhile, the defeat of Mill's amendment led to several women challenging their ineligibility to be included in the electoral roll. They argued that an 1850 statute, generally known as Lord Romilly's Act, specified that the word 'male' included females unless it was clearly stated otherwise. In June 1868 Priscilla Bright McLaren wrote to her stepson John McLaren saying, "We are writing to Miss Wigham to call a meeting of our women's committee to take a fresh action on our behalf – it is with a view to putting the names of householders on a Register." Eliza Wigham eagerly applied herself to the task – a remarkable 239 Edinburgh women put their names forward to be registered as voters.

country were beginning to ask – what bestowed on men the prerogative to define a woman's sphere? She continued. "All we ask is that you get out of our way, that you raise those barriers which impede our progress and the nation's welfare and unseal the fountains of knowledge that all may drink who thirst. Let not our daughters lower their flag till they possess that what is justly and truly their right, and he who will oppose women having a vote is himself

The first legal challenge in Scotland came from Mary Burton of Liberton Bank, Edinburgh. On 15 September 1868 Miss Burton, then 51 and a founder member of the ENSWS, appeared before Sheriff Davidson at the Midlothian Registration Court. She was the only British suffragist to conduct her own defence, and *The Scotsman* was quietly impressed: "She fought the battle for her sex. Again and again she returned to the charge, hurling Lord Romilly's Act at the head of the Sheriff." In a fiery exchange, Burton advised the judge to look up his dictionary where he would find that the word 'man' meant both man and woman. She further quoted the Bible, Shakespeare and Milton in her defence. There were, the Sheriff said, when he could get a word in, nearly 300 women in Edinburgh who wished their names to be placed on the electoral roll. His only option was to continue the case. The matter was settled at the Court of Session in October 1868, which decided that there was "a long and uninterrupted custom in Scotland limiting the franchise to males." In other words, women who had never voted were deemed ineligible to vote as they had never been voters. *The Times* described it as "the glorious uncertainty of the law." 13.

Mary Burton, sister of the historian John Hill Burton, was soon back in the news. Later in 1868 she persuaded a sympathetic assessor in Aberdeen to print on the town's electoral roll the names of women who *would* have qualified as voters. The ENSWS annual report proudly noted that the "ladies names were printed alphabetically along with those of the men," before being struck off by a Sheriff. An appeal by the committee to Aberdeen Stipendiary Court was not sustained. The women were held to be "legally" though not "morally or intellectually" disqualified – a distinction which, though meant to soften the blow, was contemptuously dismissed by the Edinburgh committee. In September 1869, Burton wrote from her cottage beneath Arthur's Seat to Lord Provost William Law, who chaired the Watt Institution and School of Arts in Chambers Street: "Sir, I shall be obliged if you will let me know whether women are admissible to the lectures of the School of Arts?" Her intervention led to an inquiry. The following month, the institution's

directors confirmed to her that women would be admitted to classes for the first time – still 23 years before Edinburgh University formally admitted woman undergraduates. Among those joining the first mixed class in what is now Heriot-Watt University was her niece, Ella Burton. 14.

The first annual report of the Edinburgh National Society in January 1868 did not divulge its membership. The level of its subscriptions suggests it had between 75 and 150 enrolled supporters, a figure that would reach 1000 in the years ahead. Its petition-gatherers had amassed upwards of 5000 names, one of the highest totals in Britain. These were presented to Parliament by Duncan McLaren. Across 1868 as a whole there were 55 petitions from Scotland, with 14,000 signatures. Edinburgh alone had therefore furnished more than a third of the signatories and a tenth of the overall British total of 50,000. Not all of them were women, of course. Edinburgh's petition was signed by hundreds of male electors, including 29 clergymen, 18 solicitors, 12 professors, 12 doctors and 12 army and navy officers. In fact, the British total included only 17,000 women signatories, a third of the names listed. This serves to identify and emphasise the importance of influential men to the cause, but it also makes it easier to understand the anti-suffrage argument that 'most' of Britain's 12 million adult women did not want the vote. The names of the 73 MPs who supported John Stuart Mill's amendment were printed as an appendix in the 1868 ENSWS report. This attracted ridicule from the *Glasgow Herald*, which claimed that the politicians were "thus held in admiration by the Edinburgh women...their names are likely to become household words, to be affectionately taught by intellectual mothers to their lisping daughters." 15.

Priscilla McLaren was certainly a household name within the wider women's movement. In 1871, McLaren addressed the Women's Suffrage Conference in London and was elected to the Central Committee of the National Society. Eliza Wigham, Mary Burton and Mrs McLaren's stepdaughter Agnes were busily touring Scotland, forging alliances and establishing committees. Burton accompanied Jane Taylour with no luggage apart from two small handbags and a hot-water bottle. She invariably dressed in a straight skirt, long cloak, and wide bonnet. She recalled the time a workman accidentally spilled paint on her clothes. To make matters worse, she was on her way to an important gathering. Among the guests were two MPs and the leading suffragist Millicent Fawcett. Concealing the splash of paint, she waited until she was shown to her room, where she washed it out. She appeared at dinner in the same outfit, smiling and serene, and collected £10 for the Edinburgh society. [16].

ENSWS members represented Scotland at gatherings of the national leadership. Priscilla McLaren often undertook the role accompanied by her husband Duncan McLaren as he fulfilled parliamentary responsibilities. Professor David Masson, the Regius Chair of Rhetoric and English Literature at Edinburgh University, also took on these duties. Masson played a prominent part in the fight for the university education of women and was the first professor to lecture to university-standard classes organised by the Edinburgh Ladies' Educational Association. The Masson Hall of Residence for female students was named in his honour. His wife Emily and daughters Rosaline and Flora were active in the ENSWS. At such meetings the pioneering Edinburgh delegates formed strong friendships with the leading figures of the Victorian movement, including John Stuart Mill and Priscilla McLaren's brother, Jacob Bright – the two politicians who had done most to promote women's suffrage in this early phase. Whether it was that the women of the Scottish capital were more enlightened, or more strongly minded, than their sisters elsewhere, or whether it was the breadth of the capital's middle classes, the principle of female emancipation appears to have had deeper roots in the city than elsewhere at this time.

Though efforts to amend the 1867 Act had failed, suffrage societies were not cowed. The 'question' had made progress; the influence of the movement was expanding; Bristol and Birmingham had started large societies and hopes were raised that political rights would not be long withheld from "one half of the intelligent community of Great Britain." The principal work of the Edinburgh National Society had evolved into arranging meetings and

Eliza Wigham, joint-secretary of the Edinburgh National Society for Women's Suffrage.

Jacob Bright, the MP for Manchester, and brother of the Edinburgh National Society president Priscilla McLaren.

speakers, circulating petitions, cultivating male support and writing to an often-bewildered Press. This resulted in 1868 in an outlay of £100 in promotion of the cause, some of it used for paid canvassers. Encouraged by its first full year, the Edinburgh society began the painstaking process of launching a larger petition – securing 1800 signatures in the Scottish capital alone by the following February and, by the middle of 1869, over 7000 names. Additionally, there were 18 individual petitions to Parliament from Edinburgh women in 1869, one of them from sisters Lilias and Agnes Craig of Carlton Street, both signatories to John Stuart Mill's petition. 17.

Jacob Bright spoke at the first public meeting of the Edinburgh National Society in Queen Street Hall on 17 January 1870 – a landmark gathering organised by his sister Priscilla, and only the second women's suffrage meeting held in Britain. It was also the largest gathering in support of women's votes ever staged. *The Scotsman* called it the 'Great Scottish National Demonstration' and reported the hall to be "filled to overflowing with women." Visitors included Central Committee members Isabella Tod of Belfast, Florence Balgarnie of Scarborough and Laura Ormiston Chant of London – all of whom had Edinburgh connections. Duncan McLaren presided, and Professors David Masson and Henry Calderwood spoke on behalf of the Edinburgh Society. Resolutions were put and seconded by male participants. No woman spoke.

It was at this important meeting that Jacob Bright proposed another women's suffrage bill, that he, along with Sir Charles Dilke, introduced to the Commons later in the year, and which was again outvoted. His speech was later published as a 12-page pamphlet. Attendees also included the Edinburgh University principal Sir Alexander Grant and its Professors David Masson and Henry Calderwood, the Edinburgh MP Dr Lyon Playfair and seven city councillors. It is significant that so many of Edinburgh's most influential men – its Lord Provost, councillors, MPs, church leaders, university academics and, indeed, Edinburgh Town Council – backed women's votes, at least for now. And yet, despite benefitting from the support of such figures, and seeing them 'hijack' its first public meeting, the ENSWS was proudly the only one of the five major British suffrage societies to not have a man on its executive committee. [18].

By early 1870, the Edinburgh National Society had been in operation for two years. In that time it had organised meetings and distributed thousands of pamphlets and handbills. It had helped to organise nearly 100 petitions containing 20,000 names – a sixth of all signatures on the 340 British petitions presented to Parliament in 1869. Over 200 qualified women householders in Edinburgh had sent in claims – all rejected – to be registered as voters under the new Reform Act. The first large-scale public meeting had been a success. Above all, the society's emissaries had set out from Edinburgh to extend its arguments and influence across Scotland, helping to form local committees and the societies to come. One newspaper commented presciently: "Patience and perseverance for a time will be needful; but the ladies and the gentlemen who are guiding this movement, are not of the class who succumb at the appearance of difficulty. There is a phalanx of brave hearts who will bear down all opposition and be ultimately victorious." [19].

Women were discovering their voices. Outraged by a newspaper's opinion that women's votes would be "controlled by clergymen" and be a "gain to Toryism," an unnamed Edinburgh contributor responded: "Anyone can assert, but can anyone prove, that men are less easily tempted than women? Those of our sex who have to fight the battle of life alone are not the most likely to be tempted with a ribbon or a toy." She signed herself, 'One Disqualified by the Wedding Ring.' The paper had the gallantry to admit that 'One Disqualified by the Wedding Ring' had shown herself "a foe worthy of our steel." It then shovelled itself into a hole by claiming that only one in 100 women wanted the franchise and that the "widows and spinsters" who would gain the vote would continue their "taste for tea-table scandal and malicious gossip, as well as for cats and parrots." [20].

On 4 May 1870, Jacob Bright's bill giving the franchise to women householders was brought up for its second reading and carried by 124 votes to 91, to gasps of surprise in the Ladies' Gallery, the tiny room with heavy metal grilles overlooking the Chamber which became a symbol of women's exclusion from Parliament. (Before 1834, women wanting to watch proceedings in the Commons had to do so via a ventilation shaft in the ceiling.) As usual the bill was deliberately 'talked out' by government supporters and made no further progress. Despite the disappointment, efforts continued to spread the suffrage message. Mary Burton joined the peripatetic crusader Jane Taylour of Stranraer on another Scottish speaking tour and helped to form committees in the north. Eliza Wigham, Eliza Kirkland and Priscilla McLaren travelled long, tiring distances to undertake engagements. At one, Mrs McLaren rejected Prime Minister William Gladstone's assertion that there was no demand for the franchise. She talked of Edinburgh being filled with supporters – 2000 at the Queen Street Hall on one occasion. She mentioned the petitions to Parliament from Scotland – 120 from towns and parishes and 200 from individual women ratepayers. She highlighted the society's speakers, praising the efforts of the Misses Wigham and Burton, and her stepdaughter Agnes McLaren. She also paid tribute to the remarkable Jane Taylour, who had addressed 41 meetings over recent weeks, from Galloway to Kirkwall – all of them "presided over by chief magistrates of burghs, sheriffs of counties, ministers of religion, and influential gentlemen." [21].

Sophia Jex-Blake was a newcomer to the ENSWS. In 1869 she applied to study medicine at Edinburgh University. Although the medical faculty voted in her favour, strongly encouraged by Duncan McLaren, the university court rejected her application on the grounds that the institution could not make the necessary arrangements "in the interest of one lady." So she advertised in *The Scotsman* for other women to join her. A second application was submitted in 1869, initially on behalf of a group of five women (with two more added later in the year to make the 'Edinburgh Seven' – Sophia Jex-Blake, Mary Anderson, Emily Bovell, Matilda Chaplin, Helen Evans, Edith Pechey and Isabel Thorne). This time, the university court approved the application.

Hostility continued, however. The women "received obscene letters, were followed home, had fireworks attached to their front door, and had mud thrown at them." Opposition culminated in the so-called 'Surgeons' Hall Riot' on 18 November 1870, when the women arrived to sit an anatomy examination and a mob of 200 students began throwing rubbish and insults at them. "The events made national headlines and won the women many new supporters, but influential members of the medical faculty persuaded the university to refuse graduation to the women by appealing decisions to higher courts. The courts eventually ruled that the women who had been awarded degrees should never have been allowed to enter the course." Their degrees were withdrawn. *The Scotsman* concluded, "The authorities of Edinburgh University seem determined not to let them win their rights by degrees." Following the setback, Dr Jex-Blake established in 1874 the London School of Medicine for Women, which "commenced with fourteen students, twelve of whom were from Edinburgh." [22].

The largest meeting ever organised by the Edinburgh National Society took place at the cavernous Music Hall at the start of 1871. The principal guest, John Stuart Mill, was greeted enthusiastically with prolonged cheering and the waving of hats and handkerchiefs by the 2000-strong audience. The ornate, pillared hall was filled to hear Mill acknowledge his welcome and generously comment that the evolving women's movement in Scotland owed "an immense debt to Edinburgh" and notably to a gentleman to whom "perhaps the cause owed the most." He meant Duncan McLaren, but added quickly, "and the ladies of his family." It was Mill's only public speech outside London, and it was reprinted in pamphlet form with the title 'Great Meeting in Favour of Women's Suffrage'. [23].

The Edinburgh National Society continued to call for votes for all women who qualified as owners or occupiers of lands or property but, as the campaign moved into the 1870s, there was a distinct transition from male-led meetings to those where the chair and principal speakers were mostly female, either prominent invitees or drawn from the branch leadership. By February 1872, the ENSWS was able to report that its outreach work had resulted in the formation of 26 local women's franchise committees across Scotland. Adopting a suggestion from Priscilla McLaren the Edinburgh branch instigated 'At Home' gatherings in the houses of those favourable to the cause. These meetings drew in women who were perhaps reluctant to attend public meetings, who had no decided opinion on the issue and who might be influenced by the opinions of the suffragists they met. Following Edinburgh's lead, 'At Homes' were introduced throughout the British suffrage movement to recruit new members and to raise funds. [24].

In May 1872, and supported by an astonishing number of petitions to Parliament, Jacob Bright moved the second reading of his Women's Disabilities Removal Bill. In a powerful appeal to the House, he highlighted the inequalities, grievances and disabilities under which women existed, and argued that their electoral exclusion was unjust as they were obliged to bear all the taxation attached to property without the rights that came with it for men. He singled out Edinburgh and said he "knew nothing more scandalous" than that every woman in the city was taxed to support a university whose door was firmly shut to one-half of the population – the same university to which the House of Commons voted large sums of money for maintenance. The opposition, on the other hand, countered that the majority of women did not want votes. The petitions which rained down on Parliament, they said, often had more male signatures than female. In any case, those who signed were a tiny proportion of the near-12 million adult women in Britain. As regards party politics, the Liberals believed that all women would vote Tory. The Tories thought the opposite – and both parties agreed that franchised women would outvote men on important matters, such as going to war, which were, in any case, 'beyond them'. And for the third time, Bright's bill was lost. [25].

It was not all doom and gloom. As 1872 ended, women in Scotland were making inroads into important areas of local decision-making. Under the Education (Scotland) Act approximately 1000 elected school boards were established and were able to begin, for the first time, to enforce attendance among children aged from 5 to 13 years. Qualified women were allowed both to vote in the elections to boards, and to stand as board members. The Edinburgh society's Flora Stevenson was one of the first two women elected in Scotland and served from 1873 until her death in 1905. In 1899 a school in Comely Bank was named in her honour and thrives today as the Flora Stevenson Primary School. It was reported that in Edinburgh's first school board elections, "one-seventh of the voters were women." Priscilla McLaren pointed out wryly that "they were not the less feminine than they were before." What better proof was there, she added, that they could exercise their voice in parliamentary elections. 26.

With the electoral arithmetic unchanged, the arguments moved into 1873. The Reform Act of 1867 had excluded one entire sex from voting, wholly and solely on the grounds of gender. The total number of voters in the United Kingdom in 1873 was about 2,600,000. If women who were householders, who occupied land and paid taxes – and who, in fact, fulfilled all the conditions required by the Act but that of sex – were added, the increase to Britain's electoral roll would have been only 300,000 – around 8000 of them from Edinburgh. Yet, according to the 1861 census, some 3,500,000, or around one third of all adult women, earned their own income. As the legislative position stood, the only classes deemed incapable of exercising parliamentary votes were infants, minors, paupers, criminals, lunatics – and women.

The Edinburgh National Society was undeterred. At its annual meeting in a well-filled Queen Street Hall, Eliza Wigham looked back on 1872 with pride. The ENSWS had staged 95 public meetings, and on every occasion but one, resolutions had been passed in favour of Jacob Bright's bill. A further 35 local committees had been established, bringing the total across Scotland to 60. Dozens of new members had enrolled. Besides the petitions from 14 Town Councils, 172 other petitions had been despatched from Scotland, with 44,749 names. The total number presented to the House of Commons in 1872 was 829, signed by 350,093 individuals, almost double the number of the previous year. It represented an enormous amount of patient and dedicated work by

An entry from the manuscript sales ledger of an Edinburgh tinmaker for an order for 25 Ballot boxes, 'japanned' in black with brass locks, dated January 1874 and presumably for the General Election which took place in January/February 1874.

A contemporary illustration depicting the unveiling of the statue to Prince Albert – with Edinburgh weather not helping the occasion.

countless women volunteers. As usual, the annual report was printed by John Greig & Son, and circulated to members. [27].

Another attempt to progress Jacob Bright's bill in May 1873 was also doomed to failure – a fourth rejection. *The Scotsman* balanced a smidgen of sympathy with its more familiar scorn: "Anyone who entered the House of Commons today would have heard a liquid babble which trilled through the chamber and would have soon discovered that it was the voice of ladies in their gilded cage, who were chattering all together like so many songbirds. Their gallery was full to overflowing, and many were disappointed in not getting in, [but] the result of the division was expected." As the debate was spun out, the Cambridge MP Patrick Smollett "sank below the level of good taste" by drawing attention to "the ludicrous names" behind the women's campaign, including, he said, Miss Becker, Miss Babb, Miss Miggs, Miss Beddie – and Mrs McLaren of Edinburgh. He expected to see, he noted haughtily, "ladies of greater social eminence." The satirical magazine *Punch* joined in the chorus of condemnation of his comments: "We understand Mr Smollett is descended from the novelist. We hope he will not descend any lower." [28].

The 1874 General Election was a disaster for the Liberals. Benjamin Disraeli's Conservatives swept to power with 350 of the 652 MPs, the party's first majority since 1841. This presented a glimmer of hope for the women's movement. Disraeli was regarded as sympathetic to the cause, whereas William Gladstone, although jettisoned as Prime Minister after six years, continued to dismiss the possibility of electoral reform. In one of his last acts as Prime Minister he refused to meet a deputation of women's suffrage leaders, including Jessie Wellstood and Eliza Wigham of the ENSWS. Mrs Wellstood, of Duncan Street, later told a conference of the National Society for Women's Suffrage in Birmingham that the key objection adopted by anti-suffragists was that few women actually wanted votes. This was not the case in Edinburgh, she said, where public interest had been "awakened." She criticised women who were "so comfortable, and so happy and easy in their circumstances" that they had become accustomed to being "subservient to men." [29].

The next annual meeting of the Edinburgh Society was held in the Bible Society's Rooms, St Andrew's Square in late February 1874. Priscilla McLaren took the chair and said, to murmurs of sympathy, that she was sorry that they had to choose another leader for their cause in Parliament, as Manchester had unseated her brother, Jacob. They had now to look to the Conservatives for help. Once again, Eliza Wigham read the report. The number of public meetings held during the year was 91, and 188 petitions from Scotland had been forwarded to Parliament. Eighteen women had now been elected to Scottish school boards. [30].

Although Jacob Bright's gas was at a peep (temporarily, as he was returned two years later), the leading societies for women's suffrage resolved to support a new bill lodged by the Cambridge MP William Forsyth, a Scottish lawyer. Forsyth's Women's Disabilities Removal Bill was introduced to the Commons the following spring, before falling on a vote, and despite 230 MPs promising in advance to support the measure. The bill was not entirely welcomed by the women's movement, as it would have been confined to unmarried women and widows who possessed the necessary property qualifications. Many married suffragists were unhappy – among them a certain Emmeline Pankhurst.

Come mid-decade, there were as many anti-suffragists raising their heads above the parapet as those campaigning for change. One anonymous *Scotsman* contributor wanted to know why women could not be content with subscribing to the funds of Edinburgh Infirmary "without presuming to interfere in its management or wanting to join its council." Even if only two were admitted, he mused, the whole council would soon be filled by women. "Why not let well alone?" he asked. "Why cannot women keep themselves in their natural and fitting place? Have they not – besides the Church – the drawing-room, the kitchen and the nursery, the croquet lawn, the ball-room, the skating pond, the concert hall, the theatre...what right have they to meddle with Ragged Schools and School Boards and, above all, with Infirmaries?" And, at a meeting in Roxburgh Free Church [now the King Khalid Hall in Hill

Square], the Rev George Macaulay told his flock that women's suffrage was "all very well, but where was it to end?" To laughter, he added that if *his* vote were to carry it, he would clear the school board and all other boards of every female member. He held that woman's place "everlastingly" should be "filled with modesty in the home." 31.

The annual Eliza Wigham feedback to the Edinburgh National Society kept up momentum and morale. The 1875 meeting was held in the Literary Institute in South Clerk Street, with Priscilla McLaren presiding. The number of petitions from Scotland had now reached an impressive 340, containing upwards of 50,000 signatures. Fourteen of them were from Town Councils and 10,000 Scottish women had sent a special memorial to the new Prime Minister "praying for his support" and reminding Mr Disraeli that he was the first member of the House of Commons to concede the right of women to representation. The Edinburgh MP James Cowan, a former Lord Provost, moved approval of Miss Wigham's report and told members the country had a large number of single women, widows and wives who had been deserted by their husbands – and who were paying taxes, bringing up their families and doing all they possibly could to keep themselves out of the poorhouse. He asked if these women were not as much entitled to vote as they were themselves. His question was met with applause and cries of 'Yes'. 32.

On March 9, Mr Cowan presented a petition to Parliament from 809 inhabitants of Edinburgh in favour of women's suffrage. On the same day the Linlithgowshire Liberal MP Peter McLagan announced a separate petition from the city. Donald Macgregor MP lodged another. It contained the names of 232 inhabitants of Leith, the port he represented. And, on March 17, the Earl of Dalkeith handed in a petition from the people of Dalkeith, Loanhead, Lasswade and Bonnyrigg. No-one could accuse the ENSWS of failing to plead their case, or of persuading others of its merits. 33.

The year 1876 ended with a visit to Edinburgh by Queen Victoria to unveil a statue to her late husband Albert. The Queen's carriage was taken in procession from Holyrood to Charlotte Square, where the statue of the Prince Consort was placed. Many thousands packed the route. In the evening fireworks and beacons lit up Arthur's Seat. Much to the women's disappointment, Victoria was strongly opposed to extending the franchise and was, "most anxious to enlist everyone who can speak or write in checking this mad wicked folly of Woman's Rights." It would have been fascinating to hear how Victorian men reconciled their allegiance to a great female Queen while no member of her sex had the vote because her laws deemed them unfit to have it. The inconsistency of men who visibly fell under Queen Victoria's spell, but dismissed the prospect of women participating in the running of the country, was not lost on Britain's 12 million adult females, including her 3,800,000 working women. 34.

The ninth annual meeting of the Edinburgh National Society for Women's Suffrage was held on the first day of February 1877 in the Royal Hotel, Princes Street. Professor William Hodgson, the university's first professor of economics, presided. Secretary Eliza Wigham rose to deliver the annual report. She was now approaching her sixties and had recently helped to launch the Penny Savings Bank in Causewayside, which she would run for many years. As before, the ENSWS membership had arranged public events and organised petitions for Parliament. The meeting agreed to ask the incoming Edinburgh Town Council to reaffirm its support for a women's bill. The council, however, decided to take no action. Though disappointed, the society dispatched James Cowan to the House of Commons where he brought before Parliament, "Petitions from the printers and publishers in Edinburgh, from inhabitants from the St Stephen's Ward, from inhabitants from Edinburgh City and from a drawing-room meeting in Edinburgh, all in favour of the Women's Disabilities Bill." 35.

On a Wednesday afternoon in June 1877 Jacob Bright moved the second reading of the Women's Disabilities Removal Bill. It was supported across the country by 799 petitions signed by 265,826 people. Mary Burton reported that the bill had attracted 1000 signatures in Edinburgh and 300 alone from Newington, "the wealthiest district, where many ladies of position, having begun to think over the matter, now take a warm interest." The bill made no progress, however. The Liberal MP Leonard Courtney succeeded in talking it out, speaking for half-an-hour in the midst of "the greatest clamour and cries of 'divide'." He was still talking at 5.45pm, when by House rules the debate was adjourned. 36.

ENSWS committee member Louisa Stevenson was at this time a leading figure in the Edinburgh Ladies' Educational Association and campaigning hard for a better education for girls and women against a crescendo of conservative male voices. She read a paper in September 1877 which demanded university access for women. She highlighted what had been done by the Universities of Edinburgh, Glasgow and Aberdeen in co-operation with voluntary associations to provide a university-standard education for women, which corresponded in many respects to that of a degree for men. Over the previous decade, the number of admissions of women for the various classes had reached 2572, an extraordinary average of over 250 for each year. It is scarcely believable that universities at this time did not recognise that the lectures, course work and examinations of these initiatives corresponded to what was being pursued on their campuses by male students. In fact, they were being taught by the same professors, albeit those with suffrage sympathies. Similarly, women were now prominent members of school and parochial boards across the city, yet councillors in Edinburgh's 13 wards frequently ridiculed the idea of allowing them to become municipal voters, far less town councillors. 37.

By 1878, the Edinburgh National Society's annual report was starting to have the repetitive sound of a drum beat. Even the indefatigable Eliza Wigham seemed to be going through the motions when she noted the 183 petitions from Scotland, although their breakdown as far as Edinburgh was concerned was of interest. One petition had come from 14 members of the Faculty of Advocates, one from 52 medical practitioners in the city, one from 35 ministers of various denominations, another from 14 publishers and printers in Edinburgh, one from 189 rectors, headmasters and teachers in the capital,

another from 912 female householders and ratepayers and 19 petitions from drawing-room meetings in the city. A petition also winged its way to Parliament signed by 212 inhabitants of Leith. To lend weight to the cause the canvassers sought signatures from different social classes and occupations – "advocates, solicitors, bankers, ministers, physicians, and headmasters." It was weary work and time consuming. Priscilla McLaren, writing to her suffrage friend Helen Taylour in 1879, captured the strain on the ENSWS membership, "Our committee women are growing too old to work, and such as are not, are invalid..." And yet, many women believed the movement's time had come. Just before Christmas 1879, the Manchester Society secretary Lydia Becker wrote to Mrs McLaren: "We have had such a meeting that I must write and tell you of it – the room, which will seat 600 or 700, was quite full of women only – all poor working women – how they listened – how they cheered – how strong and intelligent an interest they took...I feel the strength there is in those women...there is a force which, gathered together, led, organised and made manifest, is enough to lead us to victory." 38.

Optimism remained, but the opponents of women's suffrage were buoyed as yet another suffrage bill bit the dust as the 1870s drew to a close – this time voted down by 217 to 103. Alexander Beresford Hope, the Conservative MP for Cambridge University, commented that the bill, "would enfranchise foolish as well as wise virgins, and would lead inevitably to lady membership in the House." The Nottingham Tory MP George Storer held "that if the franchise were conferred on women, men would be chosen as members of Parliament solely on account of their good looks and affability." The Chester MP Henry Raikes characterised the demand for female suffrage as "hollow and insincere." He added that it was favoured by acidulated spinsters and had caused annoyance to men and created disgust among women. A Liberal, Sir Henry James, a past and future Attorney-General, said that if they gave women the Parliamentary franchise, "our councils would then be the councils of women, not to be trusted with the grave questions that came before the Legislators for settlement." Men were trained for the political world by their labours in their professions, he added, "but woman's profession was marriage." [39].

With such words ringing in their ears, and their roles defined as usual by males dictating and determining prevailing ideology and the norm, no one had to remind the women's movement that votes were as distant as ever, regardless of how many meetings were held, regardless of how many pledges of support they had.

References

1. Leah Leneman, The Scottish Suffragettes (2000), p18.
2. Martin Pugh, Women's Suffrage in Britain 1867-1928 (1980), p8.
3. Elizabeth Crawford, The Women's Suffrage Movement, A Reference Guide (1999), p708; Elspeth King, The Scottish Women's Suffragette Movement (1978), p9; The Patriot, 4 January 1847.
4. Roger Fulford, Votes for Women (1958), p45; Crawford (1999), p401.
5. Crawford (1999), p365; Leneman (2000), p23. A complete run of Edinburgh Debating Society journals from 1865 is with the National Libraries of Scotland.
6. Leneman (2000), p20.
7. Millicent Fawcett, What I Remember (1924), p120.
8. Elizabeth Ewan, Sue Innes, Sian Reynolds (Eds), The Biographical Dictionary of Scottish Women (2006), p301; Leah Leneman, A Guid Cause, The Women's Suffrage Movement in Scotland (1991), p10; https://www.socantscot.org/resource/ahead-of-their-time-a-talk-in-celebration-of-international-womens-day-by-susan-morrison/
9. The 1866 Petition List, www.parliament.uk/vote100
10. Dundee Courier, 23 May 1867; Leeds Express, 4 March 1868.
11. The Daily Review, (Edinburgh) 21 February 1867; Edinburgh Evening Courant, 6 July 1868; Leneman (1991), p12; The Suffragette, 17 January 1913; Edinburgh National Society for Women's Suffrage, 50th Report, 1918.
12. The Scotsman, 7 November 1867.
13. Liverpool Mail, 19 September 1868; Dundee Courier, 17 September 1868; Leneman (1991), p14; Woman's Signal, 5 March 1896; Fulford (1958), p58; Crawford (1999), p402.
14. Falkirk Herald, 4 November 1869; Woman's Signal, 5 March 1896.
15. Glasgow Herald, 1 January 1869.
16. Woman's Signal, 5 March 1896.
17. Edinburgh Evening Courant, 24 February 1869; Crawford (1999), p227.
18. Fulford (1958), p72; The Scotsman, 18 January 1870.
19. The Scotsman, 18 January 1870; Kelso Chronicle, 21 January 1870.
20. Dundee Courier, 6 & 7 May 1870.
21. Press & Journal, 17 May 1871.
22. https://en.wikipedia.org/wiki/Surgeons%27_Hall_riot; Scotsman, 29 February 1871; John Peacock, The Story of Edinburgh (2017), p231.
23. The Scotsman, 13 January 1871; Leneman (1991), p19; The Women's Library, LSE, PC/06/396-11/03.
24. The Scotsman, 14 February 1872.
25. The Scotsman, 2 May 1872.
26. The Queen, 10 May 1873; The Scotsman, 12 December 1873; Sarah Pedersen, The Scottish Suffragettes and the Press (2017) p23. Flora Stevenson went on to win a further nine school board elections and chaired Edinburgh School Board in 1900.
27. The Scotsman, 28 January 1873.
28. The Scotsman, 1 May 1873; Fulford (1958), p77.
29. The Scotsman, 23 January 1874.
30. Edinburgh Evening News, 25 February 1874.
31. The Scotsman, 12 January 1875; Edinburgh Evening News, 14 May 1875.
32. The North Briton, 23 January 1875.
33. The Scotsman, 2 & 10 March 1875.
34. Joyce Marlow, Suffragettes: The Fight for Votes for Women (2015), p17.
35. Edinburgh Evening News, 2 February 1877; The Scotsman, 13 April 1877; William Knox, Lives of Scottish Women (2006) p41. Knox's biography of Eliza Wigham says very little about her 30-year stewardship of the Edinburgh National Society for Women's Suffrage.
36. Women's Suffrage Journal, 2 July 1877; Dundee Courier, 7 & 18 June 1877.
37. The Scotsman, 26 September 1877.
38. Marlow (2015), p20; The Scotsman, 16 March 1878; King (1978), p11; Crawford (1999), p187.
39. The Scotsman, 8 March 1879.

RIGHT: The banner of the Edinburgh National Society for Women's Suffrage is unfurled for the first time at a meeting in St James's Hall, London, in June 1884.

The Edinburgh National Society occupied itself with charitable work as well as fighting for the vote. For example, it organised visits and raised funds for the Edinburgh workhouses. (Courtesy of the Royal College of Physicians, Edinburgh)

TWO:
THE GRAND DEMONSTRATIONS
1880-1889

"During your Majesty's reign two measures have been passed relating to the representation of the people, whereby your Majesty's own sex are still denied the rights of citizenship and the privileges of free and constitutional government. The bright example of your Majesty in the discharge of the highest political function known to the State is an irrefragable proof that the most arduous political functions are not incompatible with happiness of domestic life and the highest graces of womanly character."

Edinburgh National Society for Women's Suffrage memorial to Queen Victoria to mark her Golden Jubilee in 1887.

The 1880s began with memories of parliamentary bill after bill being lost. Women's suffrage had been introduced to legislation every year of the 1870s, apart from 1874. All had been rejected by the government, but voting figures gave no real sense of where the country's legislators stood. The majority of 33 in favour in 1870 turned into a minority of 69 the following year. The 1878 bill was defeated by 80. A year later 114 MPs were against it. One explanation is that parliamentarians took the issue lightly at first. As the years passed, and the matter returned to the Commons, it was regarded more seriously by MPs and the opposition to it was better organised. So much so that the 1870s, which had promised so much, brought women's votes no closer. 1.

Nonetheless, suffragists were determined to hansel the incoming decade with a spectacular show of support for the cause. The 'Great Demonstration' of 1880, as it was titled, was organised by the Central Committee for Women's Suffrage and announced for the wintry month of February at the Free Trade Hall in Manchester – built on the site of the Peterloo Massacre and the

scene, in years ahead, of Christabel Pankhurst and Annie Kenney's dramatic first act of militancy. The honour of presiding over this huge gathering was given to Priscilla Bright McLaren of the Edinburgh Society, whose idea for a national demonstration was now bearing fruit. And for once, all the speakers were women. The great hall was crowded, and overflow meetings were hastily arranged. Congratulatory and encouraging letters and telegrams flooded in from supporters across the country. Mrs McLaren, in opening the meeting, said that however much they laboured and petitioned, the House of Commons had turned "a deaf ear to their appeals." She was anticipating Mrs Pankhurst's justification for militancy in the century to come.

The purpose of the Grand Demonstration was to send a message to the government that women had to be enfranchised before the next general election. It asked for votes based on the municipal and school board franchise already granted south of the border. This would have disenfranchised otherwise qualified Scotswomen, as for now they were debarred from voting in council elections. The Manchester accord argued that the experience of voting in the two polls in England had shown how fit women were to become parliamentary voters. Mrs McLaren forwarded the memorial to the Prime Minister the following day along with a request that Mr Disraeli receive a deputation of women to discuss the document in person. She asked him to suggest a convenient time and place, only to be met with the frosty response through his secretary that he had no desire to see the women. Adding insult to injury, Disraeli's condescending reply told the women to make any further comments "in writing." [2.]

Earlier, in January 1880, Priscilla McLaren had presided over the annual meeting of the Edinburgh National Society at the Royal Hotel in Princes Street and made the point that the movement had grown so much that they were no longer dependent "on important public men" to steer them through their gatherings. They "could now help themselves." She had no sympathy, she said, for the aristocratic anti-suffragists – Lady This and That – who said that women should have nothing to do with politics and who believed that it was "the duty of women to suffer in patience and submission from bad husbands, bad laws, and everything which made life an agony instead of a blessing." Eliza Wigham, as usual, read the report for 1879, and when a Miss Maitland moved its adoption, she added that, "if they had had Home Rule for Scotland they would have had women's suffrage long ago, as a considerable majority of Scotch members had voted in favour of the measure." Dr Sophia Jex-Blake, Mary Burton, Louisa Stevenson and Jessie Wellstood also spoke.

As matters stood, Scotland lagged well behind England in the municipal franchise, where women had voted for town councils from 1869 after Priscilla McLaren's brother Jacob Bright had introduced the required legislation. But, in June 1881, the Municipal Elections Amendment (Scotland) Act gave council votes to women ratepayers in royal and parliamentary burghs. This was extended the following year to include Scottish women ratepayers in police burghs. The municipal vote also allowed suffragists to challenge the illogicality of being able to put their cross in a polling booth for the town councillor of their choice, but of being incapable of doing so to choose an MP. [3.]

Parliament was dissolved on 24 March 1880. The first constituencies began voting a week later and the general election continued until April 27. The focal point for suffragists was the Midlothian constituency, in which the parliamentary thoroughbred William Ewart Gladstone was standing against the sitting Conservative. Gladstone managed to convince the country that Prime Minister Disraeli's policies on the economy and foreign relations were "immoral." When votes were counted, the Liberals had secured one of their biggest-ever majorities, including 52 of Scotland's 58 seats. Disraeli resigned on April 21, and Gladstone, who had taken Midlothian by just 211 votes, became Prime Minister for a second time. The 1880 Midlothian election is regarded as the birth of the modern political campaign in Britain. It was also the first non-English constituency to be represented by a serving prime minister.

Only one tenth of Scotland's 3.7 million people voted in the 1880 general election, women among the excluded. Nevertheless, the Edinburgh society gained impetus from access to the municipal franchise and the change of government. In May, the ENSWS sent four delegates – Priscilla McLaren, Flora Masson, Miss Ramsay Smith and Louisa Stevenson – to a meeting of the Central Committee in St James's Hall, Piccadilly. With the Edinburgh leadership otherwise detained, Mary Burton presided over a public meeting at Liberton School and spoke of the disability under which women laboured. To illustrate her point, she highlighted eight villas in Liberton which carried only two votes. Six of the properties were occupied by widows. Her co-secretary Eliza Kirkland protested against the general election ballot box "being closed to women" and moved that the exclusion of females legally qualified to vote in every respect apart from their sex, was "injurious both to the persons excluded and to the community at large." A Mr Black of Liberton Mains told the large audience that women "had only to put their foot down and say, until we get our suffrage, we will pay no more taxes." His comment was met with laughter and applause, but he pursued the point: "What could the Government do with a lot of elderly ladies who would not pay their taxes?

The Synod Hall in Castle Terrace was the location of the largest women's suffrage rallies in Edinburgh and the Scottish Grand Demonstration of 1884.

They might go into the houses and distrain their goods, but then the ladies might resist. I would like to know what they would do with a lot of elderly ladies in prison?" This drew more laughter. Yet within a few years the tactic of tax-resistance would form a potent weapon in the women's armoury. 4.

Petitions continued to rain down on Parliament. In the middle of 1880 one from the Edinburgh National Society, along with another from a drawing-room meeting in Polwarth Terrace, were presented by the city's MPs. And public meetings continued to draw impressive crowds. A gathering in Queen Street Hall in October attracted 1000 women. Duncan and Priscilla McLaren's son Charles, the Liberal MP for Stafford; Lydia Becker, the leader of the early British suffrage movement; Caroline Biggs, the editor of the *Englishwoman's Review*; and the brilliant orator Helena Downing, who spoke at all nine of the Grand Demonstrations to come in the 1880s, formed part of a star-studded platform party, emphasising once again Edinburgh's importance to the national movement.

The new year of 1881 opened with Duncan McLaren's surprise announcement that he was standing down as an MP. His decision came just weeks after he had successfully steered the Married Women's Property (Scotland) Act into law, which abolished the right of administration of a married woman's property by her husband and allowed women to be the legal owners of the money they earned, and to inherit property. A former town councillor and Lord Provost of Edinburgh, McLaren had represented the city in Parliament since 1865 and had topped the poll in every election he fought. He had been returned by 17,807 of the capital's electors just nine months earlier. He said "new circumstances" brought about the decision, but his age, 81, was inevitably a factor. He also harboured the notion of providing a safe seat for his son John, which he duly filled.

The next annual meeting of the ENSWS paid handsome tribute to Mr McLaren, and also to Professor William Hodgson, the first Professor of Political Economy at Edinburgh University, who had been a faithful friend of the movement until his death in 1880. The meeting was held in the Bible Society's rooms at 5 St Andrew's Square. About 40 women attended, with Priscilla McLaren taking the chair. Eliza Wigham read the annual report, which took a hopeful view of the situation. Nine public and several drawing-room meetings had been held during the year and new committees formed. Addressing the membership, Mrs McLaren complained that the society was being ignored by the Press and she did not believe its silence was accidental, which drew prolonged applause. She pointed a finger at the *Edinburgh Evening News*, saying that it seemed "assiduously to collect painful criminal cases." She had looked through its columns for letters of approval or disapproval of the "unjust sentences" passed upon those who committed crimes on women. But there was silence. "In England they had a girl sent three months to prison with hard labour for stealing the value of 2s 6d; and in Edinburgh two drunk men, for the most cruel treatment of a woman, were sentenced by Sheriff Davidson to five months' imprisonment." She could not help exclaiming, "Alas, that flesh and blood should be so cheap when that flesh and blood is a woman's."

Suffragists regularly criticised the extraordinary discrepancies in convictions and sentencing. It was widely felt they were disproportionate. It is certainly true that the harsh treatment meted out to suffragettes contrasted strikingly with those given to convicted male criminals. There was the case of a Dundee man imprisoned for 14 days for the sexual abuse of a little girl – while Ellison Gibb, later jailed in Dundee, received six months for breaking £15 worth of windows. There was widespread anger over the five years' penal servitude imposed on Mary Leigh and Gladys Evans for setting fire to the Theatre Royal in Dublin. The Pankhursts believed its severity was designed to 'terrorise' other women who might be contemplating militant action. Further, they claimed the sentences were a desperate attempt by the government to break the spirit of the movement. In support of its imprisoned sisters, the WSPU pointed to the sentence of six months in the Second Division being served by a suffragist in Maidstone Prison for breaking £3 worth of glass, and the sentence of 15 days, with the option of a 15 shillings' fine, given to a man in Aberdeen for sexually assaulting a small girl. And when Hilda Burkitt was sentenced to two years' imprisonment for setting fire to a hotel in Felixstowe, she asked the judge to pass the death penalty, "and not waste breath."

So the campaign continued, and for the Edinburgh National Society the demands were many and varied. In November 1881, three members attended a major demonstration in Bradford organised by Lydia Becker. The chair was taken by Priscilla McLaren. Mary Burton and Mary Hope joined her on the platform fronting an audience of 3000. Closer to home, an ENSWS deputation met the Lord-Advocate John Balfour at his chambers in Parliament Square. In answer to his questions, they stated that there were over 9800 women householders in Edinburgh and that more than half of them – upwards of 5000 – had petitioned in favour of the Parliamentary franchise. This data provides the first specific evidence of the strength of support for women's suffrage within Edinburgh's population of female ratepayers. It is significant that more than half of those surveyed supported women's votes, but almost half – if they were canvassed – did not. [5].

The annual meeting of the Edinburgh Society at the start of 1882 covered routine matters and featured the usual faces. It was held again in the Bible Society's rooms and there was a larger than usual attendance. Eliza Wigham, reading the report for 1881, expressed delight that women ratepayers had been recognised. Members who were householders were reminded that they were entitled to vote for the town council from the following November and the committee "anxiously desired" that they would conscientiously exercise the "privilege." Miss Wigham next turned to the forthcoming school board elections. She expressed hope that the return of female candidates would show that women electors had "done their duty" at the polls and would be seen as capable custodians of the parliamentary vote. The report also referred to the importance of having volunteers to serve as Poor Law Guardians to care for the interests of women and children in the work carried out by Edinburgh's parochial administration. [6].

The participants of such gatherings were almost exclusively from the middle and upper classes. The Edinburgh women who appear in official records,

Female factory workers pose in their finest overalls, c1905, but many were reluctant to become involved in the campaign for votes.

Flora Stevenson.

newspapers and personal papers in the first 20 years of the Victorian campaign can be identified by family connections, or by where they lived, as being from leisured and wealthier backgrounds. Those who signed John Stuart Mill's petition, for example, mostly lived in prestigious addresses in the city's New Town, or in named mansions on its periphery. Three of them lived in Charlotte Square.

Several explanations can be offered as to why the capital's working-class women were mostly invisible in this phase of the campaign. The most plausible is the simplest; women and girls in the city's manufacturing trades – and the thousands in domestic service in Edinburgh – had no time to become involved in politics and must have considered there was little to benefit from it. Daily life was filled by a long working shift, often with domestic responsibilities afterwards, weary or not. It was a hard life with limited opportunities. For the vast majority of women, politics must have seemed a luxury accessible only to the professional and upper classes, who were protected to an extent by their class in their protests and after arrests. Moreover, to make an individual public stand was beyond the working woman's culture in the sense that it jarred with notions of respectability. In addition, the kind of protest which was seen up to 1900, that of letter writing and public speaking, was alien to a female workforce more used to its raucous factory language, public promenading and spontaneous walk-outs.

Besides, the campaign for votes was not generally concerned with votes for all women. For the most part, the leading societies argued for a franchise on the same terms as men; in other words, a limited vote for women based on property qualifications. In Edinburgh that amounted to around 9000 women from an overall population of 146,000 females of all ages in the expanding city. Thus, the vast majority of women would have remained voteless. The working classes would have had little to gain. And, while it might have been expected that the rise in the political fortunes of the Labour Party in the early 1900s would have been paralleled by a movement towards representation by working women in Scotland, it was the numerically insignificant middle classes which grasped the nettle and fought for votes.

Despite Leah Leneman's view that the wealth of experience and the organisational know-how developed in establishing unions complemented moves towards electoral equality, the connection was never made. Today's historians, for example, might be able to name no more than two Scottish working-class suffragettes, the domestic servant Jessie Stephen of Glasgow WSPU and Jenny McCallum, a Dunfermline textile worker and Women's Freedom League activist. To these might be added the unsung Ann Shanks and Annie Cuthbert of Dundee. The former bravely provided a 'safe house' for wanted militants, while repeatedly denying doing so in court; the latter, a mill worker, was a jailed London window-smasher. That is not to say that working women were not involved in the suffrage movement. More likely, their stories have been lost, or were never recorded, as is the fate of so many from poorer backgrounds in Scotland's story. [7].

Following a proposal by Priscilla McLaren, nine 'Grand Demonstrations' for women's votes took place in Britain's major cities. They began in Manchester's Free Trade Hall in February 1880 and were subsequently staged in London, Bristol, Birmingham, Bradford, Nottingham, Sheffield and Glasgow before finishing in Edinburgh's Synod Hall in March 1884. Glasgow Women's Suffrage Society hosted the 1882 Grand Demonstration, but the event was brought to life by members of the Edinburgh society who travelled to Glasgow in the first week of October to help to plan and fund the event. Mrs McLaren and Eliza Wigham were joined by Alice Scatcherd of Leeds who had spoken, so far, at six of the seven demonstrations. Priscilla McLaren said that it was often reported by the Press that women were not anxious for the Parliamentary franchise, "but if from 4000 to 5000 met to demand it," she did not see what argument they could turn to. She told Glasgow colleagues that the demonstration would be costly to organise, but she had pleasure handing over £117 which had been gathered in Edinburgh — equivalent to around £12,000 today and probably around a third of the event's cost. Elizabeth Pease Nichol had donated £50 of it. [8].

Glasgow's Grand Demonstration took place in St Andrew's Hall on November 3 and was announced as a celebration of the granting of the municipal franchise, as well as an opportunity to make the case for town council votes to be extended to parliamentary elections. Despite awful weather, the event attracted over 5000 women to Europe's largest arena. The hall was so full that "even the passages were crowded, and several hundred women failed to gain an entrance." Priscilla McLaren had difficulty accommodating the speakers, who included Alice Scatcherd, Lydia Becker, Jessie Craigen and the American women's rights pioneer Elizabeth Cady Stanton, making her first speech on British soil. There was also a remarkable Edinburgh presence on the conference platform – Mary Burton, Eliza Wigham, the Stevenson sisters, Eliza Kirkland, Miss Maitland, Mrs Paterson, Jessie Wellstood, the Misses Hope, Miss Hunter, Miss Walls, Miss Anderson and Miss Fraser – all from the capital. The proceedings were opened with a prayer offered by Miss Wigham. Mrs Wellstood spoke to support the key resolution. Flora Stevenson proposed the third resolution and a vote of thanks was delivered by Mary Burton. The importance of Edinburgh to the Victorian movement was there for all to see. [9].

Priscilla McLaren presided and told her audience: "Scotland has witnessed many a noble gathering in the cause of liberty, but never one nobler than the one I look upon tonight." Referring to the newly-won municipal vote, McLaren told them that she wished every woman householder in Scotland would regard voting with the same high moral sense of obligation as a "poor widow" in one of the manufacturing towns near Manchester, "who went to the polling booth and recorded her vote while her babe lay a corpse in the house." She thanked the women of Glasgow for "the warm and intelligent welcome" given to the speakers during the previous fortnight and said that "a match had been applied to the cold fire of the fight." She was given a standing ovation. [10].

Elizabeth Cady Stanton, who stayed with Mrs McLaren at Newington House, received a tumultuous welcome and referred to the great advance the movement had made in America. For local consumption, she expressed

The Royal Hotel in Princes Street was used for early meetings of the Edinburgh National Society for Women's Suffrage.

her delight that the municipal franchise had been conferred on the women of Scotland. Jessie Craigen, employed by Mrs McLaren as the demonstration's salaried co-ordinator, stole the show with a remarkable 'Braveheart' speech which ended with emotions running high and the vast audience on their feet. They were there, she said, "to stir the springs of life among the people, and to say with all our hearts that amongst them a freedom shall grow, and not decline." They were there to say that their future should be better than their past. Let them be faithful to their past, true to their future. Let them, she said, send up to the House of Commons the united voice of the women of Scotland. "Let us tell them that whatever they might do or might not do in England, to us at least, the daughters of women who dared to die for faith and liberty, the inheritors of a glorious and unconquered past, they should give the freedom that we claim." Elizabeth Cady Stanton recalled that Craigen

"fired bombshells into English policy, to which the audience responded with wild enthusiasm...all those on the platform rising and waving until their arms ached. I waved with the rest." [11].

Back in the capital, the Edinburgh National Society's annual gathering of 1882 took place, unusually, between Christmas and New Year's Day in the Freemasons' Hall. Again, its president Priscilla McLaren lambasted the absence of any reporting of the society's activities in the Press. She hoped women would not need to refuse to pay their taxes in order to open the ears of government, but this would be done if "the cries of women were not listened to." She said they had five of the Cabinet on their side and 172 Members of Parliament. She asked that women be taken out of the company of criminals and lunatics – which brought warm applause. Eliza Wigham read the report. Over 40,000 leaflets had been circulated, and their cause had the support of the Convention of Royal Burghs and 12 Scottish town councils, including Edinburgh. Elsewhere, the nomination of candidates for Edinburgh Parochial Board early in 1884 included, for the first time, two women, Phoebe Blyth and Katharine Robertson, who were proposed by two male doctors in the city. As there were no other candidates a vote was not required. The women's success was not welcomed by all, however. A solicitor member, A. E. Macknight, said he was a great admirer of the female sex, but he could not say he admired women when "they went out of their proper sphere." It appeared to him that the new parochial board members were "entirely out of their element, and neglecting their own duties, and intruding into matters that were not suitable for them." His view was not shared by those in the room. To shouts of "hear-hear," the chairman said he had "no doubts" that the women would be a "great acquisition" to the board. [12].

The ninth and final Grand Demonstration was held in Edinburgh in March 1884, filling the largest venue in the city, the United Presbyterian Synod Hall in Castle Terrace. It was advertised as the 'Scottish National Demonstration of Women' and the roll-call of speakers for the Saturday evening event was large and impressive. As well as the Edinburgh National Society leadership, it included Glasgow Suffrage Society's president Jessie Greig, Alice Scatcherd of Leeds, the founder of the Women's Franchise League, Edinburgh-born Isabella Tod of Belfast, who had established the North of Ireland Suffrage Society, Jane Cobden, daughter of the anti-Corn Law reformer Richard Cobden, who was treasurer of the NUWSS, and the pioneering feminist and pacifist Florence Balgarnie. All of them had spoken in Edinburgh before and would have been well known to ENSWS members.

Women were admitted free to any part of the hall, and men's tickets were available at 2/6d. All 2000 seats were taken, and hundreds more crammed into the adjacent Presbytery Hall. A thousand people were turned away, said *The Scotsman*: "The hall keeper reported that he had never seen such a sea of faces as met his view when he opened the doors." The presidency was given to Viscountess [Florence] Harberton, of the Central Committee of the National Society. The Irish suffragist had chaired previous Grand Demonstrations in London (1880) and Sheffield (1882). Lady Harberton's speech focused on "the logic" that taxation and representation went together; in other words, women who paid taxes should have a say in how they were spent. "Wealthy women are able to oppose the inconveniences of those laws," she added, "but poor women are crushed and oppressed and unable to take the first step – agitation – towards alteration and repeal." Introduced with a prayer from their Quaker secretary Eliza Wigham, Edinburgh's contributors spoke of the importance of demonstrating support for the inclusion of women in the 1884 Reform Bill. Flora Stevenson moved that a memorial be sent to William Gladstone asking him not to oppose the claims of women householders. A vote of thanks was given by Mary Burton, on which the audience rose and enthusiastically waved their handkerchiefs. They then joined in singing *Scots Wha Hae*, after which the Grand Demonstration broke up, having lasted three and a half hours. Local papers called it "a magnificent success." 13.

The year of 1884 also brought great hopes that an amendment adding propertied women to the Third Reform Bill would finally achieve the women's goal of parliamentary votes. In support, public meetings were held in the largest halls in the country – 15 in Edinburgh in one month alone – and in every case a vote in favour of the measure was carried. Politicians of all persuasions were pressed to declare themselves supportive, and this they did in such numbers that a clear majority of the House pledged to back the clause. Priscilla McLaren and three other national leaders wrote to Prime Minister Gladstone urging support for the bill and to receive a deputation. Gladstone's secretary responded icily, "He is afraid he must ask to be excused from acceding to your wishes." 14.

The writing was on the wall. All too predictably the amendment was talked out at the behest of the Prime Minister, who offered it "the strongest opposition in my power." Gladstone had revealed "for all to see the gulf that existed between himself and suffragists who were, in fact, predominantly Liberals." On June 10, the bill fell by 271 to 135. Among the 271 opponents were 104 Liberals who had pledged in advance to support the measure. It was a crushing and frustrating defeat, and instead of smoothing the path to electoral equality, the bill enfranchised many more men, and no women whatsoever. Another opportunity had come and gone. Time after time, women's votes were voted down or talked out amid jeers and mockery, or the discussion on a women's bill was never reached because a rambling, long-winded debate on some other measure had been deliberately allowed to soak up parliamentary time. Edinburgh's Jessie Methven summed up the women's annoyance: "One argument they used was that Parliament had no time – there were so many more pressing and important questions to deal with. Yet how often have we noticed that Parliament has adjourned after having sat only a few hours because there was no more business on hand?" 15.

The 1884 rejection was a serious reversal felt deeply by the whole movement, notably in Scotland where Teresa Billington recorded the huge anticipation ahead of the bill: "Crowded meetings were held, great petitions were circulated, constant propaganda was carried on by tongue and pen, so that by 1884, the year of promise, the Scottish movement was widespread and uplifted with the hope of victory." Instead, she looked back on 1884 as

"the year of disillusionment," a time in which the hoped-for advance was destroyed by the broken promises of the duplicitous MPs who had turned victory into defeat. The chicanery broke the spirit of suffragists. For the next 20 years the movement north of the border was "practically dead," she recalled. It was robbed of its energy and life. Yet she did not despair: "In Scotland the women's suffrage movement will not be marked by sudden paroxysms of growth; it will not rend up any sky-rockets of protest to illumine the sky and startle the world for a moment, but it will none the less grow and live and become potent with rebellion. For the cause of political liberty is dear to Scottish hearts." 16.

Millicent Fawcett likened the setback to "throwing the women overboard," but the movement chose to fight on. In Edinburgh, that meant persuading Liberal politicians when the opportunity arose. In September 1882 a visit by Sir Stafford Northcote, the Chancellor of the Exchequer in the previous Conservative government, presented a decent target, but he declined to pledge himself to any cause. Northcote was a guest at Hopetoun House, where he viewed the construction of the Forth Bridge, and when he arrived in the city centre to visit the Midlothian Conservative Association in Princes Street, he was met by two deputations of women and questioned again about his views on the franchise. The Edinburgh Society had prepared a memorial for him, signed by president Priscilla McLaren and joint-secretaries Eliza Wigham and Eliza Kirkland: "The injustice of the exclusion of women from the franchise is more keenly felt at the present crisis when it is proposed so largely to extend the electoral franchise to men." Dr Sophia Jex-Blake then presented Sir Stafford with a memorial signed by 314 women householders in Edinburgh and Midlothian. This stated that while they had paid their full share of tax and obeyed the country's laws, they were excluded from playing a part in the choice of those who enacted them. It also questioned the extension of the franchise to two million more male electors, "while those who are entitled to vote under the present property qualifications are still to remain disfranchised if they happen to be women." Neither memorial drew a response from Northcote, who continued to sit on the fence. 17.

The 17th annual meeting of the ENSWS took place in December 1884 in the Bible Society rooms. There was a large attendance. Jessie Wellstood, whose husband was the iron stove manufacturer and former town councillor Stephen Wellstood, stood in for Priscilla McLaren. The Liberal MP Walter McLaren, youngest son of Duncan and Priscilla, said that he considered women were now in a worse position than before, being placed on a lower level than agricultural labourers by the recent Act. He strongly pressed women householders to refuse to pay taxes until they got votes. To this, surprisingly, came murmurs of "No, no." He further urged that the women of Edinburgh should do what the men did with the one-time annuity tax, which they had refused to pay. Again, the response was shouts of "No, never." The omens were present elsewhere, but there were few signs of militancy in the venerable Edinburgh National Society. 18.

What made more of a dent in the news was a swing towards women's suffrage by Liberal and Conservative support groups. At a meeting of the 500-strong Edinburgh North Conservative Association at McLaren Academy in Hamilton Place, the lawyer James Bruce proposed pestering Conservative leaders to take steps to secure voting rights for qualified unmarried women. He faced opposition from other members, one of whom said the enfranchisement of women formed "no part of the programme of the Conservative party." Bruce's motion was carried. Over the seven years from 1885, the annual conferences of the Conservative Associations of Scotland voted to franchise women in 1887, 1890 and 1892. Conservative women also belonged to the Primrose League, founded in 1883 and taking its name from Benjamin Disraeli's favourite flower. In 1885 it formed a Ladies' Grand Council, becoming the first political organisation to give women the same status and responsibilities as men. By the mid-1880s the League had a membership in Scotland exceeding 20,000 and, in 1886, its Edinburgh branch voted to petition Lord Salisbury, the Prime Minister, to make women's votes a parliamentary measure. 19.

Supporters of the Liberal Party, meanwhile, founded the Women's Liberal Association in 1881 and, in the second half of 1885, moved towards the formation of a country-wide Women's Liberal Federation under Catherine Gladstone, whose husband was the party leader. From 1890, its annual meeting passed successive resolutions for women's suffrage. The Edinburgh Women's Liberal Association was formed in 1888, with many members of the Edinburgh National Society prominent, including Priscilla McLaren, Eliza Wigham, the Stevenson sisters, S. E. S. Mair and Mary Burton. Where Liberal Party women always had a 'little internal difficulty' was in their support of election candidates while the Liberal government itself was refusing to speak to its deputations, stalling progress and killing off bills. As the English suffragist Helen Blackburn put it, Liberal suffragists were helping men into power, who would then use that power to deny them votes. 20.

The political bombshell of 1885 was William Gladstone's shock removal from Downing Street. Benjamin Disraeli's death in 1881 had led to the emergence of Lord Salisbury (Robert Cecil) as the Conservative leader in the House of Lords, with Sir Stafford Northcote leading the party in the Commons. When Gladstone came out in favour of Home Rule for Ireland, Salisbury opposed him and formed an alliance with the breakaway Liberal Unionists, winning the June 1885 general election and succeeding Gladstone as Prime Minister. There were now 70 constituencies in Scotland and all were contested. The country's electorate had increased from 293,581 to 560,580 as a result of the 1884 Franchise Act, all men of course. The Liberal Party was again the dominant party with 51 seats, but its structure had fractured. Seven of its MPs had stood successfully as Independent Liberals, including in three of Edinburgh's four constituencies.

The 18th annual meeting of the ENSWS was held in the Royal Hotel with Mary Burton presiding. When the Lord Provost intimated that he could not attend as he felt it inconsistent with his position to take part in a "political meeting," Burton told the membership that his excuse "was very lame." He might as well say that a temperance meeting was a political meeting.

The report for the previous year was read, as usual, by Eliza Wigham. Her co-secretary Eliza Kirkland had visited 26 towns in the north of Scotland and had held interviews with 10 parliamentary candidates. Miss Wigham referred to the passing of the Franchise Act and reminded members that 800,000 qualified British women had been ignored once again. This point was taken up across the women's movement. Gladstone's 1884 Reform Act extended the 1867 legislation only to include more males. Three million men were eligible to vote in the 1880 general election. Five and a half million could vote in the 1885 election. All women and 40% of men were still without the vote. If women householders had been added, the electorate of Edinburgh would have increased from 30,000 to 38,000. 21.

ENSWS members busied themselves writing dozens of letters imploring town councils to change the situation. The response was mixed. Although many councils voted unanimously for women's votes, some swithered, while others rejected the notion out of hand. Eliza Kirkland's letter to Arbroath Town Council brought a comment from a Bailie McWattie that, "women should be better employed darning stockings." The council voted to take no action. At Hawick, Councillor Caldwell said he believed the "experiment" of allowing women to vote in municipal and school boards "had not been successful." Approval for support scraped through by six votes to five. When Perth Town Council discussed its letter, a Councillor Cowan considered "the ladies were well looked after already." His motion that they "should leave this business of women alone" was supported by 15 of the 20 councillors. The Convention of Royal Burghs was more enlightened. When it met in April 1886, a motion to extend the franchise by Councillor Pollard of Edinburgh was unanimously adopted – this despite Bailie Nicoll of Dundee suggesting that a bill to find women husbands "would be more acceptable." 22.

The sudden death of Duncan McLaren in April 1886 turned thoughts away from society activities. The popular MP had served Edinburgh for half a century, starting with a High Street shop opposite St Giles in 1824, becoming a town councillor, then Edinburgh Lord Provost in 1851 before topping the poll as one of the city's two MPs in 1865. His huge funeral procession passed through the city centre to St Giles Cathedral. Shops in Clerk Street, South Bridge and High Street closed out of respect. After the service, the procession walked, via the Mound and Princes Street, to St Cuthbert's, where he was laid to rest in front of the massed ranks of women who stood in silence in support of their bereaved president and to remember their crusading founding member and friend.

Later in the year the Edinburgh National Society welcomed Millicent Garrett Fawcett to its 19th annual meeting at Queen Street Hall. Mrs Fawcett addressed the members at considerable length. She acknowledged it was now nearly 20 years since the movement began. Despite "repeating again and again the straightforward, reasonable claim" that women who possessed the qualifications should be admitted to the franchise, she confessed she had great difficulty in understanding how it was that more progress had not been made. But she added that she had talked to an old lady who remembered the time when no woman in the Church of Scotland had any voice in its affairs, and when there were no woman teachers in the Sunday schools. She acknowledged that progress was slow and was far too often stalled, but she believed that women were making headway.

Eliza Wigham covered events for 1885 and stated that the number of MPs in favour of women's suffrage was 343, of whom 167 were Conservatives, 101 were Liberals, 32 were Liberal Unionists and 43 were Nationalists. Out of 82 town councils asked to petition in favour of a bill, only a disappointing 24 had done so. The meeting discussed opportunities which might arise from Queen Victoria's Golden Jubilee the following year. All agreed it would be widely recognised as "a most favourable time for women householders to be admitted to the rights of citizenship." A London Society visitor, Laura Ormiston Chant, remarked that she hoped "some day to see a lady Chancellor of the Exchequer" – a position not filled by a woman for another 138 years. [23].

When the Jubilee followed in 1887 the Edinburgh National Society contributed to a joint address by Britain's principal suffrage societies.

Millicent Fawcett, pictured in 1892. She would become the president of the largest British organisation for votes for women, the National Union of Women's Suffrage Societies.

It offered the Queen congratulations on her 50th year, charted important advances for women during her monarchy and included an undisguised appeal for support: "Your Majesty has been graciously pleased to assent to Acts which have restored and confirmed to women ratepayers the exercise of the municipal franchise in England and Scotland, and to the Elementary Education Acts. During your Majesty's reign two measures have been passed relating to the representation of the people, whereby...your Majesty's own sex are still denied the rights of citizenship and the privileges of free and constitutional government. The bright example of your Majesty in the discharge of the highest political function known to the State is an irrefragable proof that the most arduous political functions are not incompatible with happiness of domestic life and the highest graces of womanly character." There is no record of a reply to the joint memorial. 24.

It was not lost on suffrage supporters that 1887 also marked the 20th anniversary of John Stuart Mill's attempt to secure electoral equality for women. It meant, too, that some of the Edinburgh National Society had reached an equivalent milestone. Eliza Wigham, now 67, had spent the entire period as the society's secretary. In January 1887, Priscilla McLaren presented her with a cheque for the astonishing sum of 800 guineas – £840, or around £100,000 at today's values. It was not uncommon for men who had devoted themselves to public work to receive sizeable gestures of appreciation, but the society believed it to be the first instance on record of a testimonial of such value being given to a woman. 25.

The new year of 1888 found Priscilla McLaren again taking issue with the lack of coverage in local newspapers – as well as with what was actually printed in them. From her home, Newington House, she berated *The Scotsman* for claiming that the suffrage movement had selfishly neglected working women. She fired back: "Women have never received justice in your columns except once, when John Stuart Mill introduced the question of women's suffrage. Since then, for nearly 20 years, it has been too much the policy of your paper to ignore the question." If the Edinburgh paper had covered franchise meetings and speeches, added Mrs McLaren, it would have found, "the wretchedly poor remuneration which sempstresses receive for their long and weary work, and the evils of the 'sweating system', have been a frequent topic." She ended with a plea for fairness from the paper. "It is not from any selfish anxiety for prominence that women have for the last 20 years claimed to be made citizens of their country. They ask for political powers to increase their influence in righting wrongs wherever these exist, and they would be grateful for the aid of your powerful paper in advocating the cause they have so much at heart." To be fair, *The Scotsman*, *Edinburgh Evening News* and *Edinburgh Weekly Despatch* reported most ENSWS meetings, though editorial comment and wider analysis of the women's campaign was poor overall. 26.

In a speech to the Primrose League in Edinburgh on St Andrew's Day 1888, and completely out of the blue, the Conservative Prime Minister Lord Salisbury announced that he supported votes for women. "Do not imagine I am speaking for anybody else. But, speaking for myself only, I earnestly hope that the day is not far distant when women also will bear their share in voting for members in the political world and in determining the policy of the country. I can conceive no argument by which they are excluded." So emphatic a statement from the Prime Minister offered the strongest possible encouragement to the women's movement and Salisbury's speech was reported widely and enthusiastically by Britain's suffrage societies.

The *Women's Suffrage Gazette* immediately wrote to members of the Cabinet to ask for their opinion on the Edinburgh statement. By the next issue, they had two replies; firstly from the office of the Chancellor of the Exchequer: "Sir, in reply to your letter of yesterday's date I am desired by Lord Randolph Churchill to inform you that he has always been opposed to the extension of the Parliamentary suffrage to women." And secondly from the Secretary for Scotland: "Dear Sir, I entirely endorse everything the Prime Minister has uttered upon this subject, and I have nothing to add to it. Arthur James Balfour." 27.

So the decade was ending with some hope. And if the 500 members of the

Edinburgh National Society were looking for an appropriate Christmas gift, they might have headed to the capital's bookstalls; advertised for sale was *The Life and Work of Duncan McLaren,* in two volumes, by J. B. Mackie.

References
1. Roger Fulford, Votes for Women (1958), p71.
2. Glasgow Herald, 24 January 1880; Edinburgh Evening News, 16 February 1880.
3. Scotsman, 24 January 1880; Laura Mayhall, The Militant Suffrage Movement (2003), p18.
4. Edinburgh Evening News, 3 June 1880.
5. Edinburgh Evening News, 4 March 1881; Dundee Courier, 31 December 1881.
6. The Scotsman, 4 March 1882.
7. Norman Watson, Glasgow's Suffragettes (2023), p68. See Dundee's Suffragettes (2018), by the author, for further details on Annie Cuthbert and Ann Shanks.
8. Elizabeth Crawford, The Women's Suffrage Movement (1999), p619; Edinburgh Evening News, 4 October 1882.
9. Watson, Glasgow's Suffragettes (2023), pp12-13.
10. Leah Leneman, The Scottish Suffragettes (2000), p22.
11. Watson, Glasgow's Suffragettes (2023), p13.
12. Glasgow Herald, 29 December 1882; Portadown News, 9 February 1884.
13. Leah Leneman, A Guid Cause (1991), p27; Edinburgh Evening News, 24 March 1884; Kirkcaldy Times, 26 March 1884.
14. Joyce Marlow, Suffragettes: The Fight for Votes for Women (2015), p23.
15. David Morgan, Suffragettes and Liberals (1975), p13; Millicent Fawcett, What I Remember (1924), p28; The Suffragette, 17 January 1913.
16. Scotland and the Women's Suffrage Movement, by Teresa Billington-Greig, in The Queen, 12 September 1908; Paula Bartley, Votes for Women (1998), p12.
17. Edinburgh Evening News, 18 September 1884.
18. Idem, 27 December 1884.
19. Elizabeth Crawford, The Women's Suffrage Movement in Britain and Ireland: A Regional Survey (2006), p233; Leneman (1991), p33; Edinburgh Evening News, 14 April 1885.
20. Crawford (1999), p724; Leneman (1991), p34.
21. Aberdeen Evening Express, 5 December 1885; Scotsman, 26 December 1885.
22. Edinburgh Evening News, 16 March and 6 & 7 April 1886.
23. Glasgow Herald, 29 November 1886; The Scotsman, 29 November 1886; Leneman (1991), p32.
24. Northern Whig, 24 June 1887.
25. The Suffrage Journal, 15 January 1887.
26. The Scotsman, 24 April 1888.
27. The Queen, 8 December 1888; Campbeltown Courier, 15 December 1888.

Priscilla Bright McLaren, who was unhappy over a number of years with local reporting of the women's campaign.

By the end of the 19th century suffragists were beginning to speak in public.

THREE:
SPATS AND SQUABBLES 1890-1899

"Some of us can never forget with what difficulty we made our way from those halls intercepted as we were by the outstretched hands of hundreds of grateful women who had drunk in our words, which, they were fain to believe, promised a brighter future to women..."

Priscilla Bright McLaren, president of the Edinburgh National Society for Women's Suffrage, December 1890   1.

The Edinburgh National Society's first public meeting of 1890 filled the Wesleyan Methodist Church Hall in Nicolson Square. Despite the freshness of an incoming decade and a new venue, it was two experienced, dependable campaigners who took the floor to highlight widely-perceived political inconsistencies. Eliza Wigham raised the position of women now being allowed to vote in all local elections, while facing the "absurd" situation of being excluded from the parliamentary franchise. Mary Burton then told members that those who paid taxes should have the vote irrespective of sex, as that "had always been the basis of British representation." Priscilla McLaren and the Misses Burton and Wigham agreed to write again to the Liberal leader William Gladstone on these points. And yet, Gladstone, speaking in Edinburgh's Music Hall the following month, highlighted why the Cabinet had perhaps failed to act on women's suffrage. He said it was just one of seven major issues confronting the government. He listed temperance, the Eight Hours Bill for the working day, Disestablishment of the church, Home Rule for Scotland, agricultural allotments legislation – and women's suffrage. But the biggest problem of all, he said, was Home Rule for Ireland, and none of the others could be dealt with until "the Irish question" was out of the way. Gladstone's First Home Rule Bill of 1886 had been defeated in the Commons after a split in his own Liberal Party.

At the time of his visit to Edinburgh in 1890, he was considering a second bill for its self-government. Meantime, Irish home rule, or the lack of it, filled more newspaper columns than any other issue as the new century approached. 2.

In February 1890, the Edinburgh Women's Liberal Association was formally inaugurated at a meeting at the Oddfellows' Hall in Forrest Road. As expected, many members of the city's suffrage society were also present. It cannot be said, however, that the new association hit the ground running. When the names of the office-bearers were discussed, and a Mrs Katherine Childers – the wife of a former Edinburgh Liberal MP and Home Secretary – was proposed as president, Flora Stevenson piped up that she did not think she was much in sympathy with women's suffrage and moved that her name be removed. The debate that followed considered whether the new body was solely a Liberal Party organisation, or whether it should have a wider remit to support and promote women's rights. The association's secretary Ada Lang Todd, who was also on the ENSWS committee, defended the proposed arrangement and Katherine Childers was duly appointed president. Even with high-level Liberalism running through her family, Priscilla McLaren prickled at the decision: "Let every woman's association, of whatever party, if they seek to be a power in the State, make the possession of the franchise their first aim." She was

Ishbel, Countess of Aberdeen. (Courtesy of McCord Museum)

supported by another ENSWS member, Mary Gillies of Chirnside, who took a verbal swing at the Edinburgh Women Liberals: "To belong to this association or that, a Primrose League on the one hand or a Women's Liberal Association on the other, seems only a means of weakening and dispersing the power which should be centred on the one main object – obtaining the vote. If only the very large army of women who belong to the two great rival associations would step out of their ranks, and forgetting party interests for a time, would agree to unite for the cause of their sex, our victory would be assured. Let us have one aim, one purpose, one idea..." Gillies was pressing for a position whereby participation in the political arena would be a means to an exclusive, unequivocal end – votes for women. It was entirely the founding principle adopted in 1903 by Emmeline Pankhurst's Women's Social and Political Union. [3]

The suffrage-or-party question was raised at Liberal Party gatherings across the country. There were unmistakable signs of disquietude and a growing number of resolutions in favour of women's suffrage, or boiled down, treating men and women equally. Many were passed against the advice of office-bearers, who argued that the primary, if not the only, object of their organisation was to advance the electoral interests of the Liberal Party. Increasingly, women party workers, while remaining in sympathy with Liberal values, saw the franchise as the main goal and wished to be regarded as more than mere auxiliaries in any electoral work undertaken. When Catherine Gladstone was presented with an address by the Liberal women of Scotland there were audible grumblings in the Edinburgh audience when women's suffrage was not brought up in front of the party leader's wife.

In days following, support emerged from the unlikeliest quarter. Ishbel, Countess of Aberdeen, the head of the Scottish Women's Liberal Association and sister to the Liberal Chief Whip Edward Marjoribanks, surprised an audience in Glasgow by stating that women's suffrage was "the central and most important object to be arrived at." She said she was "heart and soul with reformers like Priscilla Bright McLaren." Predictably, Mrs McLaren welcomed Lady Aberdeen's revelation and added, "If all the members of that Association will follow their noble president's example, other associations will quickly follow, and we may hope the time for the political equality of men and women will not be so far distant as Lady Aberdeen anticipates." 4.

If Lady Aberdeen's statement came as a surprise, it was nothing to the shock which then rattled the ENSWS membership to the core. In an interview with *The Scotsman*, Mary Burton, a Liberal all her adult life, attributed "full credit" for women's advances not to the ENSWS or the wider women's movement, but entirely to the Countess of Aberdeen and women Liberals. The paper reported: "She said Lady Aberdeen came last year, and with her magic wand at once lifted women on to the political platform. Lady Aberdeen had changed the sphere of women and now political women were cropping up like mushrooms." Priscilla McLaren bristled, but did not want to tread on toes, and certainly not on Mary Burton's. In a letter to the same paper she paid tribute to her elderly friend's many achievements: "We all owe Mary Burton a deep sense of gratitude for her multitudinous labours in every good cause. Many of us have long admired her intellectual power, her woman's tenderness and her great moral courage." A 'but' was coming... "But the women, amongst whom she was one, who raised their sex to the political platform during those long and toilsome years, performed their work without the aid of party feeling. They have secured much for their sex; and neither political party, Liberal or Conservative, would have thought of bringing women out for party purposes had they not proved already how powerfully they could work in the political field." The Edinburgh Society president added that Miss Burton, "under calmer circumstances," could not have forgotten the innumerable petitions sent to Parliament, the countless public meetings held, and "those overwhelming demonstrations in so many of our large cities, where from 3000 to 6000 women have been often gathered together in the largest halls that could be obtained, with overflow meetings – all got up by women, addressed only by women, in favour of women's suffrage." She reminded Mary Burton that, "some of us can never forget with what difficulty we made our way from those halls intercepted as we were by the outstretched hands of hundreds of grateful women who had drunk in our words, which,

they were fain to believe, promised a brighter future to women." Mrs McLaren ended her gentle scolding by asking her friend if any Liberal Party meeting could compare "for a moment" with the Great Demonstration in Edinburgh in 1884, "when even the passages were crowded, and there was an overflow meeting besides, and hundreds went away unable to be admitted." 5.

Mary Burton demanded a right of reply, and there was no backing down. She insisted that the Victorian campaign had stalled, only to be revived by agitation from women Liberals: "Well do I remember the great meetings of women in Glasgow, Edinburgh, and elsewhere, and the superhuman work which a small band of earnest women did to bring together such a mass of women. It is six years ago now, and during all that time these thousands of women, although responding at the time, seemed to drop back again into passiveness, and the devoted band of women headed by Mrs McLaren felt that after all their labour the franchise for which they had worked was still in the far distance." It was when Lady Aberdeen spoke that Burton felt that women's political position "was gained." And, she added, "What has been the result of these political meetings for women? This, that a great many more thousands of women have been enrolled in political associations of various shades than ever could be got together by the women's franchise association. I quite agree with Mrs McLaren that the women's franchise movement has done much for women. In fact, it has got them everything except that one thing they asked for – and now political women are gaining that for them." 6.

One is left to wonder what the wider Edinburgh membership thought of this rift, and its public airing. Mary Burton's view, later espoused by Millicent Fawcett as she led Britain's largest law-abiding suffrage organisation, the NUWSS, was that the vote would be won by chipping away at political influencers, whether they were party leaders, MPs or senior figures. Mrs McLaren's more radical view, later championed by the Pankhursts, was that no government or political party should be supported if it did not legislate for women's votes. All should be viewed as opponents. This debate would continue into the new century ahead. As for *The Scotsman*, in the spring of 1891 its editorial decisively came out in support of women's votes. The paper blamed both Conservatives and Liberals for bringing women into politics for their own purposes, without giving them responsibility. Therefore, it concluded, "We are desirous that the suffrage should be extended to women. They enjoy the vote in the case of the Municipal and Parochial Board elections, and there is no reason why they should not have a vote in Parliamentary elections." Doubtless Priscilla McLaren spluttered into her porridge on reading her local paper's long-awaited recognition of women's rights. [7]

Not every reader approved or agreed. Nina Matheson emerged at this time as a powerful opponent. In April 1891 she wrote to *The Scotsman* "deploring" what Lady Aberdeen had said in Glasgow. She took exception to suffrage leaders giving the impression that they spoke on behalf of all women as their "accepted representatives." On the contrary, Matheson claimed that if the country "went to the polls tomorrow" a large majority of women would oppose gaining the franchise. "I can count on my fingers those who are advocates of this measure, and perhaps if the 'political women' realised in how many homes their public appearances and performances are regarded with distrust and dislike, they would be less ready to assume their favourite role and pose as the champions and mouthpieces of their quieter sisters." Of course, counter-blasting letters winged their way to *The Scotsman's* news desk. But fair play to the paper. It allowed Nina Matheson to promote her opposition in its columns, where she continued to accuse suffragists of abandoning their "legitimate sphere," as she wrote on 5 May 1891: "How many homes are neglected in the present day whilst the mistress is running from this meeting to that, from one platform to proclaim her 'wrongs' to another to proclaim her 'rights'." [8]

Nina Matheson's letters carried her name and gave her address as 'Edinburgh'. More often, those criticising the women's movement enjoyed anonymity. In her study of Scottish newspapers, Sarah Pedersen noted for the Edwardian period: "Correspondents could choose to be published under a pen name, as long as their name and addresses were made known to the editor...many letter writers on the women's suffrage issue made use of this

facility." One Edinburgh correspondent, signing himself 'G. A. S.', used language unacceptable to the modern reader as he hid behind the camouflage of his initials: "To grant Woman's Suffrage would be to impose upon women duties and responsibilities which they are quite incapable of undertaking; and which are far beyond the mental grasping power of their brains...those who are the mere scum of the sex can no more be taken as indicative of the ability of women than a penny box of soldiers can be taken as indicative of the capability of the Duke of Wellington's forces at the battle of Waterloo. These women who present before the Edinburgh public are mere moths fluttering around the candle of vain glory. To maintain that these women are the equals of men is about as rational and accurate as to say that two and two make five." Offensive, nasty language like this was unusual. Negative comments were generally restricted to placing women as managers of the household, or arguing that they were too 'impulsive' or 'emotional' or 'too weak' to engage with the political process. Nina Matheson waived her right to anonymity and was something of a lone named female anti-suffrage voice at this time, but she used decent language and her arguments would have found many nodding in agreement. Victorian anti-suffragists were mostly drawn from the restrained aristocracy and had not yet organised into the purposeful groups that would emerge in the Edwardian era, particularly when militancy required a balancing voice. [9]

The campaign was boosted in 1892 by new possibilities in the House of Commons. In April, a private member's bill was introduced by Albert Rollit, the Conservative MP for South Islington and third husband of Mary, dowager Countess of Sutherland. Rollit's Parliamentary Franchise (Extension to Women) Bill received its second reading towards the end of the month, and, for the first time in many years, it avoided being subsumed by other business. Despite government protestations a debate was allowed, and a vote took place. To surprise, it failed by only 23 votes, the division being 175 against 152. Rollit's bill was extraordinary in another respect. While gathering support at a women's suffrage meeting in St James's Hall, suffragists had what appears to have been their first face-to-face punch-up. Although unrecorded in the suffrage canon, the *London Evening Standard* called it "a free fight amongst the leading spirits of the party," and described the altercation as between those who supported Rollit's bill and "others who were bitterly opposed to it as a half-hearted measure embodying an evil principle they were sworn to combat." The *London Globe* called it a "riot." Certainly, the meeting ended in chaos – though it was mostly men who were left battered and bruised. Perhaps Priscilla McLaren would have enjoyed reading about the fate of the Press – "The reporters' table, at which some 15 or 20 journalists were seated, collapsed under the rush. Coats, hats and notebooks were trampled underfoot." 10.

The Edinburgh National Society's own wounds showed little sign of healing. In April 1892, Mary Burton made public a letter she had written to William Gladstone, the Liberal MP for Midlothian and then Leader of the Opposition. Miss Burton praised his "relaxed attitude" to women's suffrage and pledged her trust in him: "I for one am jubilant, feeling certain that you who have risked and borne so much to give to the Irish what they ask for, will give also to women what they ask. And why am I so jubilant? Because I know that the mass of women are in favour of their enfranchisement. We have now a valiant army of women willing and able to help you in the Liberal cause. And don't be afraid that we women will not be Liberals."

Once again, the linking of women's votes to the Liberal Party did not sit well at Newington House. Priscilla McLaren's response left no-one in doubt that the ENSWS – Mary Burton included – should not take sides: "We must have a political existence higher than mere service...I hope no woman will work for any candidate in Edinburgh or elsewhere who is not earnestly in favour of giving the suffrage to women." Mrs McLaren had influential friends. At the next meeting of the Edinburgh Women's Liberal Association, Louisa Stevenson tendered her resignation from the committee as she felt that had she remained, she would have been "fighting with one hand tied behind my back." 11.

The summer of 1892 was dominated by another general election. It was held in July and the Conservatives, led by Lord Salisbury, won a majority of seats. But when a vote of confidence went against him, Salisbury resigned. In his place, William Gladstone became Prime Minister for the fourth time, leading

William Ewart Gladstone.

Millicent Fawcett.

a minority government dependent on Irish Nationalist support. Mary Burton must have savoured the moment. Three of the Edinburgh constituencies were won by Liberal candidates, among them William McEwan of brewing fame. The fourth went to the Liberal Unionist Viscount Wolmer. Elsewhere, 1892 marked Keir Hardie's arrival in Parliament as a Scottish Labour MP.

Early in 1893 Millicent Fawcett arrived to speak to the Edinburgh Women Liberals. Fawcett was the acknowledged leader of the Victorian suffrage movement and had just been made president of a Special Committee created by the principal societies to collect signatures for 'An Appeal from Women of All Parties and All Classes' to be forwarded to Parliament. The women believed that no government could refuse such an all-inclusive petition representing more than half of the country's population. Among its national committee were some familiar faces – Eliza Wigham, Jessie Methven, the Stevenson sisters, Charlotte Carmichael Stopes and Priscilla McLaren – all from Edinburgh. Speaking in the Scottish capital Mrs Fawcett congratulated the Liberals on their electoral victory, but said that the women expected to work for the party to achieve such victories, "were placed in a very anomalous and ridiculous position, for while they were invited to give political work they were held to be unworthy of exercising a political vote." It was a timely reminder to Edinburgh's Liberals – including Mary Burton – to pick a side. 12.

At its annual meeting in Newington House, and once Eliza Wigham's usual report was done and dusted, Mrs McLaren told Edinburgh members that the Premier's hostility to the movement was "stimulating" support for the cause. "Even Mr Gladstone's wonderful and exalted intellect was not free from cobwebs," she joked. The 1893 report stated that Edinburgh had eight women managers on Parochial Boards. McLaren added, "We much regret that no other Scotch parishes have women managers, for there can scarcely be a more important or legitimate work for women than to care for the poor." Louisa Stevenson noted that women were now being admitted to the arts classes at Edinburgh University. Mary Lees spoke on temperance, Sarah Siddons Mair on the necessity for the vote and Dora Foster on working women.

Jessie Methven, of Great King Street, replaced Frances Simson as treasurer.

A separate committee for the Women's Suffrage Appeal was established in Scotland, with Ishbel, Lady Aberdeen as president (although she would resign early in 1894 on her husband being appointed Governor General of Canada). Special appeal books were prepared for signing and circulated around the country. Charlotte Stopes arranged the Edinburgh distribution and her organisers met at the West End Café in Princes Street. The deadline for the appeal was 31 January 1894 and by then 48,879 signatures had been collected in Scotland. Of these 16,902 were obtained in Edinburgh, roughly a third of the total. The number of signatures received across Britain at the deadline was 248,674. By the time the petition was accepted by Parliament, as far distant as 1896 due to procedural difficulties, it contained 257,796 names, 51,270 from Scotland. 13.

Meanwhile, the ENSWS continued to pile pressure on the Women Liberals to back only candidates who supported women's votes. In April 1895 the Scottish Women's Liberal Association reaffirmed its support for the franchise, but refused again to accept a resolution, proposed by the Edinburgh branch, that no woman should work at election time for a Liberal candidate who had not pledged to vote for an extension of the franchise. The issue did not go away; an unattributed front-page *Scotsman* advert on July 15 read: 'Women – Work for candidates who are in favour of Women's Suffrage'.

On 8 September 1895, Priscilla McLaren celebrated her 80th birthday. She was blessed with good health and remained the active president of the Edinburgh Society. Numerous congratulations and gifts came her way, as well as an illuminated address on parchment, bound in red leather, lined with silk and signed by the 28 office bearers of the society: "To our beloved and honoured President, Priscilla Bright McLaren – Will you permit us to take the opportunity of your birthday to offer to you our most affectionate greetings? We are very thankful you have been spared to us for eighty years, and that for a large portion of those years we have had the privilege of a close association with you... and of your wise counsels for the advancement of women in all departments. In many of these you have seen marvellous progress, and, while we would gladly

have the accomplishment of your wishes in the attainment of women's suffrage, we cannot doubt that this culminating point of justice will shortly be accorded to the women of Great Britain...We crave that the retrospect of the homes you have brightened, the hearts you have cheered, the cares you have uplifted, the woes you have solaced, the faith you have strengthened, and the love you have elicited, may give you joy in your declining days, and that you may realise the full radiance of the light at eventide, and God's own smile for ever and for ever." 14.

A lifelong supporter of women's rights, and pioneer of electoral reform, Priscilla McLaren was connected to feminist leading lights by family or friendship and it was she who first suggested holding 'At Home' meetings to embrace women who would not otherwise attend public events. She pioneered discussions on models of female citizenship and also suggested, helped to organise and led the Great Demonstrations of women which filled the largest halls of Britain in the early 1880s. She presided over the first of them in 1880 in front of 6000 women in Manchester, and at the Bradford event two years later and at both National Demonstrations in Scotland. Her speeches showed that she possessed much of the eloquence which distinguished both of her brothers, John and Jacob Bright. She had watched two of her sons, Charles and Walter, introduce women's suffrage bills in the House of Commons. And she had presided over the Edinburgh National Society from the moment it was created in 1867 to the day 28 years later that marked her 80th year.

Further celebrations took place the following year when a deputation from the ENSWS visited Raeburn Place to present Eliza Scott Kirkland with an illustrated address on her retiral from the office of honorary secretary after 20 years of service. Miss Kirkland had to relinquish the post due to ill health. The memorial was completed on vellum by Emily Paterson and signed by the committee. And, at the age of 77, Mary Burton, Edinburgh's best-known social reformer, was appointed to the St Cuthbert's Parish Council. She had spent several years by then on Edinburgh School Board and St Cuthbert's Parochial Board. To hold three important municipal appointments at this time, in addition to committee duties with the ENSWS, was a remarkable achievement and speaks volumes

Priscilla Bright McLaren, in later life.

of her useful and unselfish life. Few Edinburgh women, before or since, have worked harder for the public good.

Mary Burton had another string to her bow. She lived in a whitewashed cottage below Arthur's Seat where she recalled being inspired by her mother – "a very intellectual woman" – and after reading works by the feminist philosopher and women's rights advocate Mary Wollstonecraft. In the mid-1880s she began what might today be termed a social experiment. In Bell's Wynd, an ancient close leading from the High Street to the Cowgate, she purchased a tenement and became a 'slum landlord.' The property was seven storeys high, with a winding stone stair. Each level had four one-roomed houses which she let at from 9d to 1s 9d per week. Looking back in 1896, she recalled: "Soon after I took possession, a mother and daughter in the fourth storey had a drunken quarrel, and the daughter threw herself out of the window and was killed on the spot. In another house a drunken woman attempted to do the same thing, but I dragged her in from the window. In those days I sometimes had in one flat four such families as these – one a ticket-of-leave woman [out on parole], another with the mother in prison, another the father just out of prison, and in the fourth a husband newly convicted of a drunken assault. It soon became known that drunken, disorderly and dirty tenants would not be allowed to remain in the tenement and, as I made the place comfortable, I found that unsatisfactory tenants would reform rather than leave."

By the time of this interview, conducted with the English journalist and biographer Sarah Anne Tooley, Mary Burton had been forced by the council to sell the Bell's Wynd property, but still had around 50 families as tenants in other buildings in the Cowgate and Canongate. She was truly a pioneer in many ways. 15.

A well-filled Queen Street Hall witnessed an unusual scene in November 1896. An otherwise routine annual meeting of the Edinburgh National Society had begun with Louisa Stevenson deputising for Priscilla McLaren, who was indisposed. When hands were raised to propose and second Eliza Wigham's report, a young man in the gallery asked to move an amendment. On being told that this could be done only from the platform, he moved to the top table to propose that all women – not only those who paid rates, but all women – should be entitled to vote. This drew prolonged applause. Then, to surprise in the hall, the amendment was seconded by another young man, who told the audience that the franchise, as he understood it, ought to be given to all adult men and women. Walter McLaren gently explained that all resolutions asked that women should be treated in the same way as men. Not everyone rejoiced in such unanimity. Arch-critic Nina Matheson dashed off a letter to *The Scotsman* to complain that the women who had gathered in the Queen Street Hall had forgotten "one very important fact; that women generally do not desire the franchise." The plain truth, as Nina Matheson saw it, was that the women who "thrust themselves forcibly before the public have, by their intemperate remarks, hysterical indignations, and very great ignorance of the real state of affairs, injured the very measures they so violently advocate." 16.

Parliamentary business filled the final weeks of 1896. With a new women's suffrage bill progressing through its early stages, the five principal women's suffrage societies appointed a joint sub-committee to co-ordinate propaganda work in the House of Commons. Edinburgh was represented by Louisa Stevenson and Jessie Methven. Early in 1897 the ENSWS wrote to all Scottish MPs to remind them "to be in their places" to support the bill. When it reached the floor of the House on February 4, the Ladies' Gallery – or 'Cage' as it was scornfully known by the women – was completely filled, and dozens of female sympathisers packed the outer lobby. *The Scotsman* noted gleefully that if an MP passed across St Stephen's Hall, "he had to walk through a lane of petticoats."

The second reading of the Parliamentary Franchise (Extension to Women) Bill was presented to the Commons by the Glasgow solicitor and Conservative backbencher Ferdinand Faithful- Begg. It was calculated that it would enfranchise around half a million women. The result of the division, when it came, was the greatest triumph the advocates of franchise reform had yet seen. In a House of 385 members, 228 voted for the bill and 157 against, giving a majority of 71. It was the first important measure promoted by a private Member to pass a second reading. Cheers could be heard from the Ladies' Gallery,

The Cowgate, looking east towards the Canongate.

which was separated from the chamber by a hated grille, and beyond which women could not pass. In the outer lobby, where women had waited hours for the vote, there was unrestrained jubilation. Frances Balfour, who was in the House, described the moment in a letter to her daughter: "The galleries packed with women held their breath. The crowd of friends coming back from the Aye lobby seemed to us so great, we thought it could not be...'incredible' one woman said in my ear, then I was shaking hands with a dozen, also being kissed, and saw two sobbing. No one had dreamt of such a success." The hope now was that the bill would go forward to its committee stages where opponents could be engaged in meaningful discussions. And at a meeting the following week at the Protestant Institute on George IV Bridge, none other than the Edinburgh Women Liberals heard speaker after speaker praising the bill's unexpected progress. [17]

Then the roof fell in. When Faithful-Begg's Women's Suffrage Bill resurfaced in the House of Commons in July 1897, the government allowed an insignificant measure about insects to dominate the session and block its passage. Women across the country were dismayed, insulted and indignant at its treatment. It seemed that male politicians had a great admiration for female suffrage in the abstract. They had, however, no desire to see it in practice. Party leaders appeared content with a system in which women took on the electioneering leg-work, "but left men in charge of policy and government." Many MPs were happy to promise support, but mysteriously avoided their obligation when it came to a vote. [18]

Partly as a result of the bill's failure, but more through a long process of negotiation, the National Union of Women's Suffrage Societies (NUWSS) was formally constituted in October 1897. This led to the amalgamation of 17 of Britain's larger societies – including the Edinburgh National Society – under a central organisation. The sole objective of the NUWSS was to obtain the franchise for women. Its policies were decided by branches and, despite its Liberal-leaning membership, it pledged to support on non-party lines any women's suffrage bill placed before Parliament. (The irony was that between 1897 and 1904 there were no further bills promoting votes for women.) The new body kept the same London office previously occupied by the Central Committee. It was led by

Millicent Fawcett, who had been in the Ladies' Gallery during the debate in 1867 of John Stuart Mill's amendment, but had been too young to sign his petition to Parliament. The NUWSS executive included Priscilla McLaren, Eliza Wigham (soon replaced by Jessie Methven) and Louisa Stevenson from the Edinburgh Society. The NUWSS increasingly offered a home to constitutionalist suffragists who were uncomfortable with militant tactics, and it became by far the largest women's suffrage organisation in the country. [19]

The spring of 1898 brought the sad news that the Edinburgh Society's founding secretary, Eliza Wigham of South Gray Street, had succumbed to failing health and had decided to move to Dublin to stay with a sister. In April, members gathered in the Bible Society rooms to say goodbye and to present the 78-year-old life-long Quaker with an illuminated address, "in token of their love and esteem for her and the deep regret they feel on her leaving Edinburgh." The hall was crowded to overflowing, and speaker after speaker praised Miss Wigham's contributions to many causes, as well as her lifelong fight for women's rights. Recalling her in her simple Quaker coat of pearl grey, either at some quiet meeting or on the platform of a crowded hall, small and delicate in stature, but with a clear, strong voice "which startled as she spoke," Flora Stevenson said of her: "She had the honour of knowing Elizabeth Fry and saw much of her in connection with her visits to Scotch prisons. She was thus led to become a workhouse visitor and a member of the Parochial Board, and in these and similar capacities she has literally devoted the whole of her long life to active service. It is as a reformer that she has been forced to see the need for Women's Suffrage. Scotland has no more earnest champion of the cause." Eliza Wigham died in Dublin just over a year later. [20]

Another great servant of the society, Priscilla McLaren, was now mostly confined to her home. When the ENSWS gathered for its 28th annual meeting in Free St Andrew's Church Hall in December 1898, Louisa Stevenson, who was holding the fort for the 84-year-old president, said she was pleased that the creation of the National Union of Women's Suffrage Societies had "absolutely abolished" party politics within the movement. She then read a letter from Mrs

McLaren: "Dear friends, I am truly sorry not to be with you at our annual meeting to-day. The weight of years forbids it, but this cannot control my spirit, which is warmly with you. My friends, there is a closed door in our own land which needs to be opened, and which has been closed against one half of the nation, the women of our country, since the Reform Bill of 1832." The door was closed, she said, because of "prejudice and long custom." She spoke of the Edinburgh society's untiring work – but also of its lack of influence with parliamentary representatives. The women's efforts were taken to the House of Commons in the form of petitions only to "find a place in the waste-paper basket." Her letter ended, "Let me ask each woman present to feel it a personal duty to do all she can to unbar this heavily shut door..." [21].

Mrs McLaren's incapacity and Miss Wigham's passing seemed to signal a change of the old guard – as the Edinburgh National Society soon attracted headlines of the wrong kind. The heavy gaze of the Press fell upon it for the astonishing plea it made for the return of flogging for assaults on women. Major newspapers across the country jumped on the story. Front-page headlines screamed 'Flogging as a Remedy' and 'Wanted – the Lash'. The trouble began when an unusual memorial, signed by the Edinburgh committee, was sent to the Home Secretary Sir Matthew Ridley and to Lord [Arthur] Balfour, the Secretary for Scotland. The document was also forwarded to the Press, prefaced with a few words by Priscilla McLaren: "Flogging seems hard, but it might be merciful ultimately, as it would prove a certain deterrent, for cruel people are mostly cowards, and thus a more severe punishment might prove a blessing to the men as well as to their victims."

The ENSWS memorial noted the "serious increase" in assaults upon wives, women and girls, as well as "other forms of outrages upon them" – Victorian shorthand for sexual assaults. What made the situation worse, in the society's view, were "the totally inadequate sentences passed upon such offenders." Light sentences for domestic assaults caused widespread indignation among women generally and led the Edinburgh memorialists to demand a change to the law. As things stood, said the document, "even murderous assaults" on

Eliza Wigham (1820-1899), founding secretary of the Edinburgh National Society for Women's Suffrage. (Courtesy of Massachusetts Historical Society)

THIS WEEK: ASSAULTS UPON WOMEN.

THE Woman's SIGNAL

A Weekly Record and Review devoted to the Interests of Women in the Home and in the Wider World.

Edited by MRS. FENWICK MILLER.

No. 268, Vol. XI.   REGISTERED AS A NEWSPAPER.   FEBRUARY 16TH, 1899.   Every Thursday, One Penny Weekly.

Principal Contents of this Issue.

Assaults upon Women:
Mrs. Priscilla Bright McLaren and the Edinburgh Woman's Suffrage Society's Memorial.
Mrs. Jameson. By Emily Hill. (Concluded).
The Need of Rest. By Dr. Rachel Gleason.
St. Mary's Home for Inebriate Women.
Appeal of One Half the Human Race. By Wm. Thompson. (Continued.)
Results to Women of War and Imperialism. By Mrs. Stanton Blatch.
Our Free Circulation Fund.
Signals from Our Watch Tower:
Judicial Statistics of Intemperance in Men and Women: The New State Homes for Inebriates, Rules and Regulations; Hospitality asked for delegates to the Women's Congress; Ladies and the Board of Management of the Glasgow Royal Infirmary.
A Lady's Trip to Klondyke.
Our Short Story: The Humming Top.
Married Women and Girls in America and England.
What to Wear. (Illustrated.)
The Wolf at the Door. Verses by Mrs. Stetson.
Ladies' Work Societies.
Signals from Friend to Friend.
Current News.
Etc., etc., etc.

Popular Physicians

"If not feeling well, let these three be your doctors: Dr. Diet, Dr. Quiet and Dr. Merryman." Dr. Diet should be consulted first, as he can do most for you. Diet, indeed, is the all-important thing in gaining and retaining health.

A prudent diet should always include Quaker Oats. It is best.

THE EASY FOOD.

Quaker OATS

THE WORLD'S BREAKFAST.

PHILP'S COCKBURN HOTELS,

LONDON, GLASGOW.

12 HENRIETTA STREET, STRAND—Telegrams: "PROMISING"; 9 ENDSLEIGH GARDENS, EUSTON—Telegrams: "LUNCHEONS."

The Woman's Signal issue for 16 February 1899, taking up the Edinburgh National Society memorial with its topline 'This Week – Assaults Upon Women'.

women and girls were being dismissed with a "trifling" prison sentence or a small fine which could "scarcely be regarded either as punishment or as a deterrent, and is nothing compared with what the poor wife has to suffer." Then, it said, the "vindictive torturer" would be allowed to return to her. In calling for a change to the law to protect women, the Edinburgh Society asked the Home Secretary and Secretary for Scotland to "remember that when garrotting was a frequent crime the punishment of flogging was resorted to, the result being that the crime gradually ceased to exist." Thus, the society "reluctantly" urged that those who committed assaults on women and girls should be flogged. The memorial was signed by Priscilla Bright McLaren, Jean Miller Morrison of Douglas Crescent, Louisa Stevenson of Randolph Crescent, Ada Todd of Great King Street, Grace Millar of Eildon Street, Constance La Cour of Inverleith Row, Mary Lees of Wemyss Place, Ethelinda Hadwen of York Buildings and by ENSWS secretary Jessie Methven, of Great King Street. [22].

Despite endless hostile headlines, support for the Edinburgh proposal came from the *Woman's Signal* newspaper, which praised the society "under the courageous and wise inspiration of its venerable president" for trying to answer a serious question and offering a suggestion. The paper referred to the names of the signatories as "all honoured ones in Edinburgh – and, indeed, some of them throughout the kingdom." Its editor told readers she held the same view as that expressed by Mrs McLaren and her co-signatories.

The Scotsman, meanwhile, thought people would be sympathetic to the society's views. It was not a demand for votes, it noted, but a call to rid the country of inadequate sentences on men who brutally maltreated women. The paper, however, took issue with the society on two fronts. It did not agree, as stated in the memorial, that the Press looked lightly on sentences for serious assaults. It also pointed out that the indignation at such sentences was not confined to women. The paper then muddled its position by advancing the hypothetical case of a quarrelling household where, "the wife has been badly beaten, and it may seem that a long term of imprisonment should be inflicted. But the man is the breadwinner of the family. A bad breadwinner he may be;

54

yet, to condemn him to so many days in gaol involves the condemnation of his wife and family to so many days' starvation." Such a situation, it said, would sometimes make the magistrate "pause." The editorial continued: "There are probably few people who would not at once agree that a man who brutally maltreats a woman deserves flogging, and there is a great deal to be said for this form of punishment on the ground of its deterrent effect, as proved in the case of the garrotter. But the cases are not quite alike. Flogging has not always proved a deterrent. It has in our own day been abolished with excellent results. Its deterrent effect was questionable and its moral effect was bad. It is by no means certain that the dread of flogging would have a more restraining effect on a brute under the influence of drink and passion than the dread of imprisonment." [23].

Other contributors, such as Jane Kettle of Hampton Wick, expressed unqualified support for the Edinburgh society: "It is a matter of regret that there should be a doubt in the mind of any woman as to the wisdom and justice of such a punishment. If some of your correspondents could be brought into close personal contact with the victims of these wretches, who assault women and criminally assault girl-children, they would hardly think flogging bad enough for them…And we women, who sit secure and safe in our sheltered homes, let us imagine what an assault on a woman means – the kicks and blows, the broken ribs and blinded eyes, and these often given when an unborn babe is injured as well as a wife, the humiliations and broken hearts which may not count in the assault, but do count in life, can we think flogging too hard for this?... May the women of Great Britain join with heart and soul in helping to bring about an alteration in the law for these our injured and assaulted sisters, whose cause has been so nobly taken up by Mrs Priscilla Bright McLaren."

No response to the Edinburgh "flogging" memorial has been traced from the Home and Scotland departments of government – though it was opposed by the Humanitarian League in London. [24].

The Edinburgh National Society had lost several of its early advocates. But it had not lost its radical voice. As the 1800s prepared to give way to the new century, the need for an electoral breakthrough would be central to its role and relevancy. Against it, however, were opponents who believed the demand for women's rights was revolutionary and threatening to the bulwarks of social and domestic life. They also faced a government content to brush aside demands for the vote. Adding to the complexities, the escalating militancy of the new century would widen the ideological gap to the brave suffragists who had patiently and hopefully worked on the uphill fight for 30 years. Where, hitherto, workers for the cause had met with good-natured tolerance, soon they would have to face frightening hostility, public ostracism and ever-harsher punishment.

References
1. The Scotsman, 9 December 1890.
2. The Queen, 11 January 1890; Edinburgh Evening News, 17 January 1890; Galloway News, 31 October 1890.
3. Edinburgh Evening News, 11 February 1890; The Scotsman, 13 November 1890; Martin Pugh, Women's Suffrage in Britain (1980), p12.
4. Middlesborough Gazette, 14 November 1890.
5. The Scotsman, 9 December 1890.
6. The Scotsman, 12 December 1890.
7. Idem, 22 April 1891.
8. Idem, 28 April & 5 May 1891.
9. Sarah Pedersen, The Scottish Suffragettes and the Press (2017), p112.
10. London Evening Standard, 26 April 1892; London Evening News, 28 April 1892; Pall Mall Gazette, 27 April 1892; https://orlando.cambridge.org/people/3c33d744-9ba1-4a11-affa-cc4e168ee174
11. Edinburgh Evening News, 26 April & 17 December 1892; The Scotsman, 25 June and 23 December 1892.
12. Elizabeth Crawford, The Women's Suffrage Movement (1999), p648; Glasgow Herald, 26 January 1893.
13. Woman's Signal, 4 June 1896; Crawford (1999), p648-649.
14. The Gentlewoman, 21 September 1895.
15. The Young Woman, February 1896.
16. The Scotsman, 13 November 1896.
17. The Scotsman, 4 February 1897; Edinburgh Evening News, 10 February 1897; NRS, GD433/2/318.
18. Martin Pugh, Women's Suffrage in Britain (1980), p12.
19. Crawford (1991), pp 214 & 436.
20. Edinburgh Evening News, 20 April 1898; London Echo, 18 July 1895.
21. Woman's Signal, 29 December 1898.
22. Dundee Evening Telegraph, 30 January 1899; The Globe, 31 January 1899.
23. Quoted in Woman's Signal, 16 February 1899.
24. Idem, 9 & 17 March 1899.

The only known image of the 1907 Edinburgh procession. It is captioned, 'Suffragists leaving King's Park, 5th Oct '07, Edin.'

FOUR:
EDINBURGH'S FIRST PRISONER
1900-1907

"I looked back on all the work we had done, the demonstrations and the meetings of all kinds we had held, the letters we had written, the resolutions we had passed, and I felt it had been of no avail. We had tried every conventional way of winning our cause. We were no nearer getting what we had started out to get, and I saw that militancy was the only way."

Jessie Methven, on why she decided to leave the Edinburgh National Society for Women's Suffrage to join Mrs Pankhurst's militant WSPU. 1.

Women had no parliamentary vote as the 1900s began. But they could look back on extraordinary advances. They had emerged from the background of private life and presented themselves as candidates for positions previously the exclusive domain of men. This was not achieved without a struggle, but the Victorian pioneers fought for their rights and won them. As the new century began, women in Scotland could vote in municipal, parish council and school board elections. The Scottish universities were open, and Edinburgh University had just awarded its first honorary degree to a woman, Eleanor Ormerod, the celebrated entomologist. Women occupied prominent positions in teaching and the medical professions. Thousands were now district or hospital nurses. Civil Service exams were open to females, and in these and other areas they were now working harmoniously with men. And, according to the *Daily Express*, there were "even" modern women keen enough "to ride a bicycle, tramp a turnip field or climb a mountain ... if need be." 2.

Women had proved their ability and suitability across society. But parliamentary votes remained remote and the government aloof.

While female suffrage seemed to loom more conspicuously above the political horizon, there were just as many voices claiming that the majority of women had no desire to participate in parliamentary elections and in any case were unsuited to do so. Even as the new century began, one Scottish newspaper was keen to consign women to the "kingdom" of their kitchen: "After all is said and done, the true sphere of woman will be the home. This is her kingdom... it is of importance that the mothers of the future should be instructed in all that pertains to the making of a happy home. It is in this way that the honour of the nation will be maintained and the Empire established.**"** Thankfully such pejorative guff was increasingly uncommon. 3.

Flora Stevenson's appointment to lead Edinburgh School Board in 1900 was widely celebrated. Two decades earlier Stevenson had been the first woman from the city elected to a school board. And, at each election, "it was no unusual thing for caps to be tossed and three cheers for Flora" to be called for. Stevenson, aged 60 in 1900, began her contribution to education as a teenager when she took in disadvantaged children for school work. To help poorly nourished and impoverished families she launched the Committee for

Feeding and Clothing Destitute Children in 1879 and acted as its secretary for many years. Through this agency, thousands of needy and neglected bairns attended elementary schools – over 27,000 by 1900. She was the first woman elected an Honorary Fellow of the Scottish Educational Institute. And, of course, along with sister Louisa, she played an important and influential role in the women's suffrage movement. As the 1900s began, Flora Stevenson was a committee member of the ENSWS and sat on the executive of the National Union of Women's Suffrage Societies, travelling regularly to London and Manchester to formulate policy and hatch plans. 4.

In September 1900, the Women's Liberal Federation once again rejected a proposal to make women's suffrage a test question for Parliamentary candidates. The Liberals' fence-sitting riled the NUWSS. The following month its London leadership wrote to societies around the country with instructions to canvass candidates with four questions...

1. Are you in favour of extending the Parliamentary franchise to women ratepayers?
2. Will you, if returned to Parliament, vote for a bill in favour of women's suffrage?
3. Will you give women's suffrage a prominent place in your addresses?
4. Will you combine with others to promote legislation tending in this direction?

The Edinburgh National Society received replies from most of the city's candidates, and these were duly published:

Dr Arthur Conan Doyle [the celebrated novelist], for Central Edinburgh, responded positively: "To deny a vote to women who pay taxes is taxation without representation. 1. I am in favour of giving one. 2. Yes. 3. Have not dealt with social matters in my address. 4. Shall help when I can."

Colonel Dalrymple-Hamilton, for Midlothian, answered: "Have no objection to supporting a measure which will extend the franchise to women, but am strongly opposed to their becoming candidates for election to the House of Commons."

R. Scott Brown, for East Edinburgh, said: "1. Yes. 2. Yes, on the lines of giving women ratepayers a vote. 3. Address already published."

Sir J. Batty Tuke, for the University constituency, responded: "1. To unmarried and widowed women. 2. Up to the above point."

Sir Lewis McIver for West Edinburgh was said to be an old supporter.

Jessie Methven, secretary of the Edinburgh branch, reviewed the mostly favourable responses: "I have much pleasure in stating that in addition to those candidates, the following have also promised their support to the extension of the Parliamentary franchise to women: Mr Edwin Adam, Mr G. M. Brown and Mr McCrae. I regret to have a correction to make regarding the opinion of Sir Lewis McIver, he having written that he is not in favour of the extension of the Parliamentary franchise to women." McIver (perhaps to the women's satisfaction) unsuccessfully contested Edinburgh South at the 1892 general election. 5.

A new name entered the campaign at this time. Lady Barbara Steel was married to the new Lord Provost of Edinburgh, and in December 1900 she made the first of many public speeches on behalf of the ENSWS. Lady Steel would emerge as one of the most active of the Edinburgh suffragists, later refusing to pay her taxes and having her furniture sold off at the Mercat Cross. She would also make history as the first woman to stand for election to Edinburgh Town Council. As the year drew to a close, the society's committee issued a circular, signed by Priscilla McLaren and Jessie Methven, expressing their "keen disappointment" at the "continued indifference" shown by members of political organisations in relation to women's votes. It was intended as a public ticking-off for the Scottish Liberals, who had just passed a resolution in favour of manhood suffrage. It also accused the Liberals of political cowardice – the fear "that all will vote Tory." Jessie Methven pulled no punches in her criticism of the party's female cohort. Instead of making a stand for the principle of women's votes (which, of course, many Liberal men had preached, but not practised), she regretted and rejected the women's loyalty to the party machinery: "It is not yet too late! If they would come out now and demand a Government measure our cause would be won." 6.

The death of Queen Victoria in 1901 marked the passing of an adversary, but one whose long reign had brought significant advances in women's lives. On her accession in 1837 there had been no high schools. Now they were everywhere. There had not been one university class. In 1901 there were 2000 women graduates, 1500 students and eight honorary female graduates. In 1837 women doctors and trained nurses were unheard of. In 1901 there were 400 registered women in health service roles. There were no women's organisations at the start of her reign. Now a network of hard-working groups protected the country. Women had had no right to earnings and property. Now they owned what they had. And, in 1837, with the exception of the throne, no woman was entitled to fill any public position. Now women served on more than half of the Poor Law associations and on 236 school boards – and they had voted in their thousands in municipal elections.
The parliamentary vote was unfinished business. And, as Edinburgh welcomed five Colonial prime ministers to receive the Freedom of the City ahead of the coronation of Edward VII, it could not have been lost on the ENSWS membership that real power remained tightly in the grip of men.

Louisa Stevenson continued to deputise for Priscilla McLaren, and Jessie Methven was adjusting well to the secretary's role so long occupied by Eliza Wigham. Membership had risen again – by about 30 in 1901 – but some regulars from outlying areas had transferred to the recently formed Glasgow & West of Scotland Society. It was regretted that balloting to bring forward a private member's bill on women's suffrage had failed. There was welcome news, however, from the Scottish Women's Liberal Federation which had awakened to its influential position. At its annual meeting in Edinburgh in April 1902 it was resolved that although the association was not ready to make it a condition on candidates to support women's suffrage, it would be

The only known representation of Lady Barbara Steel from the Victorian era.

Emmeline Pankhurst and her daughter Christabel, founders of the Women's Social and Political Union.

"strongly impressed" on both the men's associations and the candidates themselves that this was the view of the majority of the federation's 10,500 members. 7.

In August 1902 the Scottish capital welcomed hundreds of delegates to the annual conference of the National Union of Women Workers. The event extended over four days and used the St Cuthbert's Halls, at the junction of Princes Street Gardens and Lothian Road. It was chaired by Lady Battersea, who had turned her homes in London into shelters for unmarried mothers and women rescued from prostitution. Sarah Mair welcomed delegates. A women's suffrage debate was chaired by Ishbel, Countess of Aberdeen. Louisa Stevenson spoke passionately on the wretched working conditions for women. After this Lady Lucy Cavendish stood up and laughingly said that she felt "like an exceedingly nervous lion in a den of Daniels" as she had doubts about giving votes to women. Her worries were promptly dismissed by Lady Frances Balfour, the president of the London Society, the largest single suffrage group in Britain, who described her speech as "a slight, and (with all respect) a very feeble opposition." Nonetheless, following the murder of her husband by Irish republicans, Lucy Cavendish devoted her time, energies and fortune to girls' and women's education. In 1965, Cambridge University named its first post-graduate college for women after her. 8.

While the Edinburgh Society continued to raise new petitions, and the capital's papers gradually lost interest in reporting them, the ground-breaking advance of 1903 was Emmeline Pankhurst's formation in Manchester of the Women's Social and Political Union (WSPU). Mrs Pankhurst, a 45-year-old widow, was already heavily involved with the local Independent Labour Party, which suggests that for a time she was content to pursue her political aims through its constitutional pathways. Indeed, it was her daughter Christabel, still only 23, who was already showing impressive platform skills and "fighting running battles" in the Press with Labour leaders over their treatment of women. Younger sisters Sylvia, then 21, and Adela, 18, shared the opinion that women's votes were best achieved through the mobilisation of working

women in the north of England. Emmeline's daughters had hinted at the direct action which would soon revolutionise the fight for equality. The WSPU also grew from the Pankhursts' dissatisfaction with both the Labour Party and the National Union of Women's Suffrage Societies; when it came to women's votes, the former was frustratingly lukewarm and the latter too cautious. The WSPU's real assets, said the Pankhursts' biographer Martin Pugh, were the energy and enthusiasm of the Pankhursts themselves: "But in 1903-1904 the WSPU was so small an organisation that expectations that it would succeed in winning the vote where others had failed seemed absurd." 9.

Led by Emmeline and Christabel Pankhurst, with Sylvia as secretary, Emmeline Pethick-Lawrence as treasurer and Annie Kenney as paid organiser, the Women's Social and Political Union resolved to limit membership exclusively to women and to keep the new organisation free from any political party affiliation. Rachel Scott, the WSPU's first London secretary, wrote to *The Labour Leader* on October 31 to announce its objective: "To secure complete equality with men, social and political." The WSPU never set out to enfranchise all women, however. With its celebrated motto, 'Deeds Not Words', it fought for votes for 'qualified women', which would give a limited franchise to females on the same property basis as males. The problem facing the WSPU, however, was akin to that which had dogged the Victorian campaigners. While it was able to persuade individual MPs to support women's votes, what had not changed was the government's refusal to allow the parliamentary process to bring them about. Many MPs were happy to pledge support, knowing their promises would never be put to the test. The WSPU, therefore, understood it had to unblock the system. That meant targeting the Prime Minister and his Cabinet – and its young volunteers were eager and determined to get on with it. 10.

The Edinburgh National Society's peaceful campaigns should not be overlooked or ignored in the fascination with the WSPU. Every name on a parliamentary petition required effort. Each conversation took time. And a negative response meant time wasted. Long and expensive journeys

Chalking pavements in advance of meetings and selling
literature was the daily routine of many supporters.
(Courtesy of London Museum)

were needed to reach locations not yet canvassed or organised. Meetings had to be arranged and staffed. Then there were the routine jobs – the duty rosters, the fund-raising, the leafleting and the spreading of the word. As one anonymous suffragette recalled: "I was told to go and chalk the pavements clearly and distinctly with 'Votes for Women,' and where and when the meeting was to be. No sooner had I finished than an irate shopman appeared with pail and brush, and proceeded to wash out my work. I repeated my notice, which met with the same treatment. 'Go to it, Suffragette, don't give in,' shouted the crowd. I made my third attempt on the flagstone just beyond his shop. Just as the angry man was raising his pail a policeman seized his arm, remarking, 'You leave her alone, that's not your ground.' 'Well done, Suffragette,' were the last words I heard as I boarded the car, my task completed. Yes, chalking and distributing bills, taking a collection or addressing the meeting, what does it matter what you do, as long as you do something to help the cause." [11].

Come 1904, the radical element of the Edinburgh National Society was continuing its calls for parliamentary candidates to support female suffrage. At the ENSWS annual meeting in February Priscilla McLaren's son Walter proposed that "women should refuse to work" for candidates who did not agree. He was opposed by Ada Lang Todd, who was deputising for his mother. Mrs Lang Todd said that what she objected to was making the support of a candidate the test of membership of a political association. She had previously refused the 'test question' as secretary of the Edinburgh Women Liberals and said that she "never for a moment" thought she should be asked to take the chair of an ENSWS meeting if the 'test question' was to be raised by the platform party, especially in the form of a resolution. As she had never seen the resolution, she protested against its being put to the meeting and threatened to leave the society if it was passed. Jessie Methven, as secretary, apologised to Mrs Lang Todd for not forwarding the resolution, but added that as she felt "so keenly in sympathy" with it, she had concluded that it was the best course for the society to adopt,

and the only practical way of gaining their aims. Mrs Lang Todd sat stoney-faced as applause for Jessie Methven rippled around the hall.

Walter McLaren moved his resolution again, supported by Mary Lees, who said she thought he "was on the right lines." Then the Rev Dr Craig moved an amendment saying that the wisest policy was to delay McLaren's proposal. Elsie Inglis, in seconding the churchman, said she did not intend to stay in a society where support for women's suffrage was to be made a test question for candidates; and if they split up the Edinburgh society, they would do "a great deal of damage" to the cause. Nevertheless, when push came to shove, Walter McLaren's resolution was adopted by 35 votes to 26. Once again, the Edinburgh society had shown its teeth – and its independence from the traditional wing of the Liberal Party. None more so than Jessie Methven, who drew praise a day or two later from a *Scotsman* contributor who said she "entirely agreed" with the ENSWS secretary. Thankfully, neither Ada Lang Todd nor Elsie Inglis carried out their threats to leave the society.

As 1905 began, women in Scotland could vote in municipal, parish council and school board elections. They could be graduates and fill many new and exciting roles. They paid taxes, too. And yet, when it came to polling day, they were debarred from placing their cross next to the name of the candidate they favoured. It is hardly surprising that growing numbers of women felt the injustice and inequity of everyday life. One meeting condemned as 'astounding' and 'disgraceful' that a householder like Flora Stevenson, the chairman of Edinburgh School Board and honorary graduate of Edinburgh University, could not vote, whereas a boy of 21 who happened to have a house could.

The Women's Social and Political Union's move from Manchester to London in 1905 got it noticed. Hundreds flocked to join. And the effect on other suffrage organisations was generally positive. The Edinburgh National Society's annual meeting in the Royal Hotel, Princes Street in February 1905, noted a significant rise in membership. Although no figures were given, the

Sarah Elizabeth Siddons Mair.

attendance of 200 women was indicative of the society's strength. The report for 1904 reported "considerable apathy" in regard to women's votes over the previous six or seven years, but that there had been "an extraordinary revival of interest." During the past 12 months, 72 women's suffrage societies had been formed, including 11 in Scotland. And when a new committee was announced, a letter from Jessie Methven winged its way to its local newspaper to encourage support for the group, and to remind readers of Edinburgh's important and continuing role in the development of the movement. But there was no public joining of the dots that the WSPU's high-profile protests had raised numbers as well as the stakes. And, for all its growing support and bullish statistics, perhaps there was an inkling within the ENSWS that it was falling behind in the march of women elsewhere. 12.

In London, Emmeline Pankhurst was busy at Westminster attempting to persuade MPs to support the idea of a new bill. She and her daughter Sylvia, then a student at the Royal College of Art, spent eight days in the Lobby working on a proposal as Parliament reconvened. But they found no-one, other than Keir Hardie, prepared to introduce such a measure if their name came out on top of the members' ballot. Eventually, the 14th name drawn, John Bamford Slack, the MP for St Albans, agreed to put forward a Private Member's Bill for women's suffrage. It was the first for eight years and its second reading was laid down for 12 May 1905. When the day came, the public galleries were crowded with expectant women who had flocked to the Commons. The first bill discussed that day concerned street lighting. The women tried to have it withdrawn to allow more time for the suffrage measure. Their appeal was turned down. They then tried to persuade government Whips to give their bill time for a full discussion, but the Whips refused. The government then allowed the Roadway Lighting Bill to 'talk out' the suffrage proposal. It was the same old story, as a rueful Mrs Pankhurst recalled: "They spun out the debate with silly stories and foolish jokes. The Members listened to the insulting performance with laughter and applause." 13.

Sad news followed at the end of September 1905 with the death at the age of 66 of Flora Stevenson, made more poignant as she had been awarded the Freedom of the City, only the second woman to receive it, just weeks earlier. Best known, of course, for her education work, and the recipient two years earlier of an honorary LLD from Edinburgh University, she was a founding member of the Edinburgh National Society for Women's Suffrage and, with her sister Louisa, presided over important meetings and spoke at major demonstrations. As she was laid to rest in Dean Cemetery perhaps the most eloquent tribute to her was by Lady Frances Balfour, the London Society president and ENSWS member: "We of a younger generation, to whom the torch has been handed, and who are equally bound to hand it on burning as brightly and hopefully as we have received it from the hands that relinquish their task, to us it must ever be a stimulus and an incentive to know that this great and gentle citizen who has passed to her rest looked for and believed in the day which should bring this right and privilege to the women citizens in her beloved country." 14.

In October 1905, Mrs Pankhurst's elder daughter Christabel and WSPU mill girl recruit Annie Kenney attended a meeting in the Free Trade Hall in Manchester to hear Cabinet ministers Winston Churchill and Sir Edward Grey. When Grey was speaking, the two women shouted, "Will the Liberal Government give votes to women?" The police were called, but Pankhurst and Kenney refused to leave the hall. During a struggle, a policeman claimed the two women kicked and spat at him. Pankhurst and Kenney were arrested and charged with assault. In court, they were each found guilty and fined five shillings, or seven days' imprisonment. Mrs Pankhurst pleaded with her daughter to let her pay the fines. Keenly aware of the political ramifications of women being jailed in his fragile Manchester constituency, Churchill also offered to pay. Pankhurst and Kenney refused and were taken to serve a week in Strangeways.

The jailing shocked the nation. No woman had ever been imprisoned for a political protest. And, for the first time, they had used violence to win the

Christabel Pankhurst – involved in the first act of militancy in 1905.

vote. But the tactics worked. Jailed suffragists were far more newsworthy than dull, drawing-room meetings. Even *The Times* gave it 500 words. In propaganda terms it was a triumph, and a crowd of more than 1000 welcomed the women's release. Overnight, sympathisers flocked to join the WSPU and the other suffrage organisations. Twenty years of peaceful protest

The Scottish Women Graduates' case convulsed the media from 1906. Frances Simson, Chrystal MacMillan and Frances Melville outside the House of Lords. (Courtesy of The University of Edinburgh)

had not produced such an effect and Christabel Pankhurst knew she had broken the mould: "Better violence than jeers, sneers, or silent contempt," she said on release. "Women," her mother Emmeline added in a memorable address to thousands of supporters, "we must do the work ourselves." And, following her daughter's release, Mrs Pankhurst urged supporters to drop political allegiances and to work only for the cause. From then, militancy was adopted as the WSPU set out to ambush, waylay and intimidate the Liberal leadership wherever possible. It was the way ahead. 15.

The Women's Social and Political Union took rooms at 45 Park Walk, Chelsea. Christabel Pankhurst, who had just finished her law degree, was made chief organiser and strategist. Adela, her younger sister, aged 21, was appointed regional organiser. Middle sister Sylvia, 24, was finishing her studies at the Royal College of Art in South Kensington. There was now a majority of MPs who supported votes for women. The government, however, remained resolutely opposed, and the WSPU set about harassing ministers, picketing meetings and causing as much disruption to government business as possible. It prompted *The Daily Mail* in January 1906 to christen them 'Suffragettes' to distinguish them (in a derogatory way) from their non-militant sisters.

Some 250 women attended the February 1906 annual meeting of the Edinburgh Society, which dwelled on the events of the previous year. It took place, once again, at the Edinburgh Café in Princes Street, with the chair occupied by Sarah Siddons Mair. Although the movement had made no progress in Parliament, a "significant increase" in membership was reported – probably taking the numbers to over 500 at this time. It was agreed to send £50 to a NUWSS election fighting fund, which had called for national donations of £1000. The visiting speaker, Esther Roper, secretary of the National Industrial and Professional Women's Suffrage Society, gave an account of the recent election at Wigan, where a male candidate had stood, unsuccessfully, entirely on women's suffrage. The Glasgow constituency of Camlachie would do the same in 1910, again without success. Edinburgh-born

Frances Melville, Warden of University Hall, St Andrews, then spoke of the agitation by women graduates to vote in the University Parliamentary elections.

This was timely. Back at the start of 1906, the Women Graduates of Scottish Universities noted: "If it can be established that one woman is competent to vote, it alters the whole aspect of the franchise for women." By then, more than 900 women had degrees from a Scottish university. As spring turned to summer, and after being refused voting papers, a case was brought by five women graduates of Edinburgh University against the Universities of Edinburgh and St Andrews with the object of having it declared that women graduates were entitled to vote at the election of a Member of Parliament for the Scottish Universities. At this time, the universities of Glasgow and Aberdeen, with one MP, and those of St Andrews and Edinburgh, with one MP, were single-member constituencies of the House of Commons. The Edinburgh National Society circulated all British suffrage societies for funds for a legal challenge. Thanks largely to the society's financial assistance, the five graduates were able to take the case to the Court of Session. The women argued that the 1868 Act specified 'person' rather than 'man' and that, as graduates, they were therefore entitled to vote in these constituencies. When, in July 1906, Lord Salvesen pronounced against the women, concluding that because only men had voted in the past, the 'unwritten constitution' meant that only men were entitled to vote, it effectively ruled that women were not 'persons.' There was an immediate outcry from the women's movement. A speedy 'crowdfunding' appeal raised the £1000 required to appeal the decision – which took the case into 1907 and then to 1908. 16.

In May 1906, the Liberal Prime Minister Henry Campbell-Bannerman consented to receiving a large deputation from across the spectrum of the women's movement. Some 350 delegates were invited to talks at the Foreign Office, including representatives from the National Union of Women's Suffrage Societies, Mrs Pankhurst's Women's Social and Political Union, Co-operative Guilds, Temperance Societies and likeminded groups, including female operatives from the textiles manufacturing towns of Lancashire and Cheshire.

Duncan and Priscilla McLaren were laid to rest in St Cuthbert's Churchyard.

The Scotsman called it "a remarkable deputation." Several women attended from Scotland, including nine from the Scottish Women's Liberal Federation. Prior to the meeting, Teresa Billington, one of the WSPU's earliest recruits, led two thousand women across central London, from the Thames Embankment to Downing Street. While their colleagues were having their hopes dashed by the Prime Minister, the procession continued up Whitehall and, after speeches in Trafalgar Square, returned to the Embankment. Beside the ancient needle named for Egypt's warrior queen, Christabel Pankhurst spoke of her anger and disappointment and urged the crowd to action. Annie Kenney asked them: "If it means prison for all of you, are you prepared to go?" A resounding chorus of 'Yes' was the reply. 17.

Having mourned the untimely death of Flora Stevenson, there was further sadness when, on 5 November 1906, Priscilla Bright McLaren passed away, aged 91, at Newington House. Following a service at St Cuthbert's Parish Church, attended by members of the various organisations she belonged to, she was interred alongside her late husband Duncan in the family vault against the high wall beside the church. Among mourners were her friends from the Edinburgh National Society, Edinburgh Women's Liberal Association, Edinburgh University Graduates, the British Women's Temperance Association and the Women's Cooperative Guild. Messages of sympathy were received from suffrage societies across Britain. The NUWSS in London forwarded a memorial to their grieving Edinburgh sisters: "That this Committee has heard with deep regret of the loss sustained by the women's suffrage movement in the death of one of its oldest and most honoured leaders. They wish to offer their sympathy to the Edinburgh National Society for the death of their revered president, and their most heartfelt condolences."

Age had not dimmed Priscilla McLaren's passion for the cause – and her willingness to embrace new methods. In 1901 she raised money for the Factory Women's Movement, the collective of millworkers fighting for votes in north-west England. And, in 1905, when Christabel Pankhurst and Annie Kenney went to jail, Mrs McLaren's influential voice was heard from the

Scottish capital speaking out in their defence: "Let us not be alarmed by what these young girls have done. It often takes what *some* would call an unwise action to rouse a nation." A year later, when she heard of the women imprisoned after trying to deliver a petition to the House of Commons, she was again deeply moved, particularly as the daughter of her old friend Richard Cobden was one of those jailed. Close to death, Mrs McLaren sent a message of "sympathy and admiration" to the jailed suffragettes in Holloway and praised their "noble courage and self-sacrifice." It was delivered to the women the day she died. The most poignant memorial at her funeral was a laurel wreath with the inscription, "With deep sympathy and regret, from the eleven women suffragists in Holloway Gaol." [18].

As 1906 ended, there were 21 suffragettes in Holloway, bringing the total number of prisoners since the women's agitation started to 42. Had Priscilla McLaren been born a little later, she might have been one of them. At WSPU headquarters, a 'Suffragette Roll of Honour' was pinned to the wall bearing the names of all those jailed for the cause. From Christabel Pankhurst and Annie Kenney in Manchester in October 1905 to Annie Fraser of Glasgow at the end of 1906, the list already included some of the greatest names in the suffrage story. But only Teresa Billington had been jailed twice – and she was now in charge of the WSPU's campaign in Scotland.

The Edinburgh branch of the Women's Social and Political Union was formed on 9 August 1906 and was the second in Scotland, after Glasgow. Teresa Billington's visit the week before breathed life into its beginnings. Billington spoke at the Mound on August 5, attracting a crowd of 400; on Leith Links on the 6th, which drew 600; at the Meadows on the 7th in front of 800 and at the Mound again the following day in front of hundreds more. The decision to start an Edinburgh branch was then taken at the Independent Labour Party rooms in the Lawnmarket on August 9. *The Scotsman* noted next day that the proceedings were private, but the *Edinburgh Evening News* stated that around 30 women were present at the meeting.

The new branch was initially called the Edinburgh and Midlothian Women's

Social and Political Union, but it was thereafter referred to as Edinburgh WSPU. Mrs Mae Clouston Grant was appointed its first president. The secretary was Mrs J. A. Young of Morningside Road, whose husband was a member of Edinburgh School Board. Elizabeth Bell, of Comely Bank Gardens, took over as secretary shortly afterwards. Mrs Johnstone, of York Place, was treasurer. Others named at this time were Morag Burn Murdoch, Esson Maule, Miss Menzies, Mrs Elizabeth Lamont and Mrs Macleod Easson. Dr Grace Cadell of Leith Walk and Isabella Cairns of Lower Broughton, seem to have started a small WSPU branch in Leith at this time, or shortly afterwards. Jessie Methven, while continuing secretarial duties for the ENSWS, apparently jumped ship early into the life of the new branch. She recalled joining immediately after Priscilla McLaren's death in November 1906. She said she believed that women had missed an opportunity in 1884 when the Reform Bill extended the franchise to more men. Had they used militancy then, she said, they would have had the vote. "I then looked back on all the work we had done, the demonstrations and the meetings of all kinds we had held, the letters we had written, the resolutions we had passed, and I felt it had been of no avail. We had tried every conventional way of winning our cause. I felt then that after all those years of conventional methods we were no nearer getting what we had started out to get, and I saw that militancy was the only way." Additionally, several members of the Edinburgh National Society attended early WSPU meetings, but appear, at least in the early days of the WSPU, to have retained their membership of the older organisation. They included Barbara Steel, Mary Gillies and Mary Lees. When Mrs Pankhurst returned to Edinburgh in October 1906 for a meeting in the Livingstone Hall, the chair was taken by Lady Steel, who also presided over an Edinburgh WSPU meeting the following month. Making her apologies for not being able to attend, Mary Lees wrote that those "who had been at work on the subject quietly for more than 30 years recognised the necessity of aggressive action." [19].

Among early supporters of the new branch was the Edinburgh teenager Cicily Isabel Fairfield. The Fairfield family had moved to Edinburgh from

Anne Cobden Sanderson – one of the signatories to the 1866 petition.

London in 1901 and lived at Hope Park Square, near The Meadows, then Buccleuch Place, both later remembered in Cicily's novels under her famous penname Rebecca West. In October 1907, Cicily wrote to *The Scotsman* pleading for support for the WSPU. Under the heading 'Women's Electoral Claims' her letter stated her opposition to "the profound national effects of the subjection of women on the nation." Was it not, she asked, the duty of every woman "to press this question before all others – and immediately?" She finished, "It is obviously incumbent on everyone whose eyes are open not only to the sufferings of women, but to the well-being of the nation, to accept the call to action of the W. S. P. U." The letter was signed Cicily Isabel Fairfield. She was just 14 years old. [20].

Meanwhile, the Haig sisters, Florence, Evelyn and Cecilia, of Comely Bank Avenue, are said to have been three of the "seven" original members of Edinburgh WSPU, but it is difficult to reconcile this with the early reporting of branch activities in the capital. The Haigs were certainly involved with the Edinburgh National Society before the WSPU had a presence in the city, so it is likely they transferred across. This adds to the picture of a group of Edinburgh activists for whom the Victorian campaign had not brought the hoped-for result, and who felt the issue had to be driven into the open through direct action. What lay ahead for them, though, was a public provoked into opposition to their new approach and increasingly unreceptive to their protests. [21].

Despite the early defections to the WSPU, there is evidence in Scotland of considerable co-operation and solidarity among and between the militant and constitutionalist societies at this time. Early 1907, for example, brought one of the most important suffrage meetings of the year when an impressive audience of 1200 at the Music Hall in George Street heard speeches by Annie Kenney, Anne Cobden Sanderson and Teresa Billington of the WSPU and Mary Lees, Sarah Mair and Lady Barbara Steel of the Edinburgh National Society. All three WSPU speakers had by then served prison sentences for militancy. Mrs Cobden Sanderson, visiting from London, was the first prominent suffragist to decamp to the WSPU. She told the audience that one of the brightest moments in the dark days in Holloway was when she and her fellow prisoners received a message of encouragement from Priscilla McLaren. Mrs McLaren, then close to death, told them that she had striven in constitutional ways for 50 years to do what the WSPU were now trying their best to bring about by unconstitutional means. It was the last letter she wrote. Mrs Cobden Sanderson told the hushed Edinburgh audience that she was prepared to go to prison again and again if the necessity arose, and she appealed to all women to join their crusade. Lady Frances Balfour, sister-in-law of former Prime Minister Arthur Balfour, took the chair and kept the peace – much to the disappointment of the local Press, who had anticipated fireworks from the suffragette newcomers of the WSPU.

Sarah Siddons Mair surely drew inspiration from the Music Hall gathering. To everyone's astonishment, the acting president of the Edinburgh National Society announced her "personal support" for militancy. She admitted that some of her friends (who knew her as Sallie Mair) had expressed surprise that after working for years on constitutional lines she now associated herself with "the new phase" of the movement. She felt "exceedingly strong that women must stand shoulder to shoulder and none of them should throw a stone at their sisters whatever their methods." She hoped that her friends who had spent decades discussing women's rights at her home in Chester Street "would give their support to other ladies working on different lines." There is no evidence that S. E. S. Mair took any part in militant action, though she remained prominent in public protests and continued to pepper the Press with letters.

Towards the end of the Music Hall meeting, a Mrs Robertson, an elderly woman and wife of a local clergyman, told the audience that she had been an advocate of women's suffrage for 25 years, but did not like the "badgering" of the government. Neither did she approve of "baiting" Mr Asquith at his London home. She wanted the Liberals left in peace. Mrs Robertson added that she was strongly in favour of the extension of the parliamentary franchise

to women taxpayers, but she was a Liberal first and a suffragist second. Teresa Billington, now just two weeks away from her marriage to the Glasgow businessman Frederick Greig, stood to respond. She said that she respected Mrs Robertson's views. She noted that Mrs Robertson had mentioned that she had been 25 years a suffragist. But Billington said she had not, and "was not going to be!" This drew laughter and the meeting ended harmoniously with Lady Steel's vote of thanks. 22.

On the last day of January 1907, the Edinburgh branch of the Women's Social and Political Union drew a full house to the India Buildings in Victoria Street for a visit by Emmeline Pankhurst, the founder of the Union. Arabella Scott, then an undergraduate at Edinburgh University, recalled the preparations for such a visit: "We would help advertise where and when Mrs Pankhurst would be speaking by the usual method of holding meetings beforehand, issuing pamphlets and chalking the pavements. If the meetings were in halls we would decorate them with the purple, white and green flags of the WSPU, or hoist and fly some at vantage points, and we would drape them over the platform. If Mrs Pankhurst was speaking outdoors we would either hire a taxi for her, or if her own car was available use that. These could be handy as a platform for her to speak from." Mae Clouston Grant presided and introduced Mrs Pankhurst, who told the Edinburgh audience that the WSPU had been formed for the express purpose of taking "practical steps" towards the enfranchisement of women. By their actions, she said, they had ended what she termed the "Press boycott on women's suffrage." The WSPU would work for no political party until they had the vote; they would help no candidate more than another; their "womanhood" was first, and party politics came after. Many Liberal women were now joining the Union, she said, and over the last 12 months the WSPU had grown to a membership of 12,000. 23.

One of those 12,000 – Isabella Cairns – was about to become the first Edinburgh woman to be jailed for the cause.

On 13 February 1907, the King's Speech to the joint Houses of Parliament contained no mention of women's suffrage. In response, 700 WSPU

Emmeline Pankhurst speaking at an outdoor meeting in Scotland.
(Courtesy of James Howie)

members attending the first 'Women's Parliament' at Caxton Hall rallied to Mrs Pankhurst's famous call to "Rise up, Women!" and marched four abreast towards the Commons. Confronted by lines of police, they were ordered to stop and told to turn back, but they continued to walk. The confrontation soon became a free-for-all. Police horses surged into the lines of women, scattering them in all directions. The women reformed into smaller groups and made repeated attempts to reach the entrances. Wholesale arrests were made as they were dragged away. Emmeline Pankhurst recalled: "They fought until their clothes were torn, their bodies bruised, the last ounce of their strength exhausted." The Press, the following day, heavily criticised the police

for using horses against defenceless women. Angry questions were asked in Parliament and Keir Hardie accused the police of "brutality." That evening, the women were bailed out by Frederick Pethick-Lawrence, and they returned to find the new WSPU headquarters at Clement's Inn a hive of activity as prospective members queued at the door.

The same Wednesday evening brought a second attack on the Commons. A detachment of WSPU approached from Caxton Hall, once again arm-in-arm and singing party songs. The police had made elaborate preparations this time. Sixty uniformed officers formed up in front of the St Stephen's and Palace Yard entrances. They were backed by a mounted patrol which kept the women and public moving. Repulsed again and again, most of the suffragists were limited to a protest outside the gate, but several made runs at the Commons and were arrested. Mrs Pankhurst recalled, "We kept Caxton Hall open, the women returning every now and again, singly or in small groups, to have their bruises bathed or their torn clothes repaired." [24].

Isabella Cairns from Lower Broughton, Leith, given as 'Bella Cairns' in court and known at home as Isabel, was the first Edinburgh suffragette to be arrested. Cairns was involved with the WSPU at Leith and had presided at a meeting in the port the previous December when Helen Fraser was the visiting speaker. This may have been the occasion when the Leith WSPU branch was formed under the leadership of Dr Grace Cadell of Leith Walk. In London for the protests, Isabella Cairns was arrested outside Parliament together with Maggie Moffat of Glasgow WSPU.

In the list of 58 arrested women, she was described as having 'no occupation'. She was released on bail before being brought to court with the others. Fifty-seven women were convicted. With Emmeline Pankhurst looking on from the back of the court, 16 first offenders were given seven days if they refused to pay their fines – which all did. A further 35 of the women were sentenced to 14 days. Two were handed 21 days and four repeat offenders received a month's imprisonment. Mary Gawthorpe was too ill to attend court and her case was adjourned.

The main entrance to the Houses of Parliament was repeatedly besieged by women suffragists.

At Westminster police court, Isabella Cairns and Maggie Moffat were convicted of disorderly conduct and fined £1 or 14 days. The magistrate said the women were directly responsible for the chaos which had occurred. Both refused to pay their fines and opted for prison, in line with WSPU policy. To the little-known Isabella Cairns, aged just 21 in 1907, went the honour of becoming the first Edinburgh suffragette to go to prison.

Another of those convicted had Edinburgh connections. Kathleen Rothwell, later described as "a well-known Edinburgh suffragette," was listed following arrest as a London woman from Battersea. She was, however, born in North Berwick in 1874 as Kathleen Paterson and her parents moved to Edinburgh when she was a child. She married Fred Rothwell in Kensington in 1906 and afterwards divided her time between London and Edinburgh. Aged 32 in 1907, she was sentenced to a £1 fine or 14 days, opted for prison and was released from Holloway, with others, on February 27. Describing herself to the magistrate as a "rebel," and laughing in a manner which drew his ire, Rothwell said she intended to "go on breaking the laws until they were able, by their own votes, to help to make them better." 25.

What we know of the prisoners' stay in Holloway can be gleaned from Cairns' fellow-prisoners Maggie Moffat and Kathleen Rothwell. Moffat was given the prison number DX27 and not allowed to wear her own clothes or have food sent in. She was not permitted to write letters or to read newspapers. At chapel each day the suffragists sat together, but conversation was limited. Moffat felt growing numbers of women – even veteran suffragists – had accepted the need for new tactics to further the women's goal: "At first there was an outcry by suffragists of the older movement against the new methods, but that has now died down. Many have declared themselves

Suffragette prisoners are released from Holloway in 1909.

very grateful to the women of the Political Union for what they were doing... although they could not see eye to eye as regards the methods adopted, and felt that they personally could not take part in the militant tactics." 26.

To Kathleen Rothwell, who wrote to newspapers as 'Kathleen Roy Rothwell, nee Paterson', we owe thanks for a rare description of prison life. On her release, she described the regime as a "soul-killing" system, one in which she was confined in a cell nine feet by seven, with only one hour's exercise per day in a yard "encircled by prison walls, into which the smoke from a chimney blows." In describing prison food, she said she felt both "starved and poisoned" when it arrived unpalatable and in greasy, smelling tins. Her cocoa was floating with fat. The bread was "as dry as dust," and no butter was allowed. She wrote of her experiences in order to make a "strong protest against this diet...its effects were dangerous to life." Rothwell, who lived in Battersea Park after moving from Edinburgh, also complained about "rude, domineering and neglectful" prison officers. 27.

On February 27, around 30 of those sentenced to two weeks were released and welcomed by supporters. Their friends formed a procession to Caledonian Road station, where they took a train to Holborn and then to a restaurant in Chandos Street. Maggie Moffat and Isabella Cairns sat down for breakfast with Christabel Pankhurst and the firebrand Edith Rigby, who later burned down Lord Leverhulme's bungalow. While the released prisoners were being entertained by their WSPU sisters, a letter was read from a woman enclosing £5. The writer said that since reading of the "cowardly action of MPs towards the deputation of women to the House of Commons," she and her sister had become income tax resisters. Another letter, signed by 'A Worn and Weary Worker for Women's Suffrage for Many A Weary Year,' enclosed a cheque for £57 towards WSPU funds. A third letter enclosed £5, and the audience was also told that the American suffragist and pioneering financier Lady Tennessee Cook had contributed another £100. Every announcement was met with enthusiastic cheering. 28.

At Westminster, Willoughby Dickinson's bill for allowing women to vote at Parliamentary elections was presented in the Commons on 26 February 1907. It proposed that in all Acts relating to qualifications and registration for parliamentary elections, whenever words occurred which used the masculine gender the same would be held to include women for the purposes of voting. Furthermore, a woman would not be disqualified from voting by reason of marriage. The government allowed a free vote, but with Liberal MPs lining up to speak of their opposition, the session ebbed away. Effectively, no Bill had any chance of success without the formal backing of the government supported by the discipline of the Whips. Disappointment was felt by suffragists of all persuasions, not least Jessie Methven, who was beginning to show her true colours despite still acting as the ENSWS secretary: "Another flagrant device used by Members to keep the subject from being discussed has been the spinning out of endless talk on trivial Bills which happened to come in front of Suffrage Bills...debated in every possible degree of uselessness until all the time at the disposal of private members was used up; and so no time was left for the vitally important measure which was to come after it." 29.

In early March 1907 Barbara Steel carried out her implied threat to withhold her Imperial taxes. Lady Steel, the widow of the former Lord Provost of Edinburgh, a Liberal Party supporter and member of the Edinburgh School Board, the Edinburgh National Society, and now the WSPU, had told various meetings that taxation without representation was "tyranny." She warned that she was willing to become a passive resister and refuse to discharge her duty as a citizen until she had been made a citizen. She also wrote to the Inland Revenue protesting against being called on to pay tax as she had "no voice in the government of the country." She told them bluntly that she would not pay. As a result, at the end of February her home in Colinton Road was visited by three sheriff officers who removed items of furniture to the value of £18. 9 shillings, the amount of inhabited property tax due. The articles distrained were an oak hall settle, a carved oak sideboard, a hallstand, seven chairs and a marble clock – which together carried a value reportedly 10 times the amount of the tax due.

On March 23 a crowd estimated at 5000 gathered at the Mercat Cross for the sale. A start was made with the most imposing item, the large sideboard. Bidding was opened by a dealer at £10 and the piece was eventually knocked down for £35. At that the auctioneer declared "the great sale" over, as the amount due had been met. Word soon spread that the sideboard had been 'bought in' by Lady Steel's friends and earmarked for return to her. At a subsequent ENSWS meeting, the Rev C. M. Black joked that the membership was delighted that Lady Steel was again in possession of her property – and the "gloomy fears" that she would soon be "languishing in the dark recesses of 'His Majesty's Palace' [Calton Prison] had not been realised." Mary Lees added that so many members of the society had prepared replacement sideboards "that a lorry could not carry them!" At the same meeting, which attracted an unusually large attendance, with standing room only – and a standing ovation for Barbara Steel – Sarah Siddons Mair was

A suffragette speaks at a public auction of the goods of Mrs Alexina McGregor of Arbroath. Note the 'No Vote, No tax' banner.

formally elected president of the society, "as one who had devoted her life to the betterment of women, educationally and politically." Dr Agnes McLaren, step-daughter of the late president, was elected honorary president, "as the committee greatly desired to maintain some link with the McLaren family." 30.

S. E. S. Mair took the chair and submitted the ENSWS annual report, mentioning that the work of petitioning was still going on as it had done for the last 40 years. She was determined not to have it said that they were "wearying in the work." Lady Ramsay, a suffragist from Aberdeen, criticised newspaper accounts of the women's behaviour during the London demonstrations. Walter McLaren broke new ground by suggesting that the Edinburgh Society should consider running its own women's suffrage candidate – something tried in Glasgow in the years ahead, earning the ridicule of the national Press. Miss Mair mentioned at the close that the

Henry Campbell-Bannerman's Cabinet. The Glasgow-born Prime Minister is seated behind the desk, with his Chancellor, Herbert Asquith, standing right foreground. The Foreign Secretary, Sir Edward Grey, stands left foreground.

Women's Social and Political Union had suggested an "orderly march" through Edinburgh in May. A little dramatic force, she remarked, had a wonderful effect upon the public, and they "would not mind a two-mile walk." 31.

As matters transpired, the procession and demonstration in the Scottish capital did not take place until 5 October 1907 – a date chosen to coincide with a visit to the city by Henry Campbell-Bannerman. Once again, the Prime Minister declined to meet the women, writing to them, "I have as much on hand on the 5th that I can undertake. Besides, I do not see that any good would arise from a deputation. I am well aware of your desires." Campbell-Bannerman appears to have been deflected from earlier platitudes by opposition from within his Cabinet. His senior ministers, including Chancellor Herbert Asquith, Home Secretary Herbert Gladstone, Foreign Secretary Sir Edward Grey, President of the Board of Trade David Lloyd-George and the

Secretary for War Richard Haldane, ranged in their views from anti-suffrage to vehemently anti-suffrage.

The Edinburgh procession was titled the National Scottish Women's Suffrage Demonstration. It was organised by the Women's Social and Political Union, but all societies and sympathisers in Scotland were invited to attend. Press appeals for support were made by the Edinburgh WSPU secretary Elizabeth Bell. Jessie Methven responded immediately to say that the Edinburgh National Society would be happy to participate and "unite" with the WSPU. Arrangements were undertaken by a committee of WSPU and ENSWS members who worked together "with an admirable enthusiasm, unity and practical wisdom." It was agreed by the societies that the widely-respected Sarah Mair would preside over a meeting planned for the Synod Hall following the parade. A triumvirate of national leaders, Christabel Pankhurst, Teresa Billington-Greig and Charlotte Despard, were invited as guest speakers, representing the militant and non-militant vanguard of the movement. Edinburgh magistrates sanctioned the route from King's Park to the Synod Hall in Castle Terrace, via the Holyrood Gate, Abbeymount, Regent Road, Waterloo Place, Princes Street and Lothian Road. Vehicles were banned, and trams and taxis halted. 32.

On October 5, massive crowds looked on as Scotland's suffragists paraded through Edinburgh in an impressive show of support for women's votes. Around 500 women travelled from Glasgow by special train – another 300 from Dundee – with the number of processionists put at 3000 by *Women's Franchise*. In a show of unity, representatives from the WSPU and constitutionalist societies walked together or completed the route by carriage or charabanc – a scene shown on the only surviving photograph of the event. The parade was headed by mounted police, followed by the Edinburgh National Society president S. E. S. Mair, who shared her carriage with Lady Frances Balfour, the president of the London Society and daughter of the 8th Duke of Argyll. The procession was reported to be half a mile long. There were veterans of the early days and "schoolgirls with hair hanging down their back." Banners were numerous. 'Scots wha hae votes – Men' contrasted with that on the next carriage, 'Scots wha hae'na votes – Women.' The familiar 'Taxation without Representation is Tyranny' was seen everywhere. The banner raised in front of the Edinburgh contingent, 'Union is Strength,' was designed by Grace Jacob of the Women's Freedom League. The women proceeded to the Synod Hall, with the streets lined "very thickly" from the Post Office onwards. It was reported that onlookers were "quiet, watchful, undemonstrative, after the characteristic Edinburgh manner." Mary Phillips described it as "just one big triumphant, glorious success."

An over-excited *Women's Franchise* estimated the watching crowd "at nearly a million," and reported, here and there, the usual witticisms flung by the man in the street, such as, "Go home and mind the baby," and "You'll get six months for this," but there was no antagonism or hostility. Instead, the popular notion of the female battleaxe – and always manly – suffragist, as depicted by the Press, in satirical cartoons and on derogatory postcards, was completely dispelled. "There was absolutely nothing in this quiet, orderly regiment of earnest women – workers in every department of life, householders and breadwinners, young and old, all united in a common loyalty to their cause – to suggest the virago of popular imagination. And so, by ancient palace and abbey, up the broad winding road, and through stately streets, the procession of women went on its quiet way." 33.

Hundreds followed the processionists to the Synod Hall and vast crowds lined both sides of Castle Terrace. When Sarah Mair took the chair, every seat was filled and the audience overflowed into the Pillar Hall below, where Barbara Steel presided over a second meeting. With Jessie Methven absent through illness, the main speaking duties for the Edinburgh society fell to Mary Lees, who followed Charlotte Despard, Christabel Pankhurst, Teresa Billington-Greig, Ethel Snowden and Emmeline Pethick-Lawrence. It was the greatest gathering of suffrage leaders ever seen outside London.

Barbara Steel was back in the news in October 1907 when she became the first woman to stand for Edinburgh Town Council, one of only four female candidates that year to take advantage of the first opportunity women had to offer themselves for election. Lady Steel stood in the city's St Stephen's Ward. At one of dozens of meetings, she said she had put herself forward as she "strongly held the opinion" that Edinburgh Town Council would never be the best town council "until there were women in it." She spoke and fielded questions on myriad subjects, including temperance, taxation, housing, wages – even the unlikely presence of gambling machines in Edinburgh ice-cream shops which offered cigarettes as prizes! Such was the novelty of a woman standing for election that her meetings were packed, and eagerly reported on by the Press. Friends from the Edinburgh Society introduced her to audiences around the ward.

St Stephen's had two vacancies for the town council, but three candidates. The polling station was at Hamilton Place Public School and 4246 voters made up the roll. The result, when it came, brought disappointment for Barbara Steel and her supporters. John Murray with 1710 votes and William Finlay with 1635 were elected to Edinburgh Town Council. Lady Steel finished third with a creditable 1124 votes. From her home in Colinton Road, she wrote to the St Stephen's Ward electors to thank them for their support: "Although unsuccessful on this occasion, I have the utmost confidence that in the near future the Municipal electors of Edinburgh, like those who elect other bodies, will avail themselves of the services of women to help in managing the many important concerns with which the wellbeing of the City is so intimately connected." The *Edinburgh Evening News* summed up the historic candidature by concluding, "Lady Steel did wonderfully well." 34.

The key event in national terms in 1907 was not the unity of purpose shown in the Edinburgh procession, but an acrimonious schism in the Women's Social and Political Union. The rift occurred when leading members of the WSPU began to question the autocratic leadership of Emmeline and Christabel Pankhurst, particularly the notion that their 'war' with the government required total loyalty and obedience, and immediate action on orders from the London hierarchy. Their differences established, Charlotte Despard, Elizabeth How-

WOMEN'S SOCIAL & POLITICAL UNION.

VOTES FOR WOMEN.

PROCESSION

OF

SCOTTISH WOMEN,

KING'S PARK TO SYNOD HALL,

On SATURDAY, 5th OCTOBER, at 3 p.m.

RISE UP, WOMEN! COME IN YOUR THOUSANDS!

A. HOSSACK, 63 BRISTO STREET EDIN.

Martyn, Dora Marsden, Anne Cobden Sanderson, Margaret Nevinson and 70 other members of the WSPU left in November 1907 to form the Women's Freedom League (WFL). Mrs Despard, who went to school in Edinburgh, became its president.

A fracture had occurred in the movement. The splintering of the WSPU had ramifications in Scotland where women had to decide the path of their future activism – to remain loyal to the sedate protest practised by the Edinburgh National Society, to follow their militant sisters as the WSPU went toe-to-toe with the government and its law enforcers – or, now, to join the Women's Freedom League, which had its own take on how to go about winning the vote for women.

References

1. Miss J. C. Methven, 'Women's Suffrage in the Past, A Record of Betrayal' in The Suffragette, 17 January 1913.
2. 'Woman in the 19th Century', Daily Express, 1 January 1901. Ormerod's portrait hangs in Old College, University of Edinburgh, proclaiming her as its first woman honorary graduate.
3. Dundee Evening Telegraph, 2 January 1901.
4. idem, 9 April 1900; Elizabeth Crawford, The Women's Suffrage Movement (1999), p655; 'The Feeding and Clothing of Destitute Children in Edinburgh', in The Poor Law Magazine, 1900.
5. The Scotsman, 2 & 4 October 1900. Arthur Conan Doyle stood for Parliament twice as a Liberal Unionist: in 1900 in Edinburgh Central and in 1906 in the Hawick Burghs, but was not elected.
6. The Suffragette, 17 January 1913; Edinburgh Evening News, 3 December 1901.
7. Edinburgh Evening News, 8 & 26 March 1902.
8. Edinburgh Evening News, 6 August 1902; Dundee Courier, 29 October 1902.
9. Martin Pugh, The Pankhursts (2001), p109.
10. Idem, p107, Crawford (1999), p726; Midge Mackenzie, Shoulder to Shoulder (1975), p12. The Pankhursts' former home in Nelson Street, Manchester is marked by a commemorative plaque.
11. Edinburgh Evening News, 10 February 1904; Women's Suffrage Record, 1 June 1904.
12. The Scotsman, 16 January 1905.
13. Idem. Motherwell Times, 13 January 1905.
14. The Scotsman, 2 October 1905. As well as an Edinburgh primary school named in her honour, in 2021 Flora Stevenson appeared on a Royal Bank of Scotland £50 note.
15. Mackenzie (1975), p20 & pp31-32.
16. Laura Mayhall, The Militant Suffragette Movement (2003), p66; Leah Leneman, A Guid Cause (1991), p42; Letter, ENSWS to other societies, 21 January 1906, The Women's Library, LSE, 9/01/0301.
17. Sarah Pedersen, The Scottish Suffragettes and the Press (2017), p55; The Scotsman, 21 May 1906.
18. Leah Leneman, The Scottish Suffragettes (2000), p22; Edinburgh Evening News, 9 November 1906; Miss J. C. Methven, 'Women's Suffrage in the Past, A Record of Betrayal', in The Suffragette, 17 January 1913.
19. The Scotsman, 10 August 1906; Edinburgh Evening News, 17 October 1906.
20. The Scotsman, 18 October 1907.
21. Miss J. C. Methven, 'Women's Suffrage in The Past, A Record of Betrayal', in The Suffragette, 17 January 1913.
22. Northern Chronicle, 9 January 1907; The Scotsman, 9 January 1907.
23. Arabella Scott, My Murky Past (Frances Wheelhouse typescript); The Scotsman, 1 February 1907.
24. Mackenzie (1975), p58 & 60.
25. Pall Mall Gazette, 14 February 1907.
26. Leneman (1991), p48. It is curious that Leah Leneman's entry in The Biographical Dictionary of Scottish Women (2006) does not specifically mention her seminal work on the Scottish suffragette movement, A Guid Cause (1991), for which she is best known.
27. Belper News, 15 March 1907.
28. Manchester Courier, 15 February 1907; London Daily News, 28 February 1907; Diane Atkinson, Rise Up Women! (2019), p66.
29. Edinburgh Evening News, 26 February 1907; The Suffragette, 17 January 1913.
30. Press & Journal, Saturday 2 & 25 March 1907. The Edinburgh Evening Despatch at this time called Lady Steel 'Edinburgh's pioneer suffragette.'
31. The Queen, 30 March 1907.
32. Women's Franchise, 22 August & 10 October 1907; Greenock Telegraph, 2 October 1907; Musselburgh News, 4 October 1907.
33. Women's Franchise, 10 October 1910; Forward, 12 October 1907.
34. Edinburgh Evening News, 7 November 1907; The Scotsman, 8 November 1907.

LEFT: A rare 'flyer' for the 1907 Women's Suffrage Procession in Edinburgh. (Courtesy of Aberdeen City Council – Archives, Gallery & Museums Collection)

Corstorphine's main street, c1908, with the unusual sight of a young girl on a bicycle.

FIVE:
CHAOS AT CORSTORPHINE 1908

"Please bear in mind that it is only in a public meeting that women can ask questions of the men whose salaries they are taxed to pay. If they attempt to carry a petition to Parliament, they are put in prison. If they call at a Cabinet Minister's house the same thing happens, and they have no representatives in Parliament as the men have, so they are compelled to put their questions in public meetings."

'A Suffragette' in a letter to the Edinburgh Evening News, 1 April 1908.

Three leading organisations campaigned for the vote as 1908 began – the NUWSS, the WSPU and the newcomers, the Women's Freedom League. From the outset the WFL was non-violent and opposed the WSPU's later targeting of private and commercial property, particularly the firing of buildings and bombings. It, too, drew its passion from 50 years of frustration, but adopted a policy of civil disobedience and passive resistance. It was particularly critical of the WSPU's 1913-1914 arson campaign – yet League members in Scotland seldom condemned their more militant sisters. Unlike the stranglehold the Pankhursts had over the WSPU, the League was run on democratic lines by committee, its aims being to widen public sympathy for women's votes across society. Yet, when push came to shove, over 100 of its members went to prison for their protests. Quickly attracting recruits, the WFL grew rapidly and soon had 60 branches with a membership of around 4000 women. It was particularly strong in Scotland, where a lack of surviving records means its activities remain under-researched. This work joins the other two in the series, *Dundee Suffragettes* (2018) and *Glasgow's Suffragettes* (2023), in revealing the League's important role. Distancing itself further from the autocratic WSPU, the League's Scottish branches frequently appointed local organisers and

had considerable autonomy. Yet, in a revealing contrast with the situation south of the border, the WFL in Scotland always had cordial relations with its militant and non-militant sisters.

By the spring of 1908, the fledgling Edinburgh Women's Freedom League had attracted members from the moderate ENSWS and defectors from the militant WSPU. They included Elizabeth Bell, Kate Moffat and Mrs Macleod Easson, who was on the cusp of becoming branch president. Alexia Jack, who had moved from her native Forfarshire to teach in Edinburgh, was appointed secretary and quickly organised a raft of activities for the 1908-1909 session, including a public meeting at the Edinburgh Café in Princes Street with Teresa Billington-Greig as principal speaker. Its ordinary and business meetings were held in the India Buildings, Victoria Street, off the Royal Mile. Annual subscription was one shilling.

A branch of the Men's League for Women's Suffrage was also started early in 1908 following a meeting at the Oddfellows' Hall in Forrest Road. Tom Johnston, the pro-suffrage editor of *Forward,* travelled from Glasgow with Teresa Billington-Greig to support its formation. Barbara Steel and Sarah Mair also spoke. Several members of the Edinburgh National Society, such as the Rev Robert Drummond of St Mark's, the solicitor Daniel Easson and the

Mary Gawthorpe on by-election duty in 1908.

FORESTERS' HALL
AFTERNOON MEETINGS
EACH
DAY 3 P.M.

THE SUFFRAGETTE MEETING

Rev Charles Black of Christ Church, Morningside, joined the new group. At a subsequent meeting, the branch agreed to affiliate to the National Men's League and announced its office-bearers. Its president was Professor Charles Sarolea, head of French at Edinburgh University; Daniel Easson was elected vice-president; its first secretary was Edward Vulliamy. In Dan Easson, especially, the women had an unswerving champion. He told the meeting that the women's movement had been going for 50 years and he now thought it was time "for militant tactics." Indeed, in 1909 he and his wife Macleod Easson launched the hitherto unrecorded militant 'Edinburgh Votes for Women Club'. Thereafter, the Edinburgh Men's League organised a programme of meetings and petitions and helped the three main women's societies with the staffing and stewarding of public events. From 1910, Edinburgh also had a small branch of the Men's Political Union, the militant male arm of the WSPU. [1]

Incidents occurred whichever organisation took its message to the people of Edinburgh. In February 1908 a Women's Freedom League meeting at Corstorphine Public Hall was so completely disrupted by Edinburgh students that it had to be abandoned. A second meeting in the village three miles west of Edinburgh was kept secret until late afternoon, "but the news found its way to the students. Residences were communicated with by telephone, and word was passed into the tutorial classes." The second meeting proceeded smoothly for about half-an-hour. Then, when Teresa Billington-Greig was delivering her address, a commotion was heard outside, marking the arrival of around 100 students from the new Corstorphine railway station. The youths brandished sticks and sang various ribald choruses as they entered the hall. The platform party took cover, leaving the students in a pitched battle with half a dozen police officers. The *London Globe* reported that doors, windows, chairs and furniture were smashed and that "the women were handed out through the broken windows." Dan Easson, one of the stewards, pointed out that the damage done at Corstorphine exceeded "all the destruction allegedly caused by women demonstrators throughout Britain." [2]

As a result of the Corstorphine riot, a self-styled 'militant Edinburgh Suffragette' wrote to *The Edinburgh Evening News* to explain events "through a woman's eyes." She said that the "male reporters" of the Press had viewed the disturbance as students "imitating" suffragette tactics. This was not the case. Moreover, "Please bear in mind that it is only in a public meeting that women can ask questions of the men whose salaries they are taxed to pay. If they attempt to carry a petition to Parliament, they are put in prison. If they call at a Cabinet Minister's house the same thing happens, and they have no representatives in Parliament as the men have, so they are compelled to put their questions in public meetings." To emphasise the difficulty women faced in getting their opinions heard, the unidentified 'Edinburgh suffragette' then described the Conference on Infantile Mortality which she had attended in London the previous week. During the opening session, the Rt Hon John Burns, President of the Local Government Board, had spoken for 15 minutes when a woman at the back of the hall shouted something. Suddenly men rose to their feet excitedly calling 'shame' and demanding that she be ejected. "Then I knew what had happened – a suffragette. It was most comical to see sober-looking men all at once become hysterical. The lady with the thirst for information allowed herself to be quietly conducted from the meeting." John Burns had just resumed his speech when again there was a woman's voice from the body of the hall. "This time he forgot the dignity of his position and toppled off his pedestal." The same process of expulsion took place, and the speech continued. Once more there was a voice from the back of the hall. "I saw a tall, handsome girl standing quite composed and calm. When I looked back at the platform there was the Cabinet Minister standing like incarnate fury, his hands clenched, his beard bristling, and his eyes blazing, and I said to myself, 'These be thy gods, O Israel.' When the handsome girl had been put out the excited men resumed their seats, and Mr Burns became once more the Cabinet Minister." [3]

Edinburgh WSPU, to whom this unidentified eyewitness likely belonged, was busy on several fronts. At one of its first public meetings in the city, in the

The Hunger Strike medal awarded to Florence Haig, showing her imprisonment for the Pantechnicon Raid of 1908. (Courtesy of London Museum)

Queen Street Hall, it introduced a graded charge for admission. The hall was well filled nevertheless to hear speakers of the calibre of Emmeline Pethick-Lawrence, who presided, Emmeline Pankhurst, recently released from her first spell in prison, the Scottish WSPU organiser Helen Fraser and the Rev Dr John Glasse, the minister of Greyfriars and a pivotal figure in the emergence of Scottish socialism. Mrs Pethick-Lawrence explained that the WSPU did not ask the vote for all women, but they demanded it on the same terms that men had it. They belonged to no party and considered it "absurd" to belong to one until they had the fundamental right of citizenship. They had no views on Tariff Reform or on the Licensing Bill or on any other political party question. They had one objective – votes for women. They would not lower the flag, she said, and if the government would not listen to their arguments, "they would protest, they would demonstrate, and more women would have to go to prison." Emmeline Pankhurst was next to speak. She said that on the occasion of her arrest there were 600 policemen to deal with 13 women. "Who made the obstruction?" she asked, to laughter and applause in the hall. Her cell door bore the words 'Unconvicted Prisoner,' and yet she wore prison clothes, ate prison food and passed 23 out of 24 hours in solitary confinement. She believed such treatment did more for their cause than any amount of public speaking. 4.

This was hardly the view held in the fashionable addresses of Edinburgh's west end. From Morningside came a rant against militancy from Dr Isabella Mears. Accusing the WSPU of "bombastic speech and a rude attitude," Dr Mears suggested that many women, as well as men, were "feeling indignant" by the actions of what she termed "agitators." Labelling the city's suffragettes as "brawlers" provoked an angry response from an anonymous 'Suffragette' who accused Mears of hindering, not helping, the cause. "In a letter in today's *Scotsman*, signed Isabella Mears LRCPL, the writer seems to forget that she would not be able to write these letters after her name except for the fight in which her forerunners took part. I remember the bitter struggle women had in their effort to be allowed to study for their medical degree. If these brave women had not had the courage to stand the abuse which was levelled at them at that time, Dr Isabella Mears would still be unable to help humanity in the way she now can." Addressing the physician's criticism of militancy, the 'Suffragette' said they had tried "sweet gentleness" in the form of drawing-room meetings and petitions "for fifty years" to no avail. Some of the petitions, she added, had been "burnt as waste paper." There was no response from Dr Mears to this or to another letter-writer who mocked her for training in London, and not Edinburgh. (Mears was actually one of Dr Sophia Jex-Blake's first students at the School of Medicine for Women in London. She was the tenth woman on the General Medical Register.) 5.

By late February, a third Women's Parliament at Caxton Hall had the predictable sequel – a WSPU march on Westminster with 50 arrests, including Emmeline Pankhurst again. Most were given six weeks in the Second Division. Sentences were becoming harsher and the defendants were warned that if their militancy continued, the authorities would consider reviving a Charles II Act which outlawed 'tumultuous Petitions either to the Crown or Parliament', which would carry a £100 fine or three months' imprisonment. When Mrs Pankhurst said she would put the threat to the test "the very next day," the authorities backed down.

Around 40 women then gathered in London for an audacious 'Trojan Horse' raid on the Commons. The plan was for the WSPU volunteers to hide in the back of two motorised furniture vans until they reached the Strangers' Entrance. Once there, they would jump out, rush in and protest until arrested. All went well until the women emerged blinking into the light, with one or two temporarily blinded and dashing off in the wrong direction. A large force of police was lying in wait. Dundee teacher Annot Wilkie recalled, "We made a rush for the doorway...We almost gained admittance when, hey presto!, scores of policemen sprang up as it seemed from the earth. We politely asked them to allow us to enter, but 'deaf as Ailsa Craig', there they stood." Wilkie, scribbling her letter while awaiting trial at Westminster police court, finished, "My name is called, so I shall write no more." 6.

The women detained in the so-called 'Pantechnicon Raid' were taken to Cannon Row police station. One of the those arrested recalled numbers swelling until women queued up to be charged, with the Scottish contingent cheering whenever one of their countrywomen appeared. Police accounts of their adventures were read from the evening papers to occasional bursts of laughter. Among those detained was Florence Haig, who had just moved from Edinburgh to London to further her career as an artist. Haig and her two sisters Cecilia and Evelyn had been founding members of Edinburgh WSPU. Another was Mary Phillips from Cardross, an active campaigner for Glasgow WSPU. At Westminster court the following day Haig and Phillips were sentenced to six weeks' imprisonment, as was Annot Wilkie. Of the 49 women sentenced, all but two – who had sick relatives – opted to go to prison. The episode was captured in rhyme by Marie Brackenbury, one of the jailed Trojans...

> Sing a song of Christabel's clever little plan,
> Four and twenty suffragettes packed into a van,
> When the van was opened, they to the Commons ran,
> Wasn't that a dainty dish for Campbell-Bannerman?
> Asquith was in the Treasury, counting out the money,
> Lloyd George among the Liberal women speaking words of honey,
> And then there came a bright idea to all these little men,
> 'Let's give the women Votes,' they cried, 'and all be friends again.'

The spring of 1908 brought political upheaval. The Prime Minister, Sir Henry Campbell-Bannerman, began to succumb to health problems. Fearing he would not survive to the end of his term, he resigned on April 3. He was succeeded by the Chancellor of the Exchequer, Herbert Asquith, with David Lloyd George replacing Asquith at the Treasury. Campbell-Bannerman died just 19 days after his resignation, aged 71. His last words were, famously, "This is not the end of me."

Prime Minister Herbert Asquith.

H. H. Asquith, MP for East Fife since 1886, was already regarded by suffragists as an implacable opponent. As early as 1892 he had nailed his colours to the mast by opposing any extension to the adult franchise. He believed there was no appetite for it and, for confirmation, "he only had to turn to his wife, Margot, and their elder daughter, Violet, who were passionate anti-suffragists." Emmeline Pankhurst regarded him as "a bluntly outspoken" opponent: "It was sufficiently plain to us that no methods of education or persuasion would ever prove successful where he was concerned. Therefore, the necessity of action on our part was greater than ever." Suffrage historian Leah Leneman was of the view that Asquith's attitude was "one of the main obstacles" to women obtaining the vote before the First World War. This was certainly the case, but to an extent his views merely chimed with an era in which the prevailing ideology placed women firmly in the home. For those like Asquith, the idea of women's suffrage contravened long-established and accepted traditions of motherhood and family life. [7.]

With a new Prime Minister in place, four parliamentary by-elections in 1908 focused the political spotlight on Scotland. The Kincardineshire election on April 25 followed the death of the sitting Liberal MP John Crombie. The campaign centred on Stonehaven, but took in several districts bordering Dundee. The following month, Dundee's citizenry went to the polls when one of the city's two MPs was elevated to the House of Lords. Montrose and Stirling were also contested early in 1908, the latter called after Campbell-Bannerman's death. All four seats were held by the Liberals.

The Kincardineshire election saw women picket polling stations for the first time in Scotland. National leaders poured into the area, and Edinburgh's WSPU, NUWSS and WFL travelled north in support. The Women's Freedom League rented a shop in Stonehaven's Allardyce Street and had committee rooms in Forfar and Montrose, where windows were decorated with "cartoons, literature and postcards of our leaders." Told to take the campaign to Stonehaven, the WSPU's Helen Wilkie reported "several pairs of curious eyes fixed on us." But soon the Union's volunteers were distributing information and literature from committee rooms in Barclay Street. At a WSPU open-air meeting in Laurencekirk, Mary Phillips – newly released from Holloway – explained why the Union had adopted militant tactics. It was, she said, because nothing else had worked. She called on electors to vote against the Liberal candidate in order to wrest votes away from the government. Phillips also spoke at Banchory, Cove and Stonehaven and presided over a meeting at the Aberdeen Fish Market at which Mary Gawthorpe also spoke. At another outdoor gathering, at the Pierhead in Torry, Gawthorpe was heckled by a man who threatened to 'knock her down' – a rare physical threat against a suffragist at this time. Conversely, Anna Munro recalled campaigning in the Mearns and being cheered by working men, one of whom stepped forward, "and gave me half-a-crown to help in the work." *The Scotsman* described "Ex-prisoner Munro" as a "tall, slight, pale complexioned young lady in a becoming picture hat and grey cloak." The Edinburgh paper's correspondent added: "The fact that the speaker has been in prison is carefully chalked up in intimations of meetings. It is found that this qualification greatly stimulates the interest." 8.

Kincardineshire folk from the borders of Aberdeen to the boundary of Dundee listened keenly to the women's message and turned up in numbers to the constituency's first-ever suffrage meetings; but, to the women's disappointment, the Liberal candidate took the seat after a straight fight with his Unionist opponent. A small, but satisfying, consolation was the reduced majority returned by Mearns' electors. There were bigger fish to fry. On 1 May 1908, Winston Churchill arrived in Dundee to seek election to the constituency made vacant by the elevation of sitting MP Edmund Robertson to the peerage. The seat was safely Liberal with a 5000 majority. Hours earlier Churchill had been defeated in North-West Manchester. Six minutes after leaving that declaration he was handed a telegram from the Dundee Liberal Association offering him the candidature at Dundee. Churchill accepted and travelled to Scotland overnight. He was greeted at the town's West Station by thousands of jubilant supporters. Already a powerful political figure, as custom dictated,

Helen Fraser of the WSPU campaigning during the Kincardineshire by-election in 1908.

his return to the Cabinet as President of the Board of Trade obliged him to put himself forward for re-election. With the WSPU and WFL pledged to campaign vigorously against every Liberal candidate, something had to give...

The Pankhursts were among 27 WSPU leaders and paid organisers who took rooms in Dundee. They included household-name suffragists such as Jennie Baines (Holloway prisoner 1906), Mary Gawthorpe (Holloway 1906, 1907), Rachel Barrett, Nellie Martel (Holloway 1906) and Mary Leigh (Holloway 1907) – with Helen Fraser, Frances Parker (Holloway 1908) and Florence Macaulay (soon WSPU organiser in Edinburgh) leading the Scottish contingent. The WSPU opened an office at 61 Nethergate and a trio of Pankhursts, Emmeline, Christabel and Adela, fronted the bid to 'keep the Liberal out'. It was the 17th by-election they had fought. The Women's Freedom League, then with 70 members in Dundee, also mobilised,

Winston Churchill – an implacable opponent of votes for women.

welcoming to the city its national president Charlotte Despard and Scottish organiser Teresa Billington-Greig and opening an office in the Cowgate. By the end of 1908 the WFL had taken part in 13 by-elections. As with the WSPU it opposed all government candidates. Dundee Women's Suffrage Society had rooms at 12 Meadowside. The branch secretary was Alice Crompton, niece of the Victorian suffragist Lydia Becker, and she welcomed NUWSS president Millicent Fawcett to Dundee. The National Union had campaigned in over 20 by-elections, and it continued to support candidates who promised votes for women.

Dundee was a Liberal stronghold. The hostile anti-suffragist Winston Churchill was the party's candidate for the city's vacant seat. East Fife, the constituency of Prime Minister Herbert Asquith, who saw no place for women in politics, lay just across the river. His predecessor Henry Campbell-Bannerman, who was never prepared to make women's votes part of government policy, had lived at Meigle, 10 miles north-west of Dundee. Herbert Gladstone, the Home Secretary who had introduced the punitive sentencing on suffragettes, had a family home 20-odd miles to the north. And while the constituency eagerly anticipated a stirring election battle, the distractive antics of the Women's Freedom League's Mary Maloney, who clanged a large dinner bell whenever Churchill spoke, dominated headlines and damaged the women's campaign. Accused by Churchill of being under the influence of drink and carried in the arms of dockers at a meeting in Peckham, Maloney arrived in Dundee to extract an apology for the "lie," attracting a boisterous crowd of 10,000 to her first meeting. Whenever Churchill spoke, Maloney's handbell completely drowned out what he said, or at least caused a noisy diversion. Churchill refused to apologise and so the skirmishes continued.

Although Maloney and her dinner bell made headlines across Britain, her noisy protests did more damage than good. Her conduct was viewed as an abuse of free speech. It also served to act as a distraction from much good election work by a coalition of WSPU, WFL and the NUWSS, who frequently ignored strategic differences to campaign side by side. It prompted the Pankhursts to write to the *Dundee Advertiser* absolving themselves and the WSPU of any responsibility. "These women are not members of the Women's Social and Political Union," they said huffily, disregarding the militancy perpetrated by their own organisation. But non-militants were also frustrated at Maloney's disruptive tactics and wrote to local papers to say so. Churchill was elected with a reduced majority, entering the Cabinet despite his youth (just 33) and the fact that he had crossed the floor to become a Liberal only four years earlier. The suffrage cause had stalled. Christabel Pankhurst noted in her autobiography that the Dundee result was a "distinct setback" to the campaign: "Our all-conquering election progress was checked." 9.

Before spring turned to summer, crowds gathered again at Edinburgh's Mercat Cross for another sale of a suffragette's goods. This time, the furniture of Miss Meredith of Roseneath Terrace, a member of the Women's Freedom League, was seized in lieu of non-payment of taxes to the value of 18 shillings. Despite the sheriff officer attempting to frustrate her friends and supporters by keeping the time of the sale a secret, then holding it early in the morning, three members of the Edinburgh WFL were up and about to distribute handbills detailing the women's grievances. A wooden 'what-not' made 6/6d, a bamboo table brought 1/6d and three chairs fetched 10/6d. There was still another chair to sell, but with the amount due to the tax authorities having been met, the auctioneer declared the sale over. All goods were bought in by friends and driven straight back to Roseneath Terrace.

That was not the end of it. Cock-a-hoop at putting the suffragettes in their place, the Edinburgh tax office then slapped a demand on the Women's Freedom League office at 33 Forrest Road. This drew a response from Alexia Jack, the branch secretary, who pointed out to them that the branch had "no trade or business, consequently no profits, and its sole income is derived from voluntary subscriptions, donations and collections from its members and sympathisers." She added that "after much hard work and not a little self-sacrifice" the branch had just enough money to pay its rent. After one of its

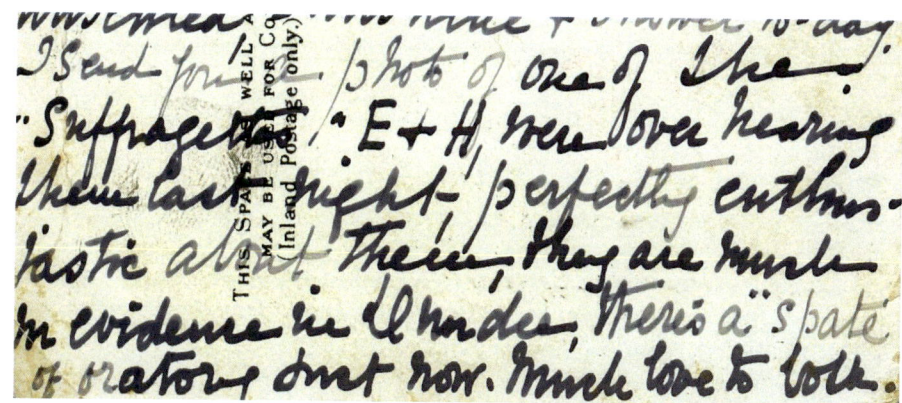

The reverse of a WSPU official postcard of Christabel Pankhurst, sent from Dundee on 7 May 1908, with the message: "I send you a photo of one of the Suffragettes. E & H were over hearing them last night, perfectly enthusiastic about them, they are much in evidence in Dundee. There is a spate of oratory just now..."

monthly bank statements showed interest of just over £1. 10s, the local income tax office demanded tax on £2. The branch refused to pay, with the result that the courts granted a warrant to sell its furnishings at the Mercat Cross. "Is it to be wondered that women are somewhat rebellious?"asked Jack. She called it "legalised robbery" – but the matter was presumably resolved by negotiation, or the tax was paid, as the branch escaped further sanction. 10.

The formal announcement of the Women's Social and Political Union's first office in Edinburgh took place in the Oak Hall of the Edinburgh Café, Princes Street in April 1908. The local WSPU leadership was present, including Jessie Methven, Morag Burn Murdoch and Miss McMillan of Corstorphine, as well as the new branch secretary Esson Maule and treasurer Evelyn Cotton Haig. On hand to lend support were Mrs John Hunter (Nellie Galbraith), Janet Bunton, Isabella Pearce and Grace Paterson – the office-bearers and leading lights of the Glasgow branch. As with their friends in the Scottish capital, the Glasgow WSPU had met in members' homes or in rented halls before finding the wherewithal to open an office at 141 Bath Street in January 1908. Now, their Edinburgh sisters had found rooms in Albert Buildings at

Alexia Jack, secretary of the Edinburgh branch of the Women's Freedom League. (Courtesy of Miss Jack's family)

24 Shandwick Place, which they intended to use as their headquarters, as well as providing a retail area to meet running costs, with a range of pamphlets, postcards, newspapers and branded goods. Mrs Hunter, the Glasgow president, congratulated the women on the opening of their first office and urged them not to be deterred by the obstacles they might face and the hostility that would come their way from the Press and public. The branch was formally opened on June 3 by Helen Fraser, Scottish Organiser for the WSPU. [11].

The Edinburgh Women's Freedom League, meanwhile, found itself swimming against the tide. In May 1908 it staged its first major meeting in the city, partnering the Men's League for such an undertaking before booking the 2000-seat Synod Hall in Castle Terrace. Firstly, Edinburgh's wayward students saw the occasion as a target for more fun. Impertinently calling itself 'The University Anti-Humbug League', its leaders issued a three-line whip calling on members to descend on the hall to oppose the suffragists, as they had done at Corstorphine. A force of 60 policemen guarded the building, with mounted officers as back-up. When the meeting began, a body of students noisily entered the gallery on either side of the platform and made their presence known with disruptive shouting and singing. They were cleared in dribs and drabs and the meeting was allowed to proceed.

Secondly, the League had invited big-hitters to the Synod Hall. Millicent Fawcett, leader of the National Union of Women's Suffrage Societies, was advertised as the principal guest. Barrister and politician Earl Russell (surprisingly as he had previously been jailed for bigamy) and Cicely Hamilton, secretary of Chelsea WFL, the first branch formed after the schism with the WSPU, were among other speakers. On the day of the meeting, Mrs Fawcett was known to be in Edinburgh, but a notice on the venue's door intimated that Amy Sanderson, another exile from the WSPU, was to take her place. The 1000-strong audience must have been further bemused when no letter of apology was read from Mrs Fawcett as the meeting began. Word spread that she had refused to speak after Women's Freedom League activists had the day before targeted 10 Downing Street. [12].

Mrs Fawcett, in fact, had sent a letter to the Edinburgh WFL secretary Alexia Jack shortly before the Synod Hall event. Without consulting the League, she had forwarded a copy to *The Scotsman*, which gleefully ran it as prominently as possible: "I must withdraw my promise to speak at the meeting. In spite of my most earnest remonstrance, the heads of the Women's Freedom League organised a disturbance at Mr Asquith's house yesterday morning, within a few hours of his making a pronouncement which, however short of what suffragists can consider satisfactory, is yet in advance on any position on women's suffrage he has yet occupied. A hostile personal demonstration against him I therefore consider ill-timed and futile, and I desire to disassociate myself and the NUWSS as emphatically as I can from yesterday's proceedings at Downing Street."

This drew a no-nonsense, bullet-pointed response, via the paper, from Alexia Jack: **"**Sir, since you without my permission have deemed it advisable to publish Mrs Fawcett's letter to me, I think it only fair to my Society and the public to give a fuller explanation of the facts.

1. Mrs Fawcett, after consultation with her committee, and knowing well that we were pledged to militant tactics, agreed to speak at this Edinburgh meeting.
2. No conditions were laid down in this agreement.
3. The meeting was convened jointly with the Men's League, an independent body not pledged to militant tactics, and who had no connection with the Downing Street demonstration, the only episode to which Mrs Fawcett took exception.
4. These facts were pointed out to Mrs Fawcett, and also that she could speak on Friday from the Men's League platform and utter publicly her protest against the London Executive of the Women's Freedom League. Further, it was shown that by adhering to her decision she was forcing the promotors of the meeting into a position of seeming dishonourable action and breach of faith, in binding them to conditions of which they were entirely ignorant and over which they had no control."

The impressive façade of Albert Buildings survives in the modern city.

Mrs Fawcett.

Miss Jack's letter concluded, "Notwithstanding these representations, Mrs Fawcett, at noon on Friday, sent her ultimatum declining to appear. The organisers, even at this eleventh hour, secured a substitute [Amy Sanderson], and advertised as prominently as they could that Mrs Fawcett would not be present at the meeting."

What we do not know in this awkward exchange is the position of the Edinburgh National Society, which was affiliated to the NUWSS, which Mrs Fawcett led. Many members of the 1000-strong ENSWS were probably hoping to hear their leader speak in Edinburgh and were as equally disappointed with her absence as their sisters in the WFL. The squabble demonstrates, once again, the tensions which surfaced between Scottish societies and the London leaderships. 13.

When Lloyd George spoke in the King's Theatre with the Secretary for Scotland alongside him in front of thousands of devoted Liberal supporters, the capital's militants decided to announce their presence in no uncertain terms. The Chancellor was cheered to the rooftops when he rose to speak. But as soon as he did so, he was subjected to the first of an extraordinary series of interruptions. A woman in the gallery began shouting for votes. When she drew breath, Lloyd George told her he agreed with her and that her "eloquence" was wasted upon him. He said he would give her the vote "tomorrow," to which the woman replied, to laughter, "Thank you." She then re-started her noisy protest and was ejected by stewards. The Chancellor resumed his speech, then – "Why don't you give women the vote?" Amid chants of "put her out," the interrupter was similarly removed. Another suffragette called out, "Does the Government intend to give women the vote?" The Chancellor replied that the franchise question had been answered by the Prime Minister, "and every sensible woman should be satisfied." She, however, was not, and was carried out. Yet another disturbance occurred. Lloyd George had just mentioned how previous governments had lost the temperance fight, when a protest sounded from the dress circle, "And your Government will be beaten, too, unless you give votes to women." Amid a melee in the seats around her, the woman was bundled away. Once again Lloyd George was interrupted, and this time the female voice came from the stalls. The Chancellor resumed his seat while the stewards escorted the dissenter out of the hall. Resuming, his use of the word 'injustice' was enough for another suffragette to demand "justice" for women. She was removed, while still shouting for votes.

Outside, the six ejected women and dozens of supporters were subjected to abuse by a crowd estimated at 1000. They were followed down Home Street, pelted with rolled-up newspapers and bits of fruit, and had to take refuge in an ice cream shop at Tollcross. Edinburgh had never seen anything like it. The mobilisation and co-ordination of WFL and WSPU activists in this early phase of militancy must have sent shockwaves across the city – not least as it involved local women and not 'imported' suffragettes from the south. No charges were brought, and the women's names are unknown. The incident, however, was plotted on the WSPU map of militancy – even the far-off *London Despatch* recognised a stushie when it saw one, and headlined Edinburgh's 'Field Day with the Chancellor'. [14].

While the city's militants were targeting Lord George, the constitutionalist National Society found itself, once again, mourning the death of one of its beloved founders, Louisa Stevenson, who passed away in May 1908 aged 73. The elder sister of Eliza and Flora, her first public duty was honorary secretaryship of the National Association for the Medical Education of Women, a large and influential body, which, under the leadership of Dr Sophia Jex-Blake, fought and won the battle to gain medical teaching and degrees for women. By 1877 she was a member of the governing council of the London School of Medicine for Women, which Jex-Blake had established three years earlier. She was the first woman to serve on an Edinburgh Parochial Board and was secretary of the Edinburgh Association for the University Education of Women. A founder member, she served on the ENSWS committee for over 20 years. She was a member of the NUWSS executive and had recently served as vice-president of the Suffrage Special Appeal Committee (Scotland).

David Lloyd George, c1907.

EDINBURGH WOMEN SUFFRAGE ORGANISERS

The Scottish contingent of the National Union of Women's Suffrage Societies to take part in the big demonstration in Hyde Park, leaving Waverley yesterday. Left to right—Miss Gordon, Miss Loudon, Miss Pressley Smith, and Miss Low. (Lemon.)

A quartet from the Edinburgh National Society for Women's Suffrage executive committee who attended the NUWSS Hyde Park demonstration in June 1908. Left to right, Lisa Gordon, Katherine Louden, Miss Pressley Smith and Alice Low.

She was awarded an honorary degree by Edinburgh University two years before her death. 15.

Two further London processions were planned for the summer of 1908. The National Union of Women's Suffrage Societies' Great Procession on June 14 brought a rallying cry to Scottish members from president Millicent Fawcett: "Join us...do not shrink from taking part in the procession and demonstration." An estimated 13,000 women walked the route from the Thames Embankment to the Albert Hall, including a large group from the Women's Liberal Federation, despite its executive deciding not to recognise the event officially. Their presence acts as a reminder that many Liberal voters and their families, especially in urban centres such as Edinburgh, supported the women's cause without relinquishing their personal political allegiances. It was the Liberal government alone which stood in the way of votes.

The second procession, a week later on June 21, was the now-famous Hyde Park 'Woman's Sunday' demonstration organised by the Women's Social and Political Union under the 'generalship' of Flora Drummond. A special train delivered the Edinburgh members, and the Scottish contingent joined Procession 'C' which left from Victoria Embankment, with the seven different processions coming together at Hyde Park. There, 80 leading suffragettes spoke from 20 different platforms formed into a circle under 700 flowing banners, some of them "mass produced and done in double-quick time" by Sylvia Pankhurst. It was estimated that 30,000 suffragettes from all over the country took part in the procession. An impressed *Guardian* reported that it "was certainly the most momentous thing of the kind that London has ever seen." The correspondent of *The Times* estimated those watching at 250,000 and said, "Probably it was doubled; and it would be difficult to contradict anyone who asserted confidently that it was trebled." But when the *Edinburgh Evening News* trotted out the old argument that the number of demonstrators was just a tiny fraction of British women, and that the "noise and vulgarity" of the WSPU was "insignificant," the militants were defended by Alexia Jack of Edinburgh Women's Freedom League: "It was members of the militant suffragists who were the initiators of the Scottish procession [in London]; the organising secretary of the demonstration was a member of the committee of the militant section in Edinburgh and is still an active member of the National Executive of the Women's Freedom League [Amy Sanderson], and, moreover, four out of five of the chief speakers that day were militants." 16.

Doctor's daughter Mary Phillips, with a roving role in the Scottish WSPU, was placed in charge of one of the columns leaving Trafalgar Square for Hyde Park. She recalled proudly that the procession she led included Keir Hardie, Bernard Shaw, H. G. Wells and Phillip Snowden. Scottish WSPU organiser Helen Fraser, speaking from one of the platforms, dwelled on the conditions endured by female workers in the textile towns of the north. She also denounced John Burns MP for his proposed parliamentary bill, which excluded married women from factory work. Fraser praised the large contingent of marchers from Scotland and felt that the vast turnout had demolished the Prime Minister's arguments. Christabel Pankhurst agreed, writing to 10 Downing Street to tell Herbert Asquith that "the WSPU had filled the park as no other franchise meeting had managed to do," and urging him to "grant votes to women without delay." Asquith, however, was unmoved by the numbers and continued to insist that there was "no evidence" that the majority of British women wanted the vote. On June 23, an Edinburgh WFL branch meeting in India Buildings heard Elizabeth Bell give an account of the London event. 17.

Before the month was out, Mary Phillips was behind bars again. She was among a WSPU cohort which besieged Parliament and was arrested when it tried to force an entry. Among the group was Florence Haig, then living in London, but one of a trio of sisters who had joined Edinburgh WSPU from the beginning. Haig and Phillips were handed three months for taking part in an illegal demonstration and sent to the familiar surroundings of Holloway – both had been jailed after the 'Pantechnicon Raid' that March.

After a delay for 'bad behaviour' Phillips was released on September 18, becoming the longest-serving suffragette prisoner in Britain up to that time.

After surviving the wild embraces of her friends, who were swathed in tartan shawls and carrying bouquets of heather in recognition of her Scottish roots, she wriggled through the crowd to mount a white heather-decorated carriage to which was harnessed a team of 12 suffragists wearing Glengarry bonnets and tartan plaids. Phillips' parents occupied the seats beside her as a Highland Pageant unfolded. The carriage was drawn to the Queen's Hall in Langham Place headed by pipers in Highland costume, while many of the women carried banners protesting at the prison 'torture'. Copies of *Votes for Women* were sold along the route. Flora Drummond, who organised the welcome, later presided over a celebratory breakfast for Phillips and stated that on October 13 the suffragettes would try to get inside the House of Commons and, "argue the question out with Mr Asquith."

Phillips herself was delighted by the reception, but hinted at the shock that many women experienced emerging from weeks and sometimes months of near-on solitary confinement to encounter on release a raucous welcome from friends and usually a slap-up breakfast: "It was all so unexpected, so delightful, so bewildering in its sudden and complete reversal of the sensations of the previous three months." Small wonder that Phillips was photographed by Special Branch in the exercise yard of Holloway looking exhausted, isolated and lost in her thoughts. 18.

Millicent Fawcett had fallen out with the Edinburgh WFL, but she still led the NUWSS and was always welcome at the affiliated Edinburgh National Society. On 13 July 1908 she was the principal speaker at a busy meeting in Queen Street Hall, where she was joined by NUWSS executive member Isabella Ford of Leeds, who was related to Elizabeth Pease Nichol of the ENSWS. Sarah Mair presided. Mrs Fawcett took the view that the huge London demonstrations a month earlier had answered many critics. She said she had then travelled to the International Women's Congress in Amsterdam where "women's votes were brought before 22 national parliaments and 29 state legislatures." Herbert Asquith's proposal to introduce a Reform Bill offered, she said, "nothing whatever for women." Men would have more

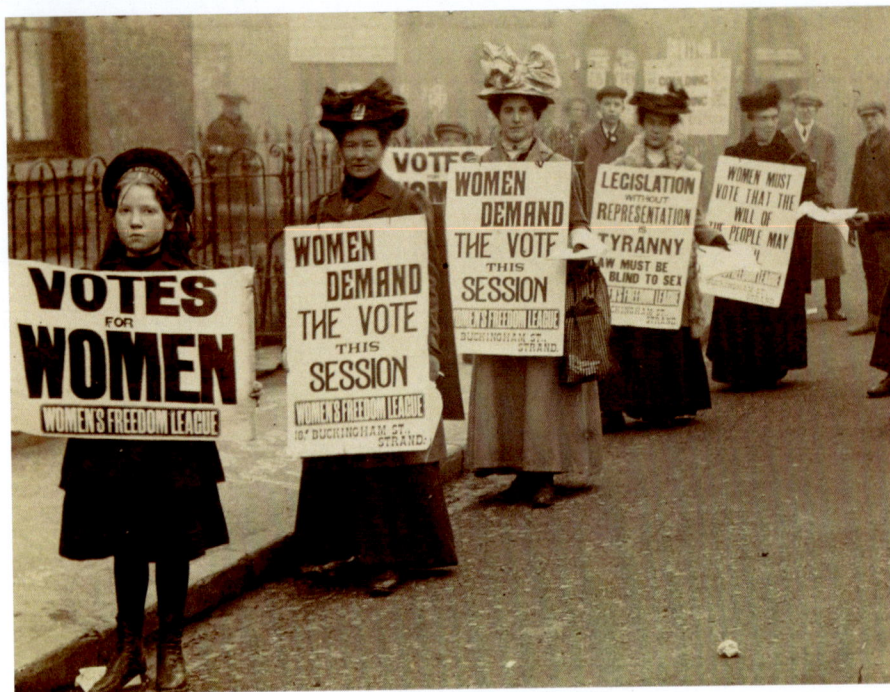

The Women's Freedom League continued its street demonstrations in the face of increased public hostility. (Courtesy of London Museum)

representation, but all women would remain voteless. Mrs Fawcett continued, "I have no faith in him, but I have faith in forces which are stronger than he, in the powers of progress and in the love of political liberty which is planted deep in every British heart." [19].

It seemed, however, no more nor no less than what had been heard at constitutionalist meetings in the previous half-century. Besides, the NUWSS was continuing to support Liberal parliamentary candidates, while the party itself was denying them votes. That was the conundrum unanswered by the NUWSS in the eyes of those following the militant path. Attempts to bring the societies together continued, however. In the middle of July, Lady Barbara Steel gave a large garden party to women suffragists at 'Boroughfield',

her home in Colinton Road. The 500 who attended included "suffragists of all kinds." Esson Maule, the incoming secretary of Edinburgh WSPU, encouraged members to attend and was later pleased to report that "small difficulties were discussed and overcome." [20].

Meanwhile, the Women's Freedom League [despite the secondary role given to them in suffrage histories] was continuing to bear the brunt of public hostility. Edinburgh members – and they now numbered 180 – faced another unpleasant experience in September 1908. An evening meeting had been arranged at the Mound. Anna Munro, who had been imprisoned in Holloway at the start of the year, was the principal speaker. A large crowd gathered, and Munro was able to talk for fully an hour without interruption. The women then moved to Chambers Street where Arabella Scott, then a League member, but later a leading WSPU militant, presided and introduced Munro once again. Mounted on a backless chair, the WFL Scottish organiser was addressing about 50 people when the first "house" of the Empire Theatre emptied. A crowd gathered, and soon the few male stewards were unable to contain a noisy and hostile element. Munro was subject to frequent interruptions, and the meeting was abandoned when the women's safety was placed in jeopardy. In the process, two of the League's linen banners were torn, some of the women were roughly handled and kicked, and Munro had to seek refuge in a shop doorway. The mob was kept at bay by members of the Men's League until the police arrived and escorted the women to the safety of their office in India Buildings.

The Women's Social and Political Union was also growing in numbers and influence in the Scottish capital. The prominence given to its recent efforts to "rush" the House of Commons and the sequel of the arrest of its leaders, drew a huge crowd to the Queen Street Hall on October 23. Every seat in the 2000-capacity hall was occupied "almost entirely by ladies." The unavoidable absence of Emmeline Pankhurst (three months in Holloway for 'inciting a riot'), was not the only disappointment. Elizabeth Robins, "a reluctant, although much-admired, speaker for the WSPU," who had been due to deputise for

Mrs Pankhurst, sent a telegram stating that she was too ill to attend. Miss Milne Chapman occupied the chair, and the main speaking duty was devolved to Mary Lees, who divided her time between the WSPU and the Edinburgh National Society. The Glasgow organiser Gertrude Conolan, Una Dugdale of London WSPU, who had a house in Aboyne, and Edinburgh WSPU member Esson Maule, who had just been appointed secretary of the Scottish Women's Social and Political Union, also contributed. Mary Lees ridiculed the idea that the recent 'rush day' in London had been a "fiasco," a term used in several newspapers. Rather, over 5000 policemen had been deployed to protect the House of Commons against a mere hundred or so women. Maule said that every time the government put one more woman in prison they were "putting one more nail into their coffin." Conolan, the final speaker, declared that for every woman who demanded the vote three years ago, "there were 100 in her place today." The distinct voice of militancy was now being heard across Edinburgh, offering an unambiguous contrast to the peaceful protests and petitions of the old National Society reported on year after year by the Misses Wigham and Kirkland. 21.

Banners were a feature of all suffrage marches and in December 1908 a four-day exhibition of some of the finest examples was staged in the Queen Street Hall. It was hosted by the Edinburgh National Society and the public was charged a shilling for afternoon entry and half of that in the evening. The banners were the work of the Artists' Suffrage League for the NUWSS and WSPU processions in London earlier in the year. Most were embroidered with silk thread, or wool, on linen and multicoloured. Over 70 banners were displayed; some of them dedicated to individual societies, others to prominent individuals in the campaign, a few to historic female figures, including Joan of Arc and Queen Victoria, and yet others to women in other fields, such as Florence Nightingale and Marie Curie. At a gathering on the first day, Sarah Mair introduced Lady Frances Balfour, daughter of the 8th Duke of Argyll and the highest ranked member of the British aristocracy to assume a leadership role in support of women's suffrage, who formally declared the exhibition

open. Short addresses on those commemorated on the banners were given by various speakers.

The Queen Street Hall was a busy place. The NUWSS had to dismantle its exhibition speedily to allow a Women's Social and Political Union meeting in the second week of December. Mary Lees presided and introduced Emmeline Pethick-Lawrence, co-leader of the Union, who told the audience that there was "no doubt" that the Government was hostile to the Women's Suffrage Bill then progressing through its early stages. She demanded facilities for its progress. If this were done, and the bill passed the Commons and was rejected by the House of Lords, then their "quarrel with the present Government was done." Loud cheers greeted her reference to the imminent release of Christabel Pankhurst from prison. So far in 1908, 124 women had been jailed. She did not know the final total, as they had not abandoned militant tactics and there were a few days left of December. This brought further cheers and foot-stamping. The Edinburgh branch was up for the fight. 22.

In mid-1908, the Scottish women graduates took their appeal to the House of Lords against the decision by the Scottish courts to refuse to allow women to vote in the University constituencies. There, two Edinburgh-born graduates, Chrystal Macmillan and Frances Simson, argued the case at length and with great ability and knowledge of legal matters. The gist of the appeal was that the Scottish women graduates were on a footing of complete equality with Scottish male graduates. The names of the women were, like those of the men, on the statutory Parliamentary voting register, established by the Franchise Act of 1868. Furthermore, in the section of the Act enfranchising Scottish graduates, the word 'person' was used, and not the word 'man'. After hearing the case, the House of Lords dismissed the appeal on the grounds that the disability of women had been "taken for granted ... not only has it been the constant tradition alike of all the three kingdoms, but it has also been the constant practice." As to the point that the women graduates were entitled to voting papers, their Lordships decreed that "they are not so entitled because the Act only says that voters shall receive them. They are not voters."

The Edinburgh banner taken to London in 1908 for the NUWSS demonstration. (Courtesy of London Museum)

The judges, all male of course, had concluded that the word 'person' in the 1868 Act meant 'male person.' Women, in other words, were not persons.

The inner workings of Edinburgh's Women's Social and Political Union are contained in a letter of December 1908 from the author and literary critic "Rebecca West", who grew up in Edinburgh as Cicily Isabel Fairfield of Buccleuch Place [later Dame Cicily]. Fairfield was just 16 at this time, and was writing to her sister Letitia: "We have had a very fine time – last Wednesday, Miss [Mary] Maloney and Louisa Walker spoke for the Men's League – I think Miss Maloney is one of the loveliest creatures I ever saw...on Thursday I went to a supper party at Mrs Easson's [of Edinburgh WSPU] to meet Miss Maloney. The occasion was the inauguration of The Votes for Women Club – a secret militant society for men and women. We come into active service first on Jan 5th when Haldane comes. We are to have a big protest meeting outside... Bushos told you about the meeting at the Mound. The crowd 'licked its lips.' The dear dainty little Scotts [Arabella and Muriel] spoke too, with Morag Burn Murdoch, Miss [Lisa] Chapman and Cecilia Haig. The Scots are magnificent workers but have not the slightest sense of humour. They said to me very solemnly, 'Could you not come to prison with us in July, Miss Fairfield?

It would be so nice and homelike if we could all go.' With best wishes for the New Year. May 1909 bring votes for Women!" [23].

The Edinburgh Votes for Women Club is not listed or mentioned in suffrage histories. Cicily Fairfield may have attended its first meeting with Dan and Macleod Easson and others, but the new club does not appear to have made an impact at the event referred to in her fascinating letter – that of the Secretary of War's speech to regimental associations at the McEwan Hall on January 5, or at Haldane's appearance at the United Service Club in Shandwick Place the same evening. There are no reports of disturbances before, during or after these meetings.

In June 1909, however, the Edinburgh Votes for Women Club had an away day, when a car decorated with a 'Votes for Women' banner was driven to Roslin. An outdoor meeting was arranged, with a question-and-answer session taken by the Eassons and a Miss Lauder. In September 1909 it was stated that the Votes for Women Club had "clubrooms" at 14 Hart Street, Edinburgh, but this was the home of the Eassons. Nevertheless, the new club must have had some pull. One meeting in September attracted 40 to Hart Street and heard speeches from Lady Constance Lytton and Isabel Kelly of London WSPU. Kelly had been recently jailed in Dundee for hijacking a Liberal Party meeting. Constance Lytton was newly released from Holloway. Lady Barbara Steel presided, and others present included Dr Grace Cadell, Mary Lees and Dr Isabel Venters, who had studied medicine at the Surgeons' Square school in London founded by Sophia Jex-Blake.

The 'secret' Edinburgh Votes for Women Club appears to have been a separate entity from the WSPU. A report in *Votes for Women* stated that on 26 February 1909, a deputation from Edinburgh WSPU attended a meeting of the Votes for Women Club at Hart Street "to explain our method of working," after which the club "decided to throw in its lot with the Women's Social and Political Union." Cicily Fairfield, meanwhile, returned to WSPU branch duties, including forming the first 'Votes for Women Corps', an organised group of Edinburgh newspaper sellers. [24].

So, the unrecorded and unique Edinburgh Votes for Women Club existed for several months – and was more than just a product of Rebecca West's wonderful imagination.

References

1. *Edinburgh Evening News, 12 February & 15 April 1908; Women's Franchise, 5 March 1908.*
2. *The Globe, 21 February 1908; Women's Franchise, 30 April 1908.*
3. *Edinburgh Evening News, 1 April 1908.*
4. *Idem, 4 April 1908.*
5. *The Scotsman, 12 & 13 May 1908; Dr Isabella Mears' obituary, British Medical Journal, 21 November 1936.*
6. *Norman Watson, Dundee's Suffragettes (2018), pp26-27.*
7. *Melanie Phillips, The Ascent of Women (2003), p235; Leah Leneman, A Guid Cause (1991), p58.*
8. *Women's Franchise, 30 April 1908; Forward, 2 May 1908.*
9. *Dundee Advertiser, 5 May 1908; Christabel Pankhurst, Unshackled (1959), p91; Dundee Courier, 13 May 1908.*
10. *Alexia Jack to The Scotsman, 31 July 1911.*
11. *Votes for Women, 14 May 1908.*
12. *Elizabeth Crawford, The Women's Suffrage Movement (1999), p264. Cicely Hamilton later formed the Women Writers' Suffrage League.*
13. *Press & Journal, 23 May 1908; The Scotsman, 23 & 26 May 1908; Edinburgh Evening News, 23 May 1908.*
14. *Falkirk Herald, 27 May 1908; London Weekly Despatch, 31 May 1908; Weekly News, 30 May 1908*
15. *The Queen, 27 October 1894; Crawford (1999), p655; Women's Franchise, 28 May 1908.*
16. *Edinburgh Evening News, 16 June 1908; Richard Pankhurst, Sylvia Pankhurst, Artist and Crusader (1979), p101; Joyce Marlow (Ed), Votes for Women (2001), p67.*
17. *Diane Atkinson, Rise up Women! (2019), p101.*
18. *London Daily News, 27 June 1908.*
19. *Edinburgh Evening News, 14 July 1908.*
20. *Women's Franchise, 23 July 1908; Votes for Women, 23 July 1908.*
21. *The Scotsman, 24 October 1908; Crawford (1999), p601.*
22. *Edinburgh Evening News, 10 December 1908; Morning Post, 18 December 1908.*
23. *Cicily to Letitia Fairfield, December 1908, Rebecca West manuscript collection, Indiana University, Bloomington, Indiana, USA. Dr Letitia Fairfield studied medicine at Edinburgh University before moving to Manchester in 1911 and joining the WSPU there. She was interviewed by Brian Harrison in 1976.*
24. *Votes for Women, 26 February 1909.*

SUFFRAGETTES

SIX:
'THE LEITH SUFFRAGE RIOT' 1909

*"I am glad to hear that you and your sister are none the worse for all you have gone through.
You are doing bravely, but I wish now more than ever that you would put yourself under Mrs Pankhurst's wing."*

Jessie Methven of Edinburgh WSPU welcoming Leith teachers Arabella and Muriel Scott on release from hunger striking in prison, and attempting to recruit them to Mrs Pankhurst's militants, September 1909.

As 1909 began, the Women's Freedom League reminded everyone that a peremptory government had 'killed off' women's votes by wrapping a facsimile Women's Bill in a white shroud, placing it into a coffin and 'burying it' in Trafalgar Square. Among the 'mourners' was Muriel Matters, recently released following her protest in the Commons where she had chained herself to the hated Ladies 'grille'. Not content with her infantry assaults, Matters had also taken to the skies in a cigar-shaped airship painted with 'Votes for Women' in large white letters to dispense 56 lbs of leaflets over Parliament from 2500 ft – which caused a paper-chase across London. A dab hand at pestering politicians in her Australian twang, she would soon be deployed on by-election duty in Scotland. Forty-two branches were represented at the League's annual conference at Caxton Hall, which began on January 9. Edinburgh-born Charlotte Despard continued as president, Glasgow's Teresa Billington-Greig as national organiser, and Amy Sanderson of Edinburgh WFL on the executive committee. The 'temper' of the conference was distinctly militant, as the resolution adopted at close of business hinted: "The Women's Freedom League recognises that the government has no intention of granting its demand for the Suffrage," and, therefore, the League would, "pursue its militant policy of opposing the government with increased vigour." [1].

A new constitutional group, the Scottish University Women's Suffrage Union, burst into life in mid-January 1909 after a meeting of women graduates at 129 Princes Street presided over by one of the Graduates' Appeal heroines, Frances Simson. The object of the Union was, "to obtain the Parliamentary franchise for women on the same terms as it is, or may be, granted to men." It was founded on non-party lines and attracted several leading suffragists. Chrystal Macmillan, its secretary, was widely known for taking the claim of women graduates to the House of Lords. Alice Smith of Leith was treasurer and organised meetings in the port. Its organiser, Frances 'Fanny' Parker, a niece of Lord Kitchener, would become one of Britain's most notorious militants. The new Union was open to men or women who had a university degree, with undergraduates welcome as associate members. Its objectives mirrored those of other societies and included: to induce public bodies and societies to petition for women's votes; to secure statements on the franchise from every candidate for a Scottish constituency; to ask questions at every political meeting addressed by an MP or a candidate; to work at Scottish parliamentary elections; to select, compile and distribute suffrage literature; to correct misstatements in the Press and to hold debates and lectures on women's suffrage. And, in its first year, the Edinburgh-based Union organised 40 meetings across Scotland. Once established, it had between 100 and 300 members.

Reflecting continued resistance to women's votes, a branch of the Women's Anti-Suffrage League was also established in Edinburgh at this time. Its first meeting in Roseburn Hall drew "a large attendance of ladies" presided over by Mrs Stirling Boyd, the incoming vice-president. The principal speaker, Mrs Archibald Colquhoun from London, said that supposing for a moment women did get the vote, the majority of voters would be female because there were a million more women than men in the country. Thus, she argued, women would dominate. She asked the Edinburgh audience to realise that they would be putting power into the hands of people who did not possess "the responsibilities." They could not force the stronger element in the community to obey the weaker, she believed. If they gave power to the majority of women, they would be trying an experiment which had "never been tried before in the history of civilisation." She believed it would amount to "a constitutional revolution." The organising secretary of the Women's Anti-Suffrage League for Scotland was given as Maud Trestrail, Carlton Hotel, Edinburgh. 2.

The Liberal Party continued to dominate Scotland's political landscape. The turnover of MPs – four by-elections in 1908, another four in 1909 – afforded suffragists every opportunity to lobby those standing for Parliament. Both the WSPU and WFL pledged to fight any Liberal candidate, whether he supported women's votes or not. This led to friction with sympathisers in the Scottish Women's Liberal Association. The NUWSS, however, supported any candidate who promised to extend the franchise to women, including Liberals. Going to the polls early in 1909 were Forfarshire, Glasgow Central, South Edinburgh and Hawick Burghs.

The South Division of Edinburgh comprised the old municipal wards of St George's, St Cuthbert and Newington (now areas around Morningside, Gilmerton, Comiston and Liberton). There were five polling stations. Dalry Public School was used for electors in St George's Ward. Gilmore Place and Bruntsfield Public Schools were polling stations for the St Cuthbert Ward. Newington Ward also used two schools, Warrender Park and Causewayside.

The total electorate was 18,789. Ahead of the March 2 election, Sarah Mair of the Edinburgh National Society made an audacious attempt to gain access to the polling stations, petitioning Edinburgh Sheriff Court to have ENSWS tables allocated to suffragists *inside* the buildings. The astonished Sheriff issued a flat refusal.

S. E. S. Mair, who had followed Priscilla McLaren as president of the ENSWS, quizzed both candidates standing in South Edinburgh. This was normal practice within the constitutionalist societies and such information was forwarded to the NUWSS in London. On confronting the men, Miss Mair found that the Liberal Unionist, Harold Cox, "whilst admitting the logic of granting the suffrage to duly qualified women, could not pledge himself to support such a measure." The Liberal, Arthur Dewar, intimated a "certain vague sympathy with the movement," but he would neither pledge himself to support a bill, nor could he do so, he said, in regard to an amendment to a future Reform Bill. Under these circumstances, the Edinburgh committee informed the National Union that neither candidate was satisfactory from the suffragists' point of view.

The South Edinburgh campaign also became a priority for the Women's Social and Political Union, whose long-held strategy called on voters to 'Keep the Liberal out'. Volunteers were delivered around the constituency by decorated carriages and, after chalking pavements, the WSPU held up to a dozen meetings each day. One, in Tynecastle Hall, attracted Emmeline Pankhurst on her latest visit to the city, and Helen Ogston, the Scottish suffragette who had gained notoriety three months earlier for interrupting David Lloyd George in the Royal Albert Hall and holding off stewards with a dog whip. Unsurprisingly, Tynecastle Hall was crowded. But, as a result of Ogston's action in London, the government rushed out the Public Meetings Act, which made interruptions at political meetings an offence. The maximum prison sentence for a conviction under the new legislation was six months, hence the women's anger that the law was a political ruse to render them silent and invisible. 3.

One report from the Edinburgh hustings told how suffragettes kept up an all-day vigil outside the Causewayside polling station, ignoring the wisecracks of small boys and shouting 'Keep the Liberal out' as men came off their shifts to cast their votes. The weather was miserable. Snow was falling and lay thick on the ground, freezing the women's feet. Most stood on rubber mats. Outside the school one woman wrapped in furs was sitting quietly at a table soliciting signatures for a petition "when a mass of snow from the school roof buried her and her petition." Passers-by rushed to her assistance and pulled her clear. "She could not be prevailed upon to leave the position to take a cup of tea until one of the Unionist workers volunteered to secure signatures. Then she gladly accepted the offer and Mr Cox's supporter got many additions to her list." More's the pity that Mr Cox came second to the Liberal. 4.

In London, meanwhile, the Women's Social and Political Union was taking stock – and adding a clock to its stock! In the five years since its inception, the WSPU calculated that it had held upwards of 50,000 public meetings. In London the Albert Hall had been filled on eight separate occasions. In Manchester, the great Free Trade Hall was often crowded. In Bristol, the Colston Hall; in Birmingham, the Town Hall; in Leeds, the Coliseum; in Liverpool, the Sun Hall; in Edinburgh, the Synod Hall and in Glasgow, the cavernous St Andrew's Hall, Europe's largest, with seats for almost 6000, were all filled to capacity. And in the spring of 1909, the WSPU opened a shop at 156 Charing Cross Road with a massive 'Votes for Women' clock outside. All hoped it was a sign of changing times.

The dust had not long settled on the South Edinburgh poll when news of Mary Burton's death saddened the city. The philanthropist, educational reformer and founder member of the Edinburgh National Society was 76 and up to the time of her passing was still busily engaged in public work. Born in Aberdeen in 1819, she had been tempted in her early years to join Florence Nightingale's corps in the Crimea, but instead threw herself into advancing the education of women in her adopted city of Edinburgh, to which she had moved in 1832. Mainly by her exertions, the Watt Institute – now Heriot-Watt

The Historic Environment Scotland plaque commemorating Mary Burton at Liberton.

University – was opened to women students two decades before access was allowed elsewhere. She served on the School, Parochial and Poor-Law Guardian boards. For the working classes, she was best known as the owner of Old Town tenements at a time when there was no organised plan for slum improvement. Here, for many years, she acted as rent collector, friend and counsellor, and as carpenter, painter and plasterer. She died on 19 March 1909, leaving a legacy of £100 to the Edinburgh National Society to campaign "for the admission of women to sit as members of Parliament, either at Westminster or in a Scottish Parliament." The city had lost a remarkable servant. 5.

Edinburgh suffragists also worked in Herbert Asquith's East Fife constituency. By distributing leaflets and chalking pavements the women advertised meetings for afternoons, which mostly attracted women, and evenings, which usually drew crowds of men and boys. At Cellardyke, a trio of speakers from Edinburgh University – Muriel and Arabella Scott and Winifred Fairfield – gave up their Easter holiday to campaign. A postcard to Arabella from Amy Sanderson at the WFL temporary office in Leven captures the spontaneity of the hustings:

"I will be in Ladybank on Friday. Will take a meeting on Friday night anywhere you like." Arabella recalled trudging around the constituency with her sister: "Muriel and I had lots of fun doing doorknocks at Ladybank, as well as speaking. Of course, in this area the people were dyed-in-the-wool Liberals, as had been their families before them. I remember one old chap came to the door who said he used to do some work for Asquith – I think he was a house painter. He proudly showed me a coat Asquith had given him. I couldn't resist shaking it and saying, 'This will get the Liberal dust out of it'." 6.

While retaining its rooms at 24 Shandwick Place, the Edinburgh WSPU branch briefly opened a shop at 100 Hanover Street. It was more a retail outlet than a centre of operations, however, and members continued to look for larger premises. Then, on 28 May 1909 it vacated both properties to move to larger and more central rooms at 8 Melville Place in Queensferry Street, opposite Randolf Crescent. It was quite an undertaking given that the branch had hosted Emmeline Pankhurst in a packed Synod Hall the evening before. Happily, the new office was quickly papered and painted in a soft shade of green and ready for Mrs Pankhurst's inspection prior to her performing the opening ceremony. That over 40 members helped with furnishings offers an idea of the membership roll at this time. The benefactors included Jessie Methven, Cecily Fairfield, Cecilia and Evelyn Haig, Margaret Maxtone Graham, Ethel Login, Margaret Murray, Ruth Calvine, Mary Lees, Florence Balgarnie and Morag Burn Murdoch. Florence Macaulay took out an advert in *Votes for Women* to alert suffragists to the move. Its readers would have noted Mrs Pankhurst's return to the Scottish capital. She had spoken at the Synod Hall in March, and now again at the end of May and would return to Edinburgh in October. Just as the Edinburgh National Society had been fundamental to the development of the Victorian campaign, so too Edinburgh WSPU, by 1909, was becoming the hub of Scotland's militant response.

The WSPU had no sooner crossed the Melville Place threshold than they were surprised and delighted to be gifted a motor car by a member, whose name was not released. A chauffeur was hired, with running costs guaranteed for six months through donations by members. A Mrs Robertson donated a new typewriter to the office – as useful as the vehicle for some. Another initiative, in June, saw John Menzies & Co agree to display *Votes for Women* advertising posters at local railway station bookstalls at a cost to Edinburgh WSPU of 2/6d a month.

The Edinburgh National Society was also on the move. In early June 1909, Elizabeth Lamond, the incoming organiser, was placed in charge of fitting out a new ENSWS office at 40 Shandwick Place. The premises replaced the Edinburgh Café, which had hosted many ENSWS branch meetings and talks. Donations were called for and a very practical Miss Houldsworth, who had already given china and £5 towards furnishing the rooms, sent a carpet-sweeper, towels, dusters and trays. Mrs Watson gave a japanned screen, and various members chipped in for a roll-top desk for the secretary. Florence Balgarnie of the London NUWSS executive, but a regular visitor to Edinburgh, gave a large table and an office chair. A novel outdoor meeting was held later in the month when Elizabeth Lamond, Lisa Gordon and Mary Low took to the sands at Portobello, hired a floating platform, handed leaflets to beach-goers and began to preach to the unconverted. The meeting lasted 45 minutes, and the crowd swelled to 80 before it was over. Suffrage newspapers were distributed and many badges were sold.

By then, the Women's Liberal Federation had established a Forward Suffrage Union, led by Marie Corbett of East Grinstead. The Union's object was to urge national Liberal organisations to support women's votes, and it threatened that unless the government incorporated a women's suffrage clause in its proposed Reform Bill, its female members would refuse to work for the party at parliamentary elections – precisely the position promoted by Priscilla McLaren two decades earlier. Moreover, by 1909, a Conservative and Unionist Women's Franchise Association was holding meetings across the country, with one group located in Edinburgh. The new association, a successor to the Primrose League, hoped to unify male and female Conservatives in favour of women's votes, but through peaceful persuasion. The association's activities were among those contained in a new paper for non-militant societies, *The Common Cause*, which was launched by the NUWSS in April 1909, priced at a penny. *The Guardian* reporter Helena Swanwick, who had spoken at 150 meetings in 1908, was appointed editor-manager.

Suffrage newspapers were fundamental to spreading the word and raising funds. The *Women's Suffrage Journal*, edited by Lydia Becker, was published between 1870 and 1890 and carried news of the late Victorian campaign. The *Women's Suffrage Record* followed in 1903 and *Women's Franchise* in 1907. By far the most important, however, were the papers associated with the WSPU, WFL and NUWSS. *Votes for Women* was edited and published by Emmeline and Frederick Pethick-Lawrence between August 1907 and 1918. It became a weekly in 1908 and was the official organ of the WSPU until 1912, when it was replaced by *The Suffragette* after the Pethick-Lawrences' break-up with the Pankhursts. In May 1908, an intriguing entry in the WSPU newspaper alluded to the forthcoming appearance of Scotland's own WSPU publication, also called *Votes for Women*. The report stated that it would appear for the first time on May 21 as a weekly penny paper. No copy of this uniquely Scottish news-sheet is known, but a hessian satchel, stencilled with thistles and bearing the name of the title, survives at Glasgow Museums. From 1909, *The Vote* was the official paper of the Women's Freedom League. Its first editor was Charlotte Despard, the WFL president. *Common Cause*, also published from 1909, was the newspaper of the National Union of Women's Suffrage Societies. In Scotland, the suffrage campaign was covered extensively by these journals and by mainstream newspapers, as well as by *The Forward* socialist paper, published from 1906. From Edinburgh came *The Only Way*, the title chosen in 1909 for Edinburgh University Women's Suffrage Society's newsletter. Rarer still is the *Aberdeen Women's Social and Franchise League Magazine*, which made its debut in March 1912, priced 2d, as a six-page paper. This may have been its first and only issue. 7.

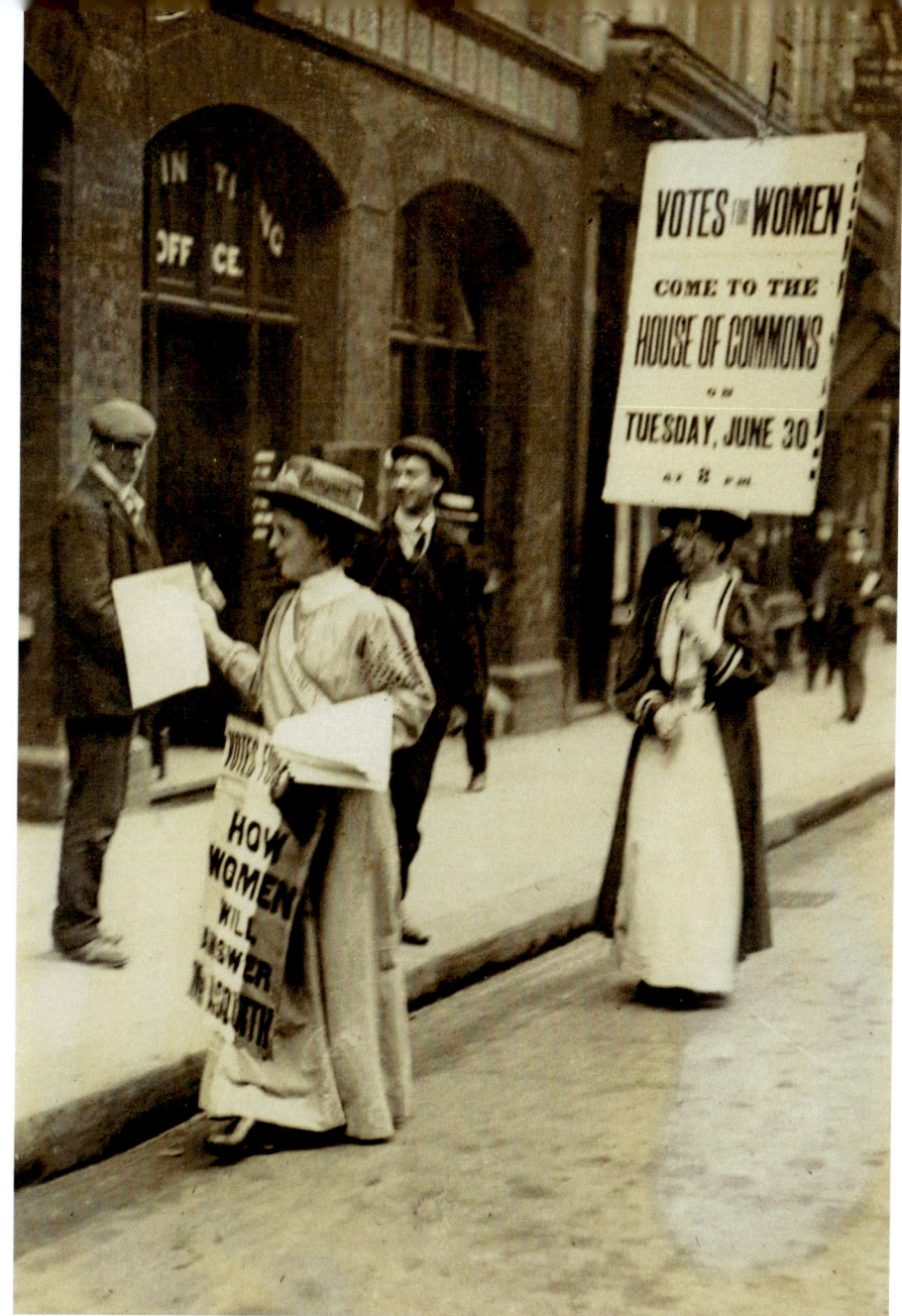

Selling newspapers was a vital – if not popular – role for suffragists of all societies. Here the women walk on the road, as they were banned from using pavements for campaigning. (Courtesy of London Museum)

Winston Churchill.

The distribution of the leading suffrage titles was significant. No records have survived, but there are reports of the Glasgow WSPU branch selling over 1000 copies of *Votes for Women* in a week. The Pankhursts talked of the paper achieving nationwide sales of 50,000 weekly, though the title itself once referred to a circulation of 40,000. And it was *Votes for Women* which announced 'The Great Scottish Demonstration' to take place in Edinburgh in October. This was hoped to be the largest suffrage procession and mass meeting ever held north of the border, with Emmeline and Christabel Pankhurst, Emmeline Pethick-Lawrence and Mary Gawthorpe named as principal speakers. Gawthorpe, an accomplished orator, was renowned for putting down hecklers. On one occasion she was pestered by a man who kept shouting, 'If you were my wife I'd give you poison." Wearied by his constant interruption, she shouted back, "Yes and if I were your wife, I'd take it." [8]

The next senior Cabinet minister to visit Edinburgh was Winston Churchill, the President of the Board of Trade. Understandably, there was a clamour for tickets for the King's Theatre event, but women hoping for a seat faced the indignity of having to sign and return a pre-printed postcard with the words, "I promise that the ticket will not be transferred to any other lady, and also that I shall in no way disturb the meeting." Local militants made their presence felt all the same. While the audience was being charmed by Mr Churchill, the WSPU staged a noisy demonstration outside. At its conclusion, Adela Pankhurst, from the back of a waggonette, urged the crowd to rush the building. The police intervened. Pankhurst and another woman refused to leave and were arrested, but liberated without charge once the meeting was over. They were the first suffragettes to be arrested in the capital and it is unfortunate that the second woman's name has been lost to history. It was possibly Florence Macaulay, the incoming organiser of Edinburgh WSPU, a former Holloway prisoner and the author of the suffragettes' marching song *The Women's Marseilles*. [9]

It would not be long, however, before Edinburgh's daughters were languishing behind bars. Whisked south to London on volunteer duty during the school holidays, the Leith teachers Arabella and Muriel Scott were arrested during a Women's Freedom League protest in Downing Street, charged with obstruction and, on 23 July 1909, paraded in front of a magistrate at Bow Street police court. One newspaper opted to describe their "light dresses and becoming hats," while a more prescient paper earmarked the sisters as "candidates for Holloway."

In court, the solemn R. B. H. Marsham heard from prosecutor Herbert Muskett that the sisters' conduct had attracted a crowd in Downing Street, and that it had become "absolutely necessary" to take them into custody. The police witness, Inspector Jarvis of Scotland Yard, told the court that the women were walking up and down in front of the Premier's house "wearing the sashes of the Women's Freedom League and carrying rolls of paper." He told them they could not stay there as they were causing a crowd to gather, around 50 people he estimated. Arabella Scott had told him that they wanted to present a petition to the Prime Minister. Jarvis had offered to deliver it for them, but they insisted it had to be presented personally (suffragists had rediscovered a Charles II Bill of Rights of 1689 that allowed petitions to be presented directly to the king or prime minister, provided no more than 10 persons were in the deputation). He had then cleared the crowd into Whitehall and placed a cordon of police across Downing Street. Jarvis then claimed that the women had continued to demand a personal interview with Mr Asquith. It eventually became necessary to take them into custody, he said, "to prevent disorder." No disturbance had occurred, however.

Younger sister Muriel spoke first on behalf of the siblings. She admitted that they had walked up and down Downing Street, then teased Mr Muskett: "Wasn't the crowd watching the submarines on the Embankment larger than the crowd in Downing Street?" Caught on the hop, Muskett stuttered, "That doesn't affect a private residence." Arabella Scott pounced to say that 10 Downing Street was not a private residence: "It is the official residence of Mr Asquith. Deputations are received and public business transacted there." Jarvis then said that he advised the crowd to "stop looking at two silly young women." Arabella told the court that there was no silliness involved "whatever." She said they were exercising their constitutional rights in presenting a petition to the Prime Minister and that the "agitation" would continue until he received a deputation. Although Muskett offered to withdraw the charge if they promised not to repeat their conduct, and the Magistrate added that he would not require them to be bound over, both defendants resolutely refused the entreaties. They were sentenced to 21 days' hard labour in the Second Division and removed to Holloway. 10.

This was not what the Edinburgh sisters wanted to hear. It was long contested by the suffrage leadership that they were political prisoners and thus eligible for First Division entitlements when convicted. This allowed them to wear their own clothes in prison, to have access to books and letters and to have free association with fellow prisoners of the same status during recreational breaks. The government, however, refused to concede that the women's actions were political. The vast majority of suffragette prisoners were therefore sentenced to the Second Division and treated as common criminals. They were denied the rights to retain their own clothes and privileges, such as writing paper and reading periods. They were allowed no visitors and were kept in solitary confinement in ill-fitting prison clothes for up to 23 hours out of 24. Little wonder suffragettes were characterised by sympathisers as 'second-class' citizens. Arabella Scott recalled, "Arriving at our cell doors, the wardresses flung them open, ordered us in then securely locked the door behind us. I was now alone in this cold, desolate cell. My only consolation was the thought that my sister was present in the adjacent cell."

Both sisters immediately adopted a hunger strike, echoing the prison protest introduced by fellow Scot Marion Wallace-Dunlop just weeks earlier. "We adopted the same policy," recalled Arabella. "We did not eat our food and we had no intention of doing so...we just played with all the juicy morsels brought to us. The pangs of hunger for the first three days were awful, but after that the body seemed to become accustomed to the lack of food.

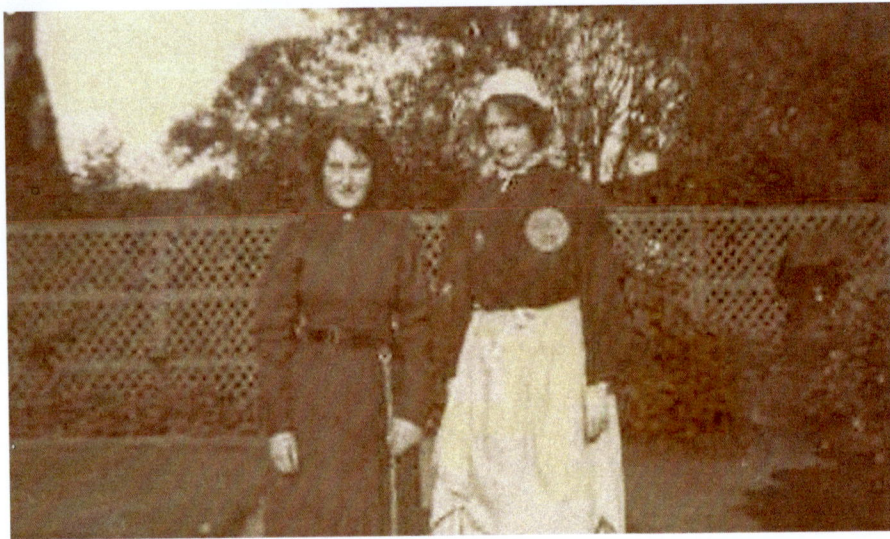

Arabella (right) and Muriel Scott pose in prison uniforms on their release from Holloway. (Courtesy of the late Frances Wheelhouse)

Then it seemed to shut off from this. The pain sets in and the agony of it is excruciating. Then, weak and ill from lack of food, we were suddenly released from prison."

Arabella and Muriel Scott were among six suffragettes released from Holloway on August 6, eight days before the expiry of their sentence. Muriel could hardly walk. "As Holloway's iron doors clanged behind us early one morning our friends from the Women's Freedom League were there to greet us," recalled Arabella. This happy scene was described by the celebrated hunger striker Lady Constance Lytton: "The moment of their coming out was thrilling. The prison doors, then a kind of courtyard to the gates, then the crowd outside. They simply ran out, rather dazed, and looking like children, some with their arms outstretched. The mixture of extreme joy and heart-tugging for those still left inside was very overcoming." 11.

Five of the six released hunger strikers were Scots, a fact not lost on the Women's Freedom League president, Charlotte Despard, who welcomed the women to Caxton Hall and praised the prominent part Scotland had played in the London protests. All had refused to take food. A slap-up breakfast appeared to revive them sufficiently for Arabella to promise "a vigorous campaign in Edinburgh" on their return. Both sisters expressed surprise at being released just two weeks into a 21-day sentence. The 'hunger fighters,' as Mrs Despard termed them, were ordered to be given their freedom after, it was thought, the king had intervened. Charlotte Despard presented them with Holloway badges, and bannerettes bearing the names of ex-prisoners were hung around the hall, large stars denoting the number of times each woman had suffered imprisonment for the cause. 12.

The Scott sisters returned to Scotland and continued their teaching posts in Leith. A supporting letter awaited them from Janie Allan of Glasgow WSPU, and a recruitment offer had come from Jessie Methven of Edinburgh WSPU: "I am glad to hear that you and your sister are none the worse for all you have gone through. You are doing bravely, but I wish now more than ever that you would put yourself under Mrs Pankhurst's wing." Muriel and Arabella Scott had pinned their colours to the WFL up to this point. On their return to Edinburgh the sisters revealed that they had met the WSPU leadership in London that July. Perhaps as a result, and after their experience in Holloway, both made the decision to concentrate future efforts entirely with the WSPU.

Arabella Scott later recalled how her headmaster in Leith had welcomed her back from 'doing time' by giving her the worst class of boys in the school. "He seemed to think I could handle them. His idea was that they would be in awe of this recent prison suffragette. When I first walked into the classroom there was dead silence, and I could see by their faces they were somewhat scared of me. But I walked in with my long blonde hair held together with a pretty black velvet bow and dressed in a lovely frock. 'Good morning,' I said, to which the lads responded with their 'good morning' and seemed surprised to see a young, slim teacher." She eventually found them "a wonderful group of boys." One legacy of their London adventure was that their mother Harriet, then living in Liberton, insisted that the sisters must never again risk arrest at the same time. Arabella recalled, "After our imprisonment in Holloway we promised our mother that we would in future not campaign together when possible. Muriel and I could then be seen at different places doing our bit." [13].

It is too often stated today that Britain's most militant suffragettes belonged to the Pankhurst-led Women's Social and Political Union. This is true for the most destructive actions, but research for the Dundee and Glasgow histories in this series has shown that often it was the activities of the Women's Freedom League that demanded the greater commitment and risk. Its members displayed extraordinary courage and determination, and won friends, supporters and success over a long period. The League's 'Great Watch', the continuous picketing of the House of Commons and the Prime Minister's house in Downing Street, placed its women at the forefront of the police crackdown over 1908-1909 and at constant threat of arrest and a long custodial sentence. At the same time, the WSPU was beginning its attacks on property, which tended to shield its activists from criminal proceedings. Indeed, it was not until the autumn of 1909 that a WSPU suffragette was jailed in Scotland. Leah Leneman felt that actions directed at the Houses of Parliament may have been more important than activism in Scotland. "But the likeliest explanation is that at this stage Scottish women faced a psychological barrier when it came to committing acts of militancy on their home ground, preferring the comparative anonymity of large-scale London demonstrations." It is clear, however, that 'opportunities' for arrest were far more plentiful in London than north of the border, particularly as the Women's Freedom League continued its petition siege of Downing Street. [14].

The WSPU confirmed a major Edinburgh procession for October 9. Flora Drummond, recruited by Mrs Pankhurst in the summer of 1905 and quickly earning the title 'The General', was named chief organiser and set up a temporary office at 63 Princes Street. It was hoped that many of the banners and flags used in the Hyde Park demonstrations the previous year would be unfurled in the Scottish capital – though members were urged to make new banners, and a size of 8ft wide by 3ft deep was recommended. Preparations

Arabella (standing) and Muriel Scott graduating MA from Edinburgh University in 1908. (Courtesy of the late Frances Wheelhouse)

Teresa Billington-Greig turned her back on the Women's Social and Political Union and the Women's Freedom League.

occupied Edinburgh's three main societies for much of the second half of 1909. All offered and gave help to Mrs Drummond. Missionaries were dispatched to outlying districts to raise funds and support. Cecilia Haig went to Dunbar, Elizabeth Roberts to Hawick and Margaret Roberts to North Berwick. The sum of £22 was raised at two 'At Homes'.

While inter-society collaboration was a distinctive feature within the Scottish movement – as confirmed by the 1907 and 1909 Edinburgh processions – internal and external rumblings and discontent surfaced from time to time. In August 1909, the Edinburgh WSPU secretary Esson Maule sent shockwaves around the local movement by announcing her immediate resignation. Maule identified "recent excesses" in militancy – a reference possibly to the arrest of Lucy Burns, Alice Paul, Margaret Smith and Adela Pankhurst after a major disturbance in Glasgow the previous week, which brought 300 police on to the streets. Miss Maule blamed the increasingly "dangerous" protests (Alice Paul had tried to gain access to the Glasgow venue from the roof). She also highlighted growing unease at the "unchallengeable orders" emanating from Emmeline and Christabel Pankhurst and addressed her concerns directly to the London leadership: "As you know, I am not antagonistic to real militant tactics, but the recent excesses in which your Union has indulged at public meetings appear to me not only futile but dangerous and wrong, being bound to raise only the hooligan propensities of the nation. Such tactics as rioting and attacking properties, so far as I can see, can only lead to a sex war; and, in fact, my opinion is that your society is degenerating from conducting a political movement into a personal quarrel with certain members of the Government. Also, the entire predominance in your Union of a few minds appears conducive to these excesses, because it takes away individual responsibility from your members." 15.

Esson Maule's comments endorsed those of Teresa Billington-Greig when she crossed from the WSPU to the Women's Freedom League. Billington-Greig's critique of militancy has been chronicled as a disagreement among suffragists, many of whom would have been deeply hurt by her comments.

Rather, she was just the first high-profile figure to publicly denounce the Pankhursts' ever-more intense militancy – others had expressed private misgivings and disenchantment with the leadership, but had not yet aired their views publicly. There was criticism, for example, of the suffering endured by many militants while the woman giving the orders, Christabel Pankhurst, had removed herself from the struggle and was safely in exile in Paris. Mary Phillips, who eventually questioned the Pankhursts' thinking, was fired by the WSPU leadership and treated to "a decidedly intemperate letter from Christabel Pankhurst." Phillips, who had been a member of the WSPU in Scotland since 1907 and had served four prison sentences, promptly embarrassed the Pankhursts by taking out a classified advert in their *Suffragette* newspaper: 'Ex-WSPU Organiser – Wants Immediate Work'. Many footsoldiers, too, thought the WSPU placed too much of an emphasis on going to prison, and were unsettled by Christabel's increasing references to being "at war." Helen Fraser, expelled in the Pankhursts' purge of October 1906, quickly found her feet in the debate again as the Scottish organiser of the National Union of Women's Suffrage Societies. Fraser was another who threw a verbal punch at the autocratic methods of the militant rivals: "The National Union believes in strengthening the hands of friends in the House of Commons and that sending men with mandates on the question from the electors is much more effective forward work for women's suffrage, though maybe slower and less showy than other methods." 16.

The women's route to votes took a disastrous turn in the autumn of 1909 with the forcible feeding of WSPU prisoners who had refused food. The tactic of hunger striking had been adopted on 5 July 1909 by the Scottish artist Marion Wallace-Dunlop, who was sent to Holloway for using stencils to print an extract from the Bill of Rights on a wall in the House of Commons... "It is the right of every subject to petition the King..." When she discovered two days later that her words had been washed off, she reprinted them. This time she was arrested. Sentenced to a month in prison, Wallace-Dunlop refused all food as a protest against the unwillingness of the authorities to recognise her

as a 'First Division' political prisoner. She was released after a fast of 91 hours.

The Pankhursts were triumphant. Here, they thought, was a manipulative tactic which would gain the liberty of jailed supporters. They assumed the authorities would not let hunger-striking women die. Their only recourse would be to set suffragettes free before the expiry of their sentence, or risk them becoming seriously ill, or worse. Arabella Scott recalled Wallace-Dunlop's stand giving suffragettes "a terrific boost for we, like many other imprisoned women all over the country, adopted the same policy." 17.

Then, on 12 September 1909, Charlotte Marsh, Laura Ainsworth and Mary Leigh were arrested while disrupting a political meeting in Birmingham. The women were sentenced to 14 days in Winson Green prison. They immediately declared a hunger strike, the strategy successfully adopted two months earlier by Wallace-Dunlop. This time they were not released and, as a repeat offender, on September 16, Mary Leigh became the first WSPU militant to be forcibly fed. The tactic of hunger striking to shorten prison sentences had backfired.

The same month, the Kinnaird Hall in Dundee played host to an important political address by the anti-suffrage Liberal cabinet minister Herbert Samuel. Rumours swept the city that militants would disrupt the meeting, resulting in the deployment of a formidable police presence around the hall. Chalked invitations on the pavement encouraged the public to: "Help the suffragettes rush Samuel's meeting." Reluctant to pass up the chance of a free evening's fun, locals massed to march with the women towards the 3000-seat hall. Soon 40 policemen faced a crowd of 1000. Tensions rose as the main speakers and guests arrived by car. With the crowd pushing from the back and the police from the front, the suffragettes urged the storming of the hall. Arrests quickly followed and five women were marched off to Bell Street police station. Two were released without charge, but for the new Edinburgh WSPU organiser Lucy Burns, Edinburgh student Alice Paul, and London activist Edith New, the evening of protest had just begun. No sooner had the trio reached Bell Street than a cell window was smashed and a hunger strike

How a newspaper portrayed Edith New, Alice Paul and Lucy Burns.

declared. Paul and Burns were veterans of Holloway and New had once chained herself to Downing Street's railings, a famous incident recalled today in many references to the militant movement.

The sequel on September 14 caused a sensation in Dundee. Crowds packed the police court to hear Burns claim that, "all constitutional methods had failed." Burns and Paul, both American students who had joined the WSPU in London, were said to have been discovered with large stones in their pockets. They were convicted of a breach of the peace and malicious mischief and fined £5, with the option of 10 days in prison. Former school teacher New was given a £3 fine or five days in jail for a breach of the peace. In common with WSPU policy, the defendants opted for the custodial sentence, ensuring Dundee the unenviable distinction of being the first city in Scotland to send suffragettes to prison.

Day after day the trio resisted all offers of food as the authorities considered whether artificial feeding should be sanctioned. Records show, however, that the Dundee prison doctor and nursing staff were reluctant to keep the prisoners long enough for the procedure to be carried out. Dr Alexander Stalker, medical officer to the prison governor, was the white knight who came to the women's aid. On 17 September 1909, he reported on the women's condition after three days of fasting and recommended "the immediate release" of Edith New, and the release of Alice Paul and Lucy Burns after five days. He added, "I have already explained why I think the recourse to forced feeding in these cases is inadmissible." [18].

For a total of 85 hours Burns and Paul refused food. Then, and without warning, the women were released on the fourth day of their sentence by order of Lord Pentland, the Scottish Secretary. Great celebrations began as the weakened suffragists were taken to Lamb's Hotel by taxi to be welcomed by Adela Pankhurst and a crowd "close on 10,000." Mrs Pankhurst and Christabel rushed north to give the leadership's blessing to the women. Thereafter, the trio recovered at the country home of Alexina McGregor near Arbroath, a suffragette 'safe house'.

Not everyone warmed to their release. An anonymous postcard to the prison governor urged the authorities to get a grip on "these female hooligans." It offered a remedy: "There is reason to believe that this starvation dodge would cease if they were put in the Infirmary ward and the food injected as is done in the case of lunacy patients." But the last words went to the suffragettes. Adela Pankhurst, with tongue firmly in her cheek, sent a postcard to the prison Governor to thank him "for your kindness" in releasing the women, and inviting him and the prison staff to attend a meeting that evening to hear her mother Emmeline speak. And, after being accused by *The Scotsman* of saying that the air in Dundee Prison was "foul," Lucy Burns wrote with speed to the Governor to say that she had said no such thing to the Edinburgh paper, adding, "As you know, it would have been most ridiculous of me to say anything against the ventilation in Dundee prison; for I broke my windows before I had time to test it!" [19].

For all the dramatic headlines, the biggest and busiest suffrage organisation was the peaceable Edinburgh National Society. As always, it focused on patient persuasion. It staged meetings, distributed literature, organised petitions and memorials and interviewed political candidates. In October 1909, the ENSWS announced a series of six lectures, a 'speaking' class, a weekly debate and training for organisers. It held 'At Home' meetings in the Edinburgh Café and put on two suffrage plays in the Queen Street Hall. It was also prepared to help smaller societies. As autumn turned to winter, it sent an organiser to Stirling to "work up" the branch there, and sent two organisers to the Liberal stronghold of Dundee to assist with the prison protest: "We have a good nucleus there of about thirty members, but we hear that Dundee is inclined to be Anti-Suffragist, so we must go; however, it is possible that it is only anti-militant and we may save it from becoming anti-everything." [20].

The highlight of 1909 was the WSPU's 'Grand Scottish Pageant' on October 5. At two o'clock, contingents from across Scotland set off from Bruntsfield Links, led by bands from Leith, Kirkcaldy, Stirling, Broxburn and Edinburgh. Some of the great banners from the historic Hyde Park demonstrations were

The Grand Scottish Pageant makes its way along Princes Street.

on show, alongside patriotic examples contributed by different Scottish societies. One was held aloft by 'Hunger Strikers' while another was titled 'Mrs Pankhurst's Banner'. Glasgow suffragists walked under a new design by Ann Macbeth, head of the embroidery department at the city's School of Art, and now a renowned artist. The banner held aloft by Perth Women's Suffrage Society is likely the rare survivor at Perth Museum. The procession was led by five girl pipers and Flora Drummond, dressed as 'The General' astride a white horse. One of the pipers, Bessie Watson, recalled going with her parents to the WSPU office in Melville Place to volunteer for the pageant. During the parade she wore "a white dress with a purple, white and green 'Votes for Women' sash, with a glengarry cap." She remembered it as a typical Edinburgh October afternoon, "dull and drizzly," and that she played her pipes at intervals along the route. [21].

The procession wound its way via Tollcross, Lothian Road and Princes Street, before reaching Waverley Market, where a mass gathering took place in a hall decked in the colours of the WSPU. One reporter thought it

The 'Jenny Geddes' float passes down Princes Street. In 1637, Geddes threw a stool at a minister in St Giles' Cathedral in objection to the first public use of the Church of Scotland's revised version of the Book of Common Prayer. (Courtesy of London Museum)

"must take rank as one of the finest – perhaps the finest – political pageant that the northern capital ever witnessed." The 1000-seat Market Hall "was filled" to hear Christabel Pankhurst's ominous defence of violence, and her mother's warning that "nothing but death will stop the individual soldier in the women's army from her fight for liberty." 22.

The Edinburgh event had its critics. A bitter letter to the Press from the president of the Young Scots Society, a group of entry-level Liberals, claimed that "in all" only 322 women marched in the procession. It stated that only 11 were behind the Dundee banner and three behind Berwick's banner. Even Glasgow and Edinburgh with a joint population of over a million "could only muster 140." He concluded, "The procession on Saturday did not represent the Scottish demand for women's suffrage, and the crowds which turned out to see it received it with withering coldness." This was a peculiar, and presumably political, observation given that *The Scotsman* put the number of people attending the post-procession meeting at "1000 seated." A further crowd of 4000 to 5000 was reported outside the hall. 23.

The peace and dignity of the Edinburgh procession was forgotten in a matter of days. A speech by Sir Edward Grey, the Foreign Secretary and local MP, at a fund-raising bazaar for Berwick Rangers Football Club, was too good an opportunity to miss. Grey had hardly shuffled his notes before Mabel Atkinson of Newcastle interrupted with the usual question. She was immediately seized by stewards and removed. Alice Paul then began shouting. She, too, was bundled out, though with more difficulty as she clung to the flower arrangement. When she attempted to re-enter the hall she was arrested and taken to Berwick police station. Elsa Gye of Newcastle was next to go. A handkerchief was thrust into her mouth and she was carried to the door. "Will you do your best to assist women?" shouted Lucy Burns of Edinburgh WSPU, which brought a repetition of the expulsion process. The four suffragettes were escorted to Berwick police station, where Alice Paul gave 63 Princes Street as her address – the office opened for the Edinburgh procession. She was charged with breach of the peace and released on bail

Mrs Pankhurst is welcomed to Waverley Market at the end of the Edinburgh procession. The banner on the right reads 'Scottish Demonstration'. (Courtesy of London Museum)

of £10. No further action was taken, however. The police abandoned the case – a decision which reportedly drew the ire of the militant.

Suffragists were often frustrated when they were denied their day – and say – in court. Emily Davison, before her death at Ascot in 1913, was furious on those occasions when charges against her were dropped. When an unknown woman paid her fine of £5 in 1910, Davison "stamped her foot in fury in the Bow Street court and refused to budge." She had wanted to go to prison. Glasgow's Janet Bunten was fined for tax evasion with the alternative of the usual week in prison. She had declared her intention of going to jail and her bags were packed. When it was revealed that her fine had been paid by an anonymous supporter, Bunten returned to the court to protest against the acceptance of the payment when it had not been made by her, or in her

VOTES FOR WOMEN.

Miss ADELA PANKHURST,

Organiser, National Women's
Social and Political Union,
4, Clement's Inn, Strand, W.C.

A WSPU propaganda postcard of Adela Pankhurst, who was prominent in many Scottish protests.

name. She was told that officials had no power to decline such payments. The staff also refused to tell her who had paid the fine. 24.

Women were by now on the warpath. Abernethy, near Newburgh, lay in Premier Asquith's East Fife constituency. On 16 October 1909 a gathering of Liberals awaited an address by Cabinet colleague Winston Churchill in a marquee in the grounds of a private house near the village. Mrs Pankhurst's daughter Adela, along with Helen Archdale of Edinburgh and the English suffragettes Laura Evans and Catherine Corbett, travelled by car to the meeting to confront their political quarry. Their efforts to speak, however, were frustrated by stewards who subjected them to a fusillade of divots and mud as their vehicle stopped at the event's entrance. The car was quickly surrounded by around 50 youthful Liberals. Some grabbed the flags which adorned the car. A placard was ripped up. A bundle of *Votes for Women* newspapers was thrown into a burn. A tyre was slashed with a knife. A handful of mud struck one woman full in the face. The rosetted stewards then tried to overturn the car. The women were thrown to the floor, narrowly escaping injury.

The unpleasant ordeal did not stop there. Several stewards then seized Adela Pankhurst by the arms and attempted to drag her to the ground. With a reported 15 policemen watching on without intervening, a steward twisted another woman's scarf around her throat, making her fight for breath. Pankhurst appealed to a lurking newspaper photographer to take a picture, "and show the people how these beasts of Liberal stewards are handling us this day." At that point, the male chauffeur managed to re-start the car and drove the women to safety. A shocked public learned of the incident from newspaper reports and letters to the Press. From these correspondents a more serious aspect to the Abernethy events emerged – that the strong force of police had failed to lift a finger to protect the women.

Within a week Pankhurst, Corbett, Evans and Edinburgh's Helen Archdale were languishing in prison and facing the prospect of the 'torture' of forcible feeding.

Two days after his visit to Abernethy Winston Churchill addressed an all-male audience of supporters in the 3000-seat Kinnaird Hall in Dundee.

The scale and importance of the event ensured local police took no chances. The entire force was mobilised. Streets were closed off and roofs searched. Mounted officers were deployed. Thousands gathered and the city was brought to a stop. Helen Archdale, daughter of former *Scotsman* editor Alexander Russell, jumped off a tram, gathered local people around her to 'rush' the barricades, and while waving the WSPU colours and shouting 'Votes for Women', made a solo dash towards the entrance. Mounted reinforcements arrived and galloped into the fray and were met head-on by the throng. It took four policemen to drag away Archdale. Hunger strike veteran Maud Joachim, niece of the famous Hungarian violinist Joseph Joachim, was then force-marched to Bell Street police station. The London suffragette Catherine Corbett followed. Four more were dragged from an attic overlooking the Kinnaird Hall. From this vantage point they had hurled stones at the hall's skylights. In the house, police detained Laura Evans and Adela Pankhurst, and two men who had barricaded the door.

The seven were taken into custody, each charged with disorderly behaviour and a breach of the peace. Charges against the men were dropped when Pankhurst confirmed they had not been told what was to happen (both were members of the Men's Political Union and probably knew exactly what was planned). The five women admitted the offences. Archdale, the only Scot, gave her name as "Archdale or Russell" and her address as 63 Princes Street, Edinburgh. She was 33 years old. She told the court that women "would continue to protest as long as they had life left." Each was fined £2 with the alternative of 10 days in prison. They defiantly opted for jail, refused to wear prison clothes, and on being taken to the cells, immediately adopted a hunger strike. The women also penned a cheerful note to the *Votes for Women* newspaper: "Dear Scotch Members – Just before we go to prison we send you our love and greetings and ask you to keep the flag flying..." 25.

The jailings brought a swift reaction from the WSPU. Flora Drummond was despatched to Dundee and led hundreds behind her 'war wagon' to the prison. As the hours and days passed and the stand-off continued,

Helen Archdale. (Courtesy of the National Portrait Gallery)

a concerned *Dundee Courier* noted, "The five suffragettes in Dundee are very hungry. For almost sixty hours not a particle of food has touched their lips." Then, on October 21, two friends paid Helen Archdale's fine to secure her release, but were told in a message from Archdale that she would not agree to it being paid, and that she would stay in prison. After hunger striking for four days, the women were liberated on October 24. They had spent 102 hours in prison – with Archdale said to have lost one and a half stones during her incarceration. She had to be supported by friends outside and assisted into a cab. Catherine Corbett later paid tribute to the courage of the Dundee people, who had kept the riot going for three hours – "They were glorious." 26.

Flora Drummond, posing as the WSPU's 'General'.

This time, government records show a clear desire by the authorities to forcibly feed the prisoners. Three days before their release, the Scottish Office in Whitehall, which was in charge of the prison service in Scotland, sent a telegram, followed by a letter of confirmation, to the Prison Commissioners in Edinburgh advising: "Dundee prisoners should, unless medically certified unfit, be fed under medical supervision if and when necessary." 27.

This statement contradicts various suffrage histories which give credit to the Scottish authorities for resisting the practice adopted in England. What stopped forcible feeding taking place in Scotland was not the refusal of the political and prison authorities, but the reluctance of the prison medical staff to carry it out. In a letter on October 23, the prison governor told the Prison Commissioners: "Professor Stalker and Doctor Buist have carefully examined each of the five females tonight and both doctors consider it would be inadvisable to feed them by force." Remarkably, the authorities were prepared to offer enhanced payments to medical personnel willing to carry out the controversial procedure. An internal memorandum from the Commissioners' secretary David Crombie reveals that Dr Stalker was having trouble finding nurses to help with the 'treatment'...and so, "I impressed on him the desirability of getting one or two, even at increased fees." Despite a nurse being brought from Perth, Dr Stalker appeared determined not to carry out the treatment. To the Commissioners on October 24 he reported, "Visited the five suffragettes today in company with Dr Buist and signed certificates recommending that the five should be liberated when convenient." The women were set free the same afternoon. 28.

Militancy brought headlines and the WSPU believed, good or bad, that they helped to pile pressure on the government. They also impacted upon the activities of other societies, who frequently complained of the "damage" done by the Pankhursts' strategy. Elsie Inglis of the ENSWS regularly wrote to the Edinburgh papers to distance her organisation from acts of violence. There was also scathing criticism in the Press. The *Edinburgh Evening News*, for example, openly questioned the women's sanity. "There is little doubt that some of these women are in a state of chronic hysteria. They are not responsible for their actions when their nerves give way. Meantime the cause of women's suffrage is rapidly falling in public esteem, as day by day gangs of hysterical women, supposed to be educated, prove their absolute unfitness to take a sane view of political conditions." This was typical of newspaper coverage, which appeared willing to report on – if not agree with – the views of the old constitutionalist organisations, but rejected out of hand the hardline policies of the WSPU and, to an extent, the softer civil disobedience of the Women's Freedom League. 29.

Militancy also added impetus to those who disputed the aims and claims of the suffrage societies. At a meeting in the Music Hall in November 1909, the Edinburgh Women's Anti-Suffrage League heard its president, the Marchioness of Tweeddale, claim that militancy had boosted their membership. The "strides the League has made in point of numbers" had allowed the branch to send an anti-suffrage petition of 15,000 signatures to the House of Commons. Among those present were the best-selling novelist Mrs (Mary) Humphry Ward and a roll-call of the aristocracy, including the Dowager Lady Kinross, Lady Christison, Lady Fraser and Lady Russell. The speakers told the audience that their presence showed "their disapprobation of the conduct of their sisters" who were "unsexing themselves." This was characteristic of the arguments adopted by anti-suffragists; not only were militants demonstrating that they were "unfit" to participate in how a government was run, they were also disgracing their sex by rejecting accepted (as they saw it) notions of womanly behaviour and respectability. 30.

Contrast that with the next meeting in Edinburgh when the WSPU drew a huge audience of women to the King's Theatre to welcome Christabel Pankhurst and Flora Drummond. The branch chair Florence Macaulay introduced Pankhurst as "the inventor and evolver of the militant methods." In a popular touch, Mrs Drummond presented mementoes to the five girl pipers from Broxburn who had headed the Edinburgh procession earlier in the month. She said they were frequently told that women should not have

The novelist and leading anti-suffragist Mary Augusta Ward, who used her married name Mrs Humphry Ward.

Christabel Pankhurst – faced a heckler in an Edinburgh audience.

the vote because they could not be soldiers. Her response was that men should not have the vote because they could not be mothers. Christabel Pankhurst then addressed statements made by Mrs Humphry Ward at the anti-suffragette meeting in the Music Hall. She said the anti-suffragists were "not the enemy." She blamed the government. Most unusually, the WSPU chief strategist and co-leader was heckled by a woman in the Edinburgh audience. Pankhurst told her that had she been at a Liberal meeting she would have been thrown out. The interrupter replied, "I am not doing the same thing you did. I am interrupting a meeting that has to do with women's suffrage. You interrupt meetings that have to do with something else." Pankhurst replied that, logically speaking, a Cabinet Minister could not speak on any political question that was not connected with votes for women. This drew applause. The woman was not finished. "I have not brought 20 people here to carry on one after the other. I am here alone." To this, Pankhurst replied, "We have often had one suffragette at meetings, but she had been thrown out all the same. You will make a good suffragette yet!" Pressed for her name after the meeting, the woman said she was Mrs Arthur Somervell. She further admitted that she was a member of the Anti-Suffrage League. In truth, she showed a bit of bottle taking on Christabel Pankhurst single-handedly. None of the Cabinet did. [31]

Somervell's questions reflected a wider resentment across Scotland at decisions made by the WSPU leadership. The Pankhursts appear to have begrudged the independent activity of Scottish branches and their habit of employing local organisers and moved swiftly to bring them into line with London. The previous year the Scottish organiser Helen Fraser had been dumped by the WSPU hierarchy. The Pankhursts were certainly aware of Fraser's popularity and her steady steering of the WSPU membership in Scotland before replacing her in 1908. When told that London was intending to exercise greater control over the branch network and likely now to employ headquarters- or English-based organisers in the four Scottish WSPU offices, Fraser refused to toe the Pankhurst line and was effectively sacked. Whatever their merits, the edicts from London killed off the notion of an independent Scottish militant movement, and the WSPU followed through with its intention to embed headquarters' organisers across the Scottish network. Gertrude Conolan arrived to take up the position in Glasgow. In Aberdeen, Caroline Phillips was controversially ousted and replaced from London by Ada Flatman. And for a short time in 1914 the Welsh militant Mary Allen, the first woman to receive a WSPU hunger strike medal, was sent north to take over in Edinburgh despite strenuous objections, with Christabel Pankhurst calling the Edinburgh branch "cantankerous." 32.

Prime Minister Asquith remained the biggest stumbling block to women's votes. As 1909 drew to a close, he accepted an invitation from Edinburgh Town Council to the Freedom of the City – though no date for the ceremony was arranged. Nonetheless, it prompted Alexia Jack, secretary of the local Women's Freedom League, to write to the Lord Provost to claim that since he had become Prime Minister, Mr Asquith had "persistently insulted" them, particularly in his refusal to receive deputations. Instead, Miss Jack conveyed the Edinburgh WFL's view that he was "unworthy of the high honour of being enrolled as a citizen of this ancient city." The other suffrage societies weighed in. Before November was out, four deputations descended on Council Chambers to argue the case. The women had to wait two hours while councillors attended to other business, and even then, a further discussion took place as to whether the deputations should be received. The Town Clerk pointed out that they had received letters protesting against the award from the Women's Social and Political Union, the Women's Freedom League, the Scottish University Women's Suffrage Union, the Edinburgh University Women's Suffrage Society and the Edinburgh National Society for Women's Suffrage – and now, he told them, four deputations of women were waiting outside. Sir William Brown, the Lord Provost, asked if any good purpose could be served by hearing the deputations. Some councillors answered that they should be heard; others said they should not, and one councillor suggested they knew what the women were going to say anyway. Eventually the council

voted 24 to 21 to hear the women, and Sarah Mair for the NUWSS, Alexia Jack for the WFL, Florence Macaulay for the WSPU and Frances Simson of the Universities' Union were allowed to plead their case. At this time the Edinburgh University Women's Suffrage Society brought out its own paper, *The Only Way*, edited by Kate Macrae. It was priced at a penny, or 2d per copy by post. The first issue contained a portrait of Chrystal Macmillan – and the *Song of the Anti-Suffragist*...

Oh, let me be your doormat, do!
I only ask
To lie and bask;
I have no brain, or spine, like you. 33.

Before the year was out, suffragettes were languishing in Calton Prison after the city's first jailing of the 40-year campaign. The drama began at a meeting in Leith on December 6 at which Sir Edward Grey, the Foreign Secretary, was the principal guest. The Gaiety Theatre was crowded, enthusiastic and noisy. Some 2500 people had crammed in, including a number of women, despite care being taken to ensure that the tickets "did not get into the hands of suffragists." The WSPU distributed hundreds of handbills ahead of the meeting inviting local men to join the protest. Elaborate preparations were made to keep protesters away from the event. Police and stewards were vigilant and ready. Outside, streets were patrolled by plain-clothes policemen and uniformed officers. As the start of the event approached, a boisterous crowd of around 700 gathered in adjacent streets, including "members of the Women's Freedom League and the WSPU" – but the women were heavily outnumbered by the "men of Leith" who had answered the call to arms.

Edith Hudson was blamed by *The Scotsman* for causing the ensuing rumpus. It accused the Edinburgh nurse of "waving the Union tricolour above her head," and encouraging a howling mob to follow her down the Kirkgate. She reportedly led the crowd to the front of the theatre, where a line of police

Edith Hudson of Edinburgh WSPU – one of the first two suffragettes to be imprisoned in the city. (Courtesy of the Mary Evans Picture Library)

was drawn up across the road. She attempted to force her way through and was promptly detained, the paper said. The crowd rushed the police line and a struggle ensued. The situation became so threatening that the police drew their batons. A fight started, and several of the townsfolk were injured. Uniformed officers forced a passage through the melee and eventually escorted Hudson to the police station. *The Scotsman* noted their progress: "Policemen and prisoner all bore traces of the scuffle. The latter, however, though somewhat exhausted, was still shouting 'Votes for Women'." One man

was also arrested. Later, stones were thrown through the Leith Post Office window. Labels attached to the missiles carried the message, 'Taxation without representation is tyranny.' A woman was arrested at the scene. During the course of the evening all three were bailed to appear at Leith police court the following morning. 34.

Next day, a Saturday, Baillie Philip Dresner, an Edinburgh pawnshop proprietor, opened proceedings against the trio. Around 20 women took seats in the public gallery, many wearing WSPU badges, but the court was visibly packed with the men of Leith who "showed their sympathy with the women very emphatically." The first case called was that of Robert King, a young engineer from Newhaven who appeared with a bandage around his head. He was charged with the assault of two police officers. He pleaded not guilty, and the case was continued. At his trial the following Thursday, he was found not proven – a verdict welcomed with cheers and clapping from Leith's working men.

Both women were advised by Dan Easson of the Men's League, a solicitor, but he was limited to providing them with copies of the complaint against them. The *Edinburgh Evening News* said the defendants "stated their motives with calm deliberation and took their punishment unflinchingly." Edith Hudson, who gave her address as the WSPU office in Edinburgh, was charged with conducting herself in a disorderly manner and committing a breach of the peace. She said she had no intention of causing a riot; her presence had been political. She would have gone peacefully and asked her question without a disturbance, but the government would not allow her to do that. To hissing in the court she was found guilty and fined £5 with the alternative of 30 days' imprisonment.

Elsie Roe Brown of Archibald Place, Edinburgh was charged with malicious mischief. On a table in the centre of the courtroom was a stone with a label attached, which was said to be the missile she had used in her attack. She was fined £3, or 15 days, for breaking a window at Leith Post Office in Constitution Street by throwing stones wrapped in paper. One pane was broken. She said she wanted to draw attention to the government's dishonourable action in trying to suppress the women's movement. In throwing the stone she had taken care to see that no one would be hurt. Both women opted to go to prison and were removed to Calton Prison in Edinburgh where they refused to take food.

That night, an impromptu meeting of the WSPU at the foot of Leith Walk passed a resolution protesting at the arrests and the severity of the sentences imposed on the two women. Lucy Burns said they knew that the two prisoners meant to protest inside Calton Prison just as their friends were doing outside. The first step, she said, would be a hunger strike. The women would refuse to take any food in the prison, and Burns calculated that by Saturday at the latest they would have reached "the fainting stage." If they were not released by then, it would be obvious that they were being forcibly fed, and that Scotland "was as bad as England." She appealed to the large crowd to accompany the WSPU to the walls of the prison "to give to Miss Hudson and Nurse Brown an encouraging cheer and to show them that the sympathies of the people of the district were with them."

The Women's Freedom League also staged a protest meeting, packing out the Edinburgh Café in Princes Street. Referring to the riot at Leith, the League's Mrs Dobbie said that women were entitled to be admitted to a public meeting as well as men. If that right had been conceded in Leith, Edith Hudson would have committed no offence. She also said that women contributed quite as much as men to the salary of the Cabinet Minister who spoke at Leith. She accused the police of completely losing their heads – "as they always did." There was further condemnation of the sentences at a meeting of the Men's League in the Livingstone Halls, South Clerk Street. Councillor Bruce Lindsay, who presided, called them "vindictive and of a nature of revenge." 35.

There are fascinating sub-plots to what the *Edinburgh Evening News* named 'The Leith Suffrage Riot'. The first occurred when, out of the blue, Elsie Roe Brown was released on December 7, the day after her incarceration, her £3

fine having been paid anonymously. The WSPU let it be known that the fine had been settled "without her knowledge" and called it "a scandal." It took steely courage to embark on a protest knowing that a prison term was almost inevitable. But many suffragettes cheerfully took clothes and other essentials into court, expecting to face the penalties of their actions. Roe Brown had prepared herself for this sacrifice and must have felt crushed, even humiliated, when it was denied to her. On her release, she told a WSPU meeting that she had been subjected to "the great indignity of being forcibly stripped and dressed in a prisoner's uniform marked with the broad arrow of common criminals." Miss Chapman, chairing the meeting, welcomed Nurse Brown and said they would see if Scotland would adopt the cruel and illegal practice of forcible feeding in relation to Edith Hudson, who was continuing her protest in Calton Prison by refusing food. She asked for three cheers for Hudson.

Later, however, Flora Drummond brought the devastating news to a WSPU meeting in Leith that Roe Brown after her conviction had been dismissed from the Edinburgh nursing home where she worked – despite a brave stand by her matron and fellow Edinburgh WSPU activist Florence McFarlane, who resigned in protest. It was also stated that other nurses at the home had also resigned in protest. The *Edinburgh Evening News* added that "Miss McFarlane was known throughout the country as one of the best matrons in Edinburgh." 36.

For women such as Elsie Roe Brown to act in an unconstitutional way jarred with notions of respectability. It took commitment and, at times, astonishing single-mindedness. Many followed orders without a care for the consequences, which often involved individual acts of great daring and personal sacrifice. Even at the height of the burnings and bombings in 1913-1914, when public anger and hostility forced many suffragists into hiding, WFL and WSPU volunteers continued to sell *The Vote* and *Votes for Women* on street corners. Many suffered abuse and violence. Elsie Roe Brown probably considered fully the action she intended to undertake at Leith – but to lose one's job in Edwardian Britain left no safety net of alternative

The 'Foot of Leith Walk' was popular with suffragists as a location for outdoor meetings.

income. It must have come as a terrible shock to the wider suffrage movement, attracting equal measures of sympathy, condemnation and outrage.

Edith Hudson was liberated a day later, on December 8, with Edinburgh WSPU telling the Press that it had no idea how her freedom had come about – but that if her fine had been paid, "it was against the will of Miss Hudson." *Votes for Women* reported that Edinburgh WSPU remained extremely sceptical and suspicious. The branch believed the fine had been paid by the authorities to enable the prison staff to avoid force feeding the two women. Cecilia Haig, of Edinburgh WSPU, wrote to *The Scotsman* to suggest that

they might have been paid by the police, prison authorities or government, as "it would not suit this so-called Liberal Government to have many suffragettes in prison at this time." She cited a similar situation in London, where Mrs Pankhurst's fine was paid anonymously and with suspicious timing. It was, said Haig, paid without her knowledge, and by whom nobody knew, and against her wishes. "Several fines have been paid lately by unknown persons," she added. Official records, however, suggest that the fine was paid by Hudson's mother. In a note to the Prison Commission the Governor recalled, "When it was intimated to her that her fine was paid, she made no objection & remarked that it was just like her mother to be so determined." [37].

Secondly, it was revealed in court that 27 plain-clothes police officers had been deployed in Leith's Kirkgate for Edward Grey's meeting. This was strongly criticised as excessive and unnecessary in an editorial in the *Edinburgh Evening News*: "It is a matter for consideration whether, had 20 of these 27 plain-clothes constables been in uniform, there would have been any disturbance at all. In so considerable a departure from the usual practice, the Leith authorities tried an experiment which had unfortunate results. It is one which we trust will not be repeated." Having said that, the uniformed and covert policemen were not entirely distinguishable from each other, since all the plain-clothes officers also carried batons!

Thirdly, and finally, a claim was made by the Kirk Session of South Leith against the Town Council for compensation for damage done to the railings in front of Kirkgate Church, which had been pulled away during the disturbance. It is not known who won that Battle of Leith!

References

1. London Evening Standard, 4 January 1909: Women's Franchise, 14 January 1909.
2. The Scotsman, 18 January 1909; Edinburgh Evening News, 28 January 1909.
3. The Scotsman, 9 March 1909; Edinburgh Evening News, 23 February & 3 March 1909.
4. Western Times, 5 March 1909.
5. The London Echo, 18 July 1895; Elizabeth Ewan, et al, The Biographical Dictionary of Scottish Women (2006), p54.
6. Courier, 17 April 1909; Amy Sanderson to Arabella Scott, 29 July 1908, private collection; https://hgsheritage.org.uk/Detail/objects/SUFL27
7. Votes for Women, 6 August 1909; Elizabeth Crawford, The Women's Suffrage Movement (1999), pp458-460.
8. Diane Atkinson, Rise up Women! (2019), p53.
9. Evening Telegraph, 14 July 1909; Western Times, 19 July 1909.
10. Sheffield Evening Telegraph, 24 July 1909.
11. Arabella Scott, My Murky Past (Frances Wheelhouse typescript); Laura Mayhall, The Militant Suffragette Movement (2003) p105; Ian McDonald, Vindication! A Postcard History of the Women's Movement (1989), p46.
12. Idem. Leah Leneman, A Guid Cause (1991), p78.
13. Arabella Scott, My Murky Past.
14. Leneman (1991), p88.
15. Edinburgh Evening News, 26 August 1909; Courier, 25 August 1909.
16. Atkinson (2019), p433; Dundee Courier, 12 February 1909.
17. Arabella Scott, My Murky Past; Votes for Women, 21 May 1908.
18. NRS HH16/36 Report from James Crowe, Governor of HM Prison, Dundee, to Prison Commissioners, Edinburgh, 15-17 September 1909; NRS, HH16/36, Report by Dr Stalker, Medical Officer to the Governor of HM Prison Dundee, to the Prison Commissioners, Edinburgh, 17 September 1909.
19. NRS, HH16/36, Letter, Lucy Burns to Governor HM Prison, Dundee, 18 October 1909; Postcard, Adela Pankhurst to the Governor, 18 September 1909; anonymous postcard to Governor, 14 September 1909. For full details of the arrests and imprisonments, and the government's response, see Norman Watson, Dundee's Suffragettes (2018), pp52-56.
20. Common Cause, 7 October 1909.
21. People's Story Museum, Edinburgh, Votes for Women, nd, c1995, pp6-8.
22. Votes for Women, 22 October 1909.
23. Edinburgh Evening News, 11 October 1909; Scotsman, 11 October 1909.
24. Berwick Advertiser, 15 October 1909; Edinburgh Evening News, 14 October 1909
25. Atkinson (2019), p179.
26. Idem, p178; Courier, 21 October 1909; Dundee Evening Telegraph, 21 October 1909.
27. NRS HH16/619. Letter confirming telegram, Under-Secretary, Scottish Office to Scottish Prison Commissioners, 21 October 1909.
28. NRS HH16/619, Minute by D. Crombie, Secretary to the Prison Commissioners, 23 October 1909.
29. Edinburgh Evening News, 29 October 1909.
30. Idem.
31. Northern Whig, 1 November 1909.
32. Leneman (1991), p195.
33. Edinburgh Evening News, 15 & 16 November 1909; Ross-shire Journal, 17 June 1910.
34. The Scotsman, 6 December 1909.
35. Edinburgh Evening News, 4, 6 & 17 December 1909; Western Times, 7 December 1909; The Scotsman, 7 December 1909.
36. Atkinson (2019), p208; Edinburgh Evening News, 8 & 13 December 1909; Dundee Courier, 13 December 1909. NRS, HH16/38, Minutes of exchange between Governor, Edinburgh Prison and the Prison Commissioners, 9-10 December 1909.
37. The Scotsman, 9 & 10 January 1910; Votes for Women, 17 December 1909.

Arrested women are led away.

SEVEN:
SISTERS ARE DOING IT 1910-1911

"No longer does he jeer; he watches the Suffragists in respectful silence, reads their banners with appreciation, and regards their leaders with something very like respect."

The change in male perceptions of suffragettes in a report on a major demonstration on Calton Hill, June 1910.

The New Year could not come round quickly enough for the beleaguered authorities – yet 1910 brought only further opportunities for suffrage protest. There were two general elections, in January and December. The first to take place, between January 15 and February 10, allowed the constitutionalist societies to grill each candidate in turn, energised suffrage supporters and provided hours of work for branch volunteers. The three main Edinburgh societies hired local halls, printed pamphlets, handbills and posters for distribution, and offered visiting speakers to other constituencies, which partly explains the constant focus on fund-raising. The WSPU and WFL were always busy trying to 'Keep the Liberal out' and travelled in numbers to campaign in Herbert Asquith's East Fife constituency and against Winston Churchill in Dundee.

At the start of January, the Edinburgh National Society launched an appeal from Shandwick Place, naming it the 'Ten Thousand Shilling Appeal Fund' in the hope of raising £500 for election work. Sarah Mair took the reins. On January 22, Mair wrote from her home in Chester Street to complain about *The Scotsman's* account of electioneering in Leith, particularly the "not unnatural failure on the part of the 'mere man' reporter to discriminate between women wearing scarfs of red, white and green and others distinguished by purple, white and green." As usual, Miss Mair was grumpy

that the paper's coverage had confused the ENSWS with the WSPU. It was rather a petty complaint, given that neither candidate at Leith supported women's votes.

Elsewhere, the ENSWS took part in a National Union of Women's Suffrage Societies' initiative to gather signatures from male electors supportive of votes for women – still the only voters' petition collected on the day of a general election. Across the country, the Liberals lost nearly 100 seats to the Tories and emerged from the January poll with no overall majority. Governing with the consent of Irish Nationalists and a few Labour MPs, the Prime Minister sacked Herbert Gladstone and replaced him with Winston Churchill as Home Secretary. The new Asquith/Churchill alliance sounded warning bells across the suffrage movement. Both men believed women's votes would mean a million new Tory voters and they had no intention of allowing any extension to the franchise that included females. 1.

The headline news of early 1910 was Emmeline Pankhurst's dramatic decision to call a surprise truce and suspend militancy. In a carefully worded statement, the WSPU said it would instead support a Conciliation Committee, which had been established in January from over 50 MPs, many of them favourable to women's votes, to report to Parliament on a process towards a Women's Franchise Bill acceptable to all parties. The Women's Freedom

Lucy Burns of Edinburgh WSPU. (Courtesy of the US Library of Congress)

League followed quickly in announcing a suspension of its militant protests. The WSPU and WFL wanted to offer the government an opportunity, in an atmosphere of peace and calm, to introduce facilities for women's votes. In the meantime, both continued with propaganda work – meetings, rallies, 'At Homes' and the distribution of pamphlets supportive of a proposed Conciliation Bill. The National Union of Women's Suffrage Societies also placed its 22,000-strong army on alert to support the progress of the Conciliation Committee's work. The NUWSS sensed that women's votes were within reach. Reflecting its optimism, president Millicent Fawcett recalled, "We disposed of hundreds of our 'Pass the Bill' badges, and we had to send back to the office for more." 2.

The Edinburgh societies took stock. Even the proactive WSPU had time to contemplate the future. Margaret Fraser Smith told the city's branch that the suspension of militancy could bring a reduction in the heavy sentences that were taking their toll on younger members. Whatever might lie in the future, she hoped there would be no more forcible feeding and that "it would not be necessary for any more women to go to prison." The truce also benefitted membership numbers. Edinburgh WSPU secretary Florence McFarlane noted for the last week of March that 15 newcomers had signed on, with 12 the week before and, after a visit from Emmeline Pethick-Lawrence earlier in the month, "20 names had been sent to London." 3.

The WSPU's busy Edinburgh office remained at 8 Melville Place in Queensferry Road. The new organiser sent north by the Pankhursts, the American Lucy Burns, was a previously jailed firebrand, joining the WSPU in May 1909 while on holiday in London, and being imprisoned in June, July and September that year – quite an achievement! A branch library had been started to add to the Union's funds and to make suffrage literature available. Books were signed out at the Thursday evening meetings and a penny, paid in advance, was charged weekly. Jessie Methven donated half of the stock, and over 50 books were available on women's suffrage, including bound volumes of the WSPU newspaper *Votes for Women*.

The WSPU was not alone in advancing numbers. The Edinburgh National Society's recruitment drive also brought impressive results. Its 1910 annual report showed that the membership had more than doubled in 1909, rising from 384 to 854 – though any benefit accrued from the publicity surrounding militancy was left unsaid. The branch had arranged 111 meetings and started 10 new societies. And now, in 1910, it was doing what it had done since 1867, canvassing male electors in favour of woman's suffrage. Altogether the Edinburgh society held meetings in 12 constituencies, organised petitions in 10 of them, and helped in the high-profile Dundee campaign. The ENSWS was still led by S. E. S. Mair, with Elsie Inglis and Chrystal Macmillan as vice-presidents. Its office remained at 40 Shandwick Place.

In the spring of 1910, the Women's Freedom League opened the 'Edinburgh Suffrage Shop' at 33 Forrest Road. From the banners on the walls to the flower arrangements, the League's green, white and gold sparkled throughout. The centre was used for meetings, talks and fund-raising projects. It served as a gathering space, staged exhibitions and sold books, pamphlets, newspapers, baking and crafts. Its formal opening on May 14 featured a cellar transformed into a 'Holloway Cell' where members could be 'booked in' for sixpence. Grace Jacob of Dalkeith Road, the Edinburgh WFL branch president, was an elementary schoolteacher. Alexia Jack, another teacher, was secretary. Its salaried organiser was Madge Turner. In early January, Alexia Jack shared several platforms with the Scottish WFL organiser Anna Munro. At one meeting in Cupar, in the Prime Minister's constituency, Jack was scathing of the wealthy Dundee jute baron Sir James Caird for donating the huge sum of £10,000 to the Free Trade movement while, she said, the condition of the 30,000 millgirls in Dundee – including 2000 in Caird's own Ashton Works – was "disgraceful." [4].

Following on from a period of comparative quiet as the suffragette 'truce' was honoured, and while the country mourned the death of King Edward VII, the Parliamentary Franchise (Women) Bill – or Conciliation Bill – was introduced to the House of Commons as a Private Member's Bill by the Labour

MISS ANNA MUNRO, Secy. Scottish Council, 30 Gordon Street, Glasgow.

Anna Munro, Scottish Organiser for the Women's Freedom League.

The Daily Mirror

THE MORNING JOURNAL WITH THE SECOND LARGEST NET SALE

No. 2,265.   SATURDAY, NOVEMBER 19, 1910   One Halfpenny.

VIOLENT SCENES AT WESTMINSTER, WHERE MANY SUFFRAGETTES WERE ARRESTED WHILE TRYING TO FORCE THEIR WAY INTO THE HOUSE OF COMMONS.

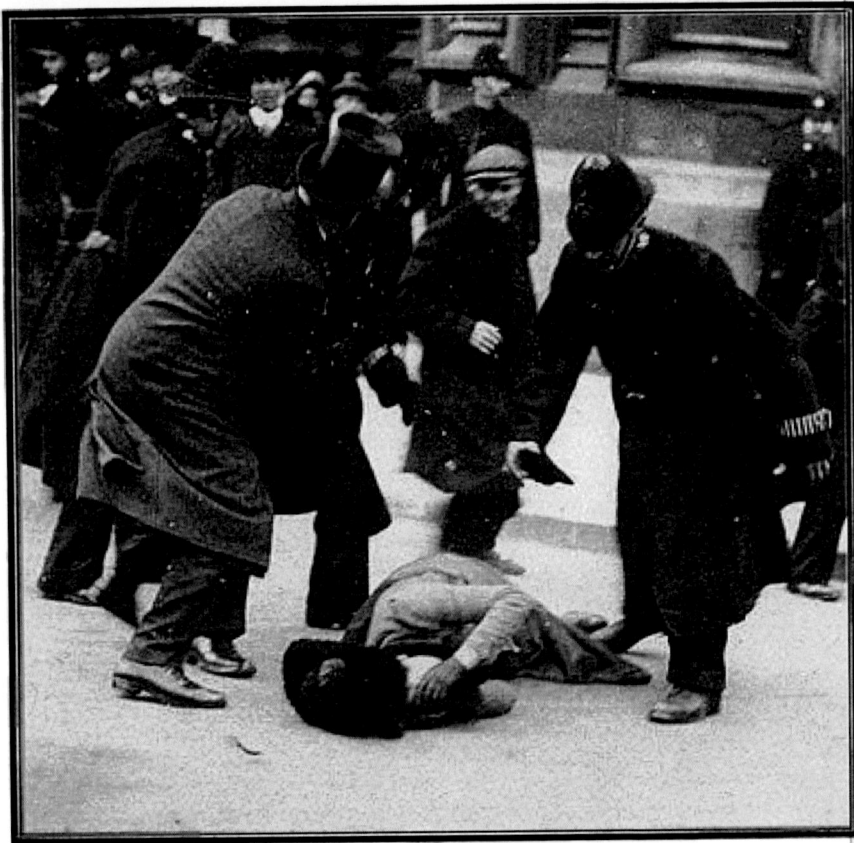

The shocking front page of the Daily Mirror showing Ada Wright lying injured on the pavement during the Black Friday violence. The Government ordered the photograph to be withdrawn.

MP David Shackleton. The bill proposed to enfranchise women occupiers only – around a million of them – but still only 1 in 13 women. It effectively took the municipal register as it existed and applied it to Parliamentary elections. A married woman would not be deprived of the vote because she was married; but the bill provided that a husband and a wife from the same property could not both vote. The measure had the support of the suffrage societies and MPs from all parties in the House. Shackleton referred to it as giving women a start as Parliamentary electors, and believed a more detailed bill would enfranchise many more females. No opposition was presented at this stage and the measure was given a formal First Reading on June 14.

Dozens of meetings were held in support of the bill, notably Lisa Gordon's and Elizabeth Lamond's efforts on two wheels to tour Borders constituencies by bicycle to muster support. The largest demonstration took place in London on June 18, a six-mile-long 'Prison to Citizenship' march of 10,000 suffragists. The WSPU made up the majority of participants, but seldom marched in isolation. The occasion brought together several of the main societies and speakers from 40 platforms, with a large group of Scottish Women's Freedom League members opting to wear "our tartan, heather and thistle." The National Union of Women's Suffrage Societies did not take part officially, but members illustrated the complexities of the Scottish suffrage movement by travelling south to show solidarity. Women Liberals also participated. There was some discord, however, when *Votes for Women* described the event as 'The March of England's Women.' Irate Scots put them right.

To coincide with the London procession, Scottish suffragists organised a mass meeting on Calton Hill in Edinburgh and advertised it with chalked pavements and a sandwich-board parade along Princes Street. Although this demonstration was organised by the WSPU, other suffrage societies participated, including the Women's Freedom League, the Edinburgh National Society for Women's Suffrage, the Scottish University Women's Suffrage Union and the Edinburgh Men's League. Ahead of the event, the ENSWS reported, "We are negotiating with the Women's Liberal Federation and the

Conservative and Unionist Franchise Association in hopes that they will both help us." Supporters gathered on Calton Hill in their thousands, with brass bands, pipers, waggonettes, flags and banners. Four platforms were erected and speeches were made by Barbara Wylie and Eunice Murray of the WFL, Chrystal Macmillan of the Universities' Union, Jessie Methven of Edinburgh WSPU and Dr Elsie Inglis for the Edinburgh National Society. But heavy rain dampened the women's enthusiasm and many trudged home wrapped in their 'colours'. Despite the downpour, the demonstration was said to have helped to change the attitude of 'the man in the street': "No longer does he jeer; he watches the Suffragists in respectful silence, reads their banners with appreciation, and regards their leaders with something very like respect." 5.

In the autumn of 1910, a branch of the Church League for Women's Suffrage was established in Edinburgh. Its secretary, Alice Robertson of Drummond Place, quickly issued a programme of 'drawing room' gatherings. The League had been founded in England the previous year "to band together, on a non-party basis, suffragists of every shade of opinion who are Church people in order to secure for women the vote in Church and State, as it is or may be granted to men." The first Sunday of every month was observed by members for prayer towards its objective. In years ahead, a Scottish Churches League for Woman Suffrage would be formed, with its headquarters in Edinburgh. As far back as 1867, of course, the ENSWS had benefitted from the support of several of the city's influential clergymen.

At this time, prayers for divine intercession must have been made many times for the successful passage of the Conciliation Bill, which safely negotiated its Second Reading on July 12 by 299 votes to 189. But this great advance was relegated from newspaper headlines by the darkest and most disturbing day in the history of the women's suffrage movement.

On 18 November 1910, and following an angry breakdown between the House of Commons and House of Lords over that year's budget, Herbert Asquith called a snap general election for December and said that Parliament would be dissolved on November 28. Enraged by the sudden decision to

How the police behaviour was seen by those sympathetic to the women's cause.

give no more time to the Conciliation measure, 300 women at an 'indignation' meeting in Caxton Hall marched menacingly to Parliament Square to 'have it out' with Asquith directly. Outside the Commons they were met with extreme force by massed ranks of police, who had expected trouble. The ensuing battle entered suffrage history as 'Black Friday' – a day that earned its name from the violence meted out to female protesters, some of it sexual, by scores of Metropolitan Police and crowds of agitated bystanders.

Dozens of women were cruelly assaulted as they attempted to break through the police lines. In a six-hour battle they were roughly handled, hurled to the ground and beaten, with sullen, hostile onlookers jeering and goading the police on. Banners were torn down and trampled into the grass to the threatening encouragement of the taunting mob. Over 150 women were assaulted. Many were injured, some severely. At least 29 were sexually molested. Long-time suffrage supporter Henry Nevinson, a *Daily News* journalist, recorded the scene: "Here I saw one of the most famous doctors rush against the police at the very front. Flung savagely back, she instinctively tidied her scarf and rushed again. Here a writer, equally famous, was caught bodily off her feet and dashed upon the pavement...there, a hospital nurse almost succeeded in breaking the line till she was caught by the throat and driven back into the seething contest." A shocked *Daily Record* told its Scottish readers the protest was different from any other it had ever seen: "The women were jostled, the people jeering and yelling with delight at their discomfiture." The *Daily Mirror* added that the police "seemed to enjoy the proceedings." 6.

Despite Black Friday's orchestrated brutality, 115 women and four men found themselves arrested. Six women from Edinburgh were among them. The battered and bedraggled were taken into custody, most charged with obstructing the police, and some with assault. Many reported being struck or manhandled. Others bore the physical marks of beatings. Some were still in shock. The Press generally took the side of the suffragettes. A sensational *Daily Mirror* front page photograph showed Ada Wright prostrate at a policeman's feet, seemingly unconscious. The government ordered the picture to be suppressed and the negative destroyed. The same issue contained a letter from the vice-president of the Royal College of Surgeons, another eyewitness: "The women were pushed about in all directions and thrown down by the police. Their arms were twisted until they were almost broken. Their thumbs were forcibly bent back, and they were tortured in other nameless ways that made one feel sick at the sight. I was there myself and saw these things done." Meanwhile, a Scottish doctor had her hands full. Dr Flora Murray, now commemorated on a banknote, was working in London and had set up a unit to treat women injured in clashes with police, or during protests at meetings. She was present outside Parliament on Black Friday, ministering to the injured and patching countless wounds. A member of Kensington WSPU, Murray later acted as the house doctor at a secret

nursing home to which hunger-striking prisoners were taken, one of her most weakened 'patients' being Kitty Marion after she had been forcibly fed 232 times in 14 weeks. 7.

Six members of Edinburgh WSPU were arrested, charged and convicted of obstructing the police on Black Friday or the day following, when women took out their anger on West End windows. All chose to go to prison apart from Dr Grace Cadell, who was allowed to return to her patients in Leith...

- Florence McFarlane had moved with her parents and sisters to Edinburgh in the 1880s where her father John launched a Liberal-leaning newspaper, the *Scottish Leader*. McFarlane entered nursing around 1890 and by 1901 she was the matron of a private hospital in the city. In December 1909 she made a brave stand when she resigned from her post rather than dismiss one of her nurses, Elsie Roe Brown, who had taken part in a militant protest. McFarlane was 33 when she travelled south to join WSPU comrades, one of them her sister Edith of Wimbledon WSPU, who had also been arrested on Black Friday as Mrs Edith Begbie. Both sisters were convicted of obstructing the police and sentenced to 14 days, with Edith further charged with throwing stones at Winston Churchill's windows in Ecclestone Square.
- Lilias Mitchell, from Leith, where her father ran a timber business, was convicted of obstructing the police and assaulting a constable with a stone. Mitchell described it as "my first real and horrid plunge into militancy." She wrote of the rowdy scenes prior to her arrest and how the sight of a policeman gripping a girl by the throat "roused my indignation and undoubted fighting spirit, for I knocked off his helmet." In court, a police constable gave evidence that Mitchell had struck him with a stone on the helmet. He had taken the stone from her, and she had remarked, "I have plenty more ammunition." She was sentenced to a fine of £2 or 14 days. She chose jail.

- Dr Grace Cadell of Leith Walk was charged with slapping a police officer on the face. She admitted that she had put her finger under the strap of his helmet, but denied assault. She said she was willing to apologise as she "had to get home to my patients." Her apology was accepted, and she was discharged.
- Edith Hudson, then 38, appeared before Herbert Muskett at Bow Street police court on November 23, charged with obstruction. With Muskett's words ringing in her ears that the "lenient" sentences so far passed down seemed to be having no effect, she was given 14 days in Holloway. She had been sentenced to 30 days at Leith the year before.
- Cecilia Wolseley Haig of Comely Bank Gardens, with her sisters Florence and Evelyn, were members of Edinburgh WSPU. Their parents, Helen and James Haig of Berwickshire, supported women's suffrage and a grand uncle had been imprisoned in 1819 for a speech in favour of electoral reform. It was reported that the imprisonment of her sister Florence in London in 1908 emboldened Cecilia to volunteer for militant duties. She had donated to WSPU central funds as early as April 1908.
- Evelyn Cotton Haig was an artist, specialising in miniatures. She studied in Edinburgh and Paris and exhibited at the Paris Salon and Royal Academy. She was brought into Edinburgh WSPU by her sisters Florence and Cecilia in 1908 and was later branch treasurer. With her sister Cecilia she ran the 1909 East Edinburgh election campaign for the WSPU and helped to organise that year's Edinburgh procession. Both Cecilia and Evelyn Haig received 14 days. Their sister Florence, who had a studio in Chelsea by this time and was secretary of Chelsea WSPU, does not appear in the lists of Black Friday arrests, but had already served two terms in Holloway. [8.]

Despite being nursed by her sisters over subsequent months, Cecilia Haig died from kidney cancer at Brook Street Hospital, London on 31 December 1911, just over a year after Black Friday. She was interred at Highgate Cemetery.

Representatives of the WSPU and the Men's League were present, and among the wreaths was one in the familiar colours of Mrs Pankhurst's Union.

Five days later, on 5 January 1912, *Votes for Women* marked Cecilia Haig's life with an 'In Memoriam' tribute and claimed her death was the result of injuries sustained on Black Friday. "Another name has been added to the roll of those who have given their lives for the cause of women's emancipation. Miss Cecilia Wolseley Haig, after a year's painful illness brought on in consequence of the terrible treatment to which she was subjected on Black Friday, passed from this life on Sunday last. When she went on the Deputation, on November 18, 1910, Miss Haig was entirely unaware of the presence of any illness, and, indeed, felt quite well. But on Black Friday she was not only subjected to assault of a most disgraceful kind but was also trampled upon."

Sylvia Pankhurst also claimed the Edinburgh suffragette had died because of the beating she had received on Black Friday. "I saw Cecilia Haig go out with the rest; a tall, strongly built, reserved woman, comfortably situated, who in ordinary circumstances might have gone through life without receiving an insult, much less a blow. She was assaulted with violence and indecency, and died in December 1911, after a painful illness, arising from her injuries." And on 14 January 1912, the WSPU leader-in-waiting Annie Kenney planted a commemorative tree in tribute to the Edinburgh suffragist, with the inscription: "In memory of Cecilia Wolseley Haig. Died 31 December 1911 as a result of injuries received when on a delegation to the Prime Minister on 18 November 1910." [9.]

It is, of course, impossible to say today whether Edinburgh has a suffragette 'martyr'. No source from November 1910 can be traced describing Cecilia Haig's injuries or the sexual assault hinted at by *Votes for Women* and Sylvia Pankhurst. What is certain is that Cecilia Haig's life ended when she was just 55. Her death certificate stated kidney cancer as its cause. Others who knew her – including two figureheads of the militant movement – blamed the injuries and trauma she endured on November 18. It is doubtful if *Votes for Women*, still carefully edited by Emmeline and Frederick Pethick-Lawrence at

this time, would have attributed blame to the Black Friday authorities without the Haig family's knowledge and, likely, Florence Haig's consent.

Among others injured or assaulted on Black Friday were Elizabeth and Agnes Thomson of Hartington Place, Edinburgh. Both had joined the WSPU in June 1909 after hearing Mrs Pankhurst speak in the Synod Hall. They had travelled to London and had been allocated to one of the 12-strong duty groups. Elizabeth Thomson recalled, "Some of the policemen were a very rough lot, and burly men. They shoved us and pushed us, and when we held on to the railings they pulled our hands off...one man struck me a blow on the back, and after an hour and a half we were driven down a side street [by police], and so we returned to Caxton Hall." The sisters then joined Emmeline Pankhurst and 20 to 30 women for a march on Downing Street. During the resulting crush, "some of those in the front were knocked over. Agnes fell with five ladies on top of her. She was severely bruised but almost miraculously not suffocated, as the ladies were so careful not to hurt each other."

At that point Elizabeth became detached from her sister, and when they eventually found each other, Agnes admitted to her that she had feared "I was killed as she could not find me." We can only imagine that emotional reunion in such extraordinary circumstances. "My sister was feeling her fall, and my back was rather bad, so we decided not to do any more and told Mrs Pethick-Lawrence so. We then went back to our lodgings. Next morning we decided to go home to Edinburgh by the 10 o'clock train." The sisters had previously hosted temperance and philosophical society meetings at their home, but were shunned on return to Scotland. "After that, of course, no one would accept an invitation to our house." Public protests such as those being vividly reported from London breached taboos of women's sex and class and risked the reputation and professional success of otherwise respectable women, especially those from better-off, conservative families. Several militants –

LEFT: All the women detained were released on the orders of the Home Secretary, Winston Churchill.

including Ethel Moorhead and Frances Parker – were ostracised by their families, who found it impossible to condone their actions. 10.

Black Friday became a public relations disaster for the government. As events unfolded, Winston Churchill decided not to bring criminal proceedings against those arrested, raising the immediate suspicion that, in avoiding trials, the Home Secretary was attempting to suppress evidence of police misconduct which might come to light in court. But all charges were dropped and the women were released, batch by batch, from Bow Street and Cannon Row police stations. Many still carried bags of clothes, having anticipated spending the next week or two away from home. One of them, apparently, had let out her house for a month.

Lord Lytton's Conciliation Committee thereafter undertook interviews with 135 witnesses, nearly all of whom described acts of violence against the women, with 29 of the statements listing details of sexual assault. An Irish suffragette swore on oath that her undergarments had been torn off. Another told of having her breasts clutched by police "in as public a manner as possible" and how her skirt was lifted up. Another woman told the committee: "I saw an Inspector run from the cordon over to me. He furiously struck me with his fist and felled me to the ground. I got up…and he felled me again. Blood was flowing from the first blow I received." Demands for a public inquiry were rejected by Churchill, but Black Friday's viciousness led to a change in approach. Unwilling to risk further violence, the WSPU resumed previous forms of direct action, such as stone-throwing and window-smashing, where the perpetrators, by and large, avoided capture and the possibility of injury. Deputations to Parliament were also stopped. Not for the first time it was left mostly to the Women's Freedom League to continue the terrifying task of interrupting meetings and facing the wrath of an increasingly-hostile public. 11.

The fall of the Conciliation Bill enraged Edinburgh suffragists. Women queued to join the city's suffrage societies, and quickly took to the streets. A joint demonstration of the Men's League, the WSPU, the Women's Freedom League and the Universities' Union was held in the various streets off Princes Street. At St David Street and the Mound the crowds numbered 500 and 1000. Women stood on orange boxes or spoke from the backs of waggonettes. The *Edinburgh Evening Dispatch* appeared to feel the women's pain. It wondered how they would nurse their "hot indignation." Everyone, it said, thought the bill was certain to go through. Now the country would face the women's anger…"The Suffragettes we know, and their methods we know, and we may take it for granted that the Premier and his colleagues have unpleasant times ahead." 12.

On November 22, just five days after Black Friday, Prime Minister Asquith announced that should the Liberals be returned in the December election, parliamentary time would be allowed for a Conciliation Bill to be put to Parliament. The WSPU was angered that his announcement was for the 'next parliament' rather than the next session, and 200 suffragettes invaded Downing Street, where scuffles again broke out with the police. Over 150 women were arrested. The following day another march on Parliament was met by police cordons and a further 18 protesters were detained. With the continued fall-out from Black Friday, and in the knowledge that it was not a 'good look' to jail hundreds of women ahead of a general election, charges against most were quietly dropped.

Black Friday survivors were back on active duty before the year was out. David Lloyd George arrived in Edinburgh to address an assembly of Liberals at the Synod Hall. While the Chancellor was speaking, a window at the rear of the platform was broken. A stone was lowered on a string. Attached to it was a label with the words, "For the Chancellor – to the greatest hypocrite of modern times, autocrat, and traitor. Lloyd George, free women and then advocate democracy." The women responsible, Florence McFarlane of Edinburgh WSPU and Annie Cuthbert of the Dundee branch – both hurt on Black Friday – then locked themselves into a side room. Both were arrested. They were liberated on £1 bail, but it was stated the next morning that no charge would be brought against them. Once again, a Cabinet minister preferred not to have his day in court.

MR. H. H. ASQUITH.

Freedom of Edinburgh.

LONDON, December 21.

The freedom of the city of Edinburgh was conferred upon the Right Hon. H. H. Asquith yesterday. In his speech on the occasion, Mr. Asquith urged the cities to grapple with social questions. The Earl of Rosebery was present at the ceremony.

The Edinburgh freedom ceremony for Mr Asquith was widely reported - this mention from New Zealand.

If suffragettes expected sympathy after their brutal treatment in London, it failed to materialise. Following his visit to Edinburgh, the Chancellor was tracked to Penicuik by Muriel and Arabella Scott and Morag Burn Murdoch of Edinburgh WSPU. Muriel Scott succeeded in getting to his car and shouted for votes into its open window. Police dragged her away. A crowd of around 2000 then turned on the suffragettes. The women were hemmed in with nowhere to go. A policeman who rushed to assist was pushed aside. A member of the Men's League called for volunteers to protect the trio, and a cordon was formed around them to allow the women to reach their car. Two attempts were made to overturn the vehicle before its terror-stricken occupants were able to return safely to Edinburgh.

On December 20, the day after polling returned him to power, Herbert Asquith received the Freedom of Edinburgh. He was accompanied to the ceremony by his wife Margot and daughter Elizabeth. Strict precautions were taken, not least as Ethel Moorhead had walloped his Home Secretary with an egg a fortnight earlier. Five hundred tickets for the ceremony were allocated to women, but made available only through town councillors. Each ticket-holder's name had to be submitted to the Town Clerk. The invitation was then issued in the woman's name and it was non transferrable. The *Midlothian Journal* was concerned – though not because of the explicit discrimination against women: "Ladies, through no fault of their own, but because of the shrieking sisterhood, were debarred from that free gift of tickets to which they have been accustomed on previous occasions." The audience of 3000 did not see the squads of police outside every entrance, with a dozen mounted officers held in readiness in a lane behind the hall. Despite the precautions, two unnamed suffragettes "succeeded for a few minutes in diverting attention and stimulating the anger and irritation of the audience." Both were ejected. Two male supporters were also removed. By and large, however, the protest was restricted to Women's Freedom Leaguers walking or driving up and down Castle Terrace parading banners decrying Asquith and his government. But, surprisingly, there was no formal demonstration and the event passed off without incident. [13].

Down south, the angry and frustrated WSPU and WFL leaderships issued separate Christmas-time calls-to-arms. "We are forced into resuming our vigorous agitation justified by the position of outlawry to which women are at present condemned," said the League. The WSPU's statement was equally emphatic: "As the Prime Minister will not give us the assurance that women shall be enfranchised next year, we revert to a state of war." The government – and the country – must have dreaded the new year to come.

As matters transpired, however, nationwide celebrations for King George V's coronation brought a continuation of the suffragette truce. Despite the fall of the Conciliation Bill, the women's campaign had won the backing of 150 local authorities, and more than a million people had pledged support. But, adding to a sense of foreboding within the movement was the continued failure of measures in the House of Commons – while even the arch anti-suffragist Prime Minister had received the Freedom of Edinburgh with hardly a murmur.

The most dramatic news of early 1911 was Teresa Billington-Greig's decision to walk out on the Women's Freedom League. Her unexpected departure was marked by a blistering attack on the militant movement which soured her relationship with many former comrades in the League and WSPU – and left just as many bewildered. Her article in the monthly *New Age* magazine, *The Militant Suffrage Movement: Emancipation in a Hurry*, left little room for doubt that she now regarded the Pankhurst strategy as misguided and flawed. "I believed in it, worked in it, suffered in it, rejoiced in it, and I have been disillusioned." Thus began her tirade.

Writing from her home in Bishopbriggs, she explained her change of heart: "I think the sacrifices asked are neither good nor necessary, nor legitimate, and I cannot continue to make them." Billington-Greig claimed that there were two objects of militancy: the early winning of Parliamentary votes; and the assertion of a woman's right to be herself. She had worked for the first object, but believed in the second. She had become convinced that the greater role of women in society was being sacrificed in the haste for immediate votes. "I can do better work for this greater end, and use my powers to greater advantage as a free-lance feminist than as a member of the Freedom League. Hence my resignation." 14.

Suffragists were shocked by Billington-Greig's undisguised attack on the Pankhursts, and the Edinburgh WSPU was placed on the defensive. At its next meeting in the Arts Halls, George Street, Margaret Fraser Smith said the Press was now saying that the WSPU "were under the domination of self-appointed autocrats." That was not so, she added. Their leaders "were the best and finest women in the world." Her words attracted applause, but murmurings, too. The branch had just captured the services of Frances 'Fanny' Parker from the Scottish University Women's Suffrage Union. Parker, a niece of Lord

Kitchener, would become in the years ahead "an inspiring and dangerous schemer" with "an exquisite madness." 15.

The Women's Freedom League was also holding to the 1910 truce. The Edinburgh branch president was Sarah Munro and its secretary Alexia Jack. The WFL Edinburgh Suffrage Shop at 33 Forrest Road was run by Caroline Dalziel and Miss Thompson of Rosslyn Crescent. Incomings and outgoings were looked after by its treasurer, Miss M. A. Wood of Great King Street. The programme of meetings and day-to-day propaganda was placed in the hands of assistant secretary Helen McLauchlan. At one function, suffrage recitations were given by Mary Williamson and *The Awakening* was sung by past president Grace Jacob. Among visiting speakers early that year was Alison Neilans, a member of the WFL executive who was then in charge of the Clyde Campaign for the Glasgow headquarters of the Scottish WFL. In March 1911, the League took part in a special women's suffrage religious service in the Synod Hall conducted by three ministers from different denominations. A choir drawn from the various suffrage societies led the singing. The new Edinburgh NUWSS secretary, Katherine Loudon, composed a hymn for the occasion, which was sung just before the close ...

Sin and suffering, shame and sorrow,
Need and want against us stand:
Open ills and shrouded evils
Breathe their poison o'er the land:
Lord, that we may serve our country
Put the weapon in our hand. 16.

The highlight of early 1911 was an extraordinary attempt by suffragists to disrupt the National Census. The plan was for women to spend Census Sunday on April 2 in the houses of sympathisers. If an enumerator called at a house where women had gathered, they would not be admitted – nobody would be at home. A notice outside would say simply 'No Vote – No Census'.

Census night at the Café Vegetaria in Nicolson Street. The woman at the back is impersonating Winston Churchill. (Courtesy of the National Library of Scotland)

In towns across the country, women occupiers filled their homes with as many friends as they could squeeze in. In the morning they were instructed to return their census papers with the words, 'No votes for women, no information from women'. The government threatened legal action, but none was taken.

The census boycott was a Women's Freedom League initiative and they promoted it from February 1911. But if the clock is turned back to October 1910, the idea was also discussed at a Women's Social and Political Union meeting in Edinburgh. After addresses by three Edinburgh suffragettes, Margaret Fraser Smith, Lucy Burns and Edith Hudson – all active WSPU militants and ex-prisoners – the topic of tax resistance came up. During the discussion an unnamed woman in the audience asked the speakers if they would consider, "If there was any way in which they could annoy the Government with regard to the census?" As the laughter in the hall subsided, the woman said she "would be prepared to walk about all night to keep the census work back, and to carry a kettle of tea with her." There were further chuckles at this. The Edinburgh WSPU organiser Lucy Burns then said that the suggestion was "a very good one" and would be considered. 17.

In any event, great preparations were made for the Census Day protest. 'Boycott' meetings were held by the Women's Freedom League and Eunice Murray, in one rousing speech, called upon all who were not already involved to support the "new anti-government subterfuge." Copies of The Census Act were sold and collections taken. But while the Women's Social and Political Union and the Women's Freedom League actively encouraged opposition to the population count, the non-militant Edinburgh National Society expressed disapproval of the tactic. On learning of the plan, president Sarah Mair issued a public rebuke; "Now, unpleasant as is always the task of finding fault with one's neighbour...I feel it is incumbent on me to draw attention to the fact that the large National Union, of which our Society is a branch, does not look with favour on the policy adopted by certain other suffragists attempting to spoil the census returns." In years ahead, the ENSWS never strayed from its constitutionalist opposition to militancy, though it might also be said that its grassroots members seldom criticised their more pugnacious Edinburgh sisters.

The Press, of course, was outraged. The Edinburgh Evening News called the census evasion "nonsensical." The city's Evening Dispatch thought it "foolish and misguided." The Dundee Courier saw it as "fatuous" and "silly." The Herald in Glasgow claimed sarcastically that the tactic was simply a ruse for women to conceal their age. One Edinburgh resident railed that the "tomfoolery" had gone far enough. As for the £5 penalty facing women evaders, "They have been shown too much leniency and it is high time that these would-be martyrs and heroines were pulled up and brought to their senses." Cynics also took delight in pointing out that the census evasion coincided with April Fool's Day. The last word went to the satirical magazine Punch – it claimed that the women had simply "taken leave of their census." 18.

The boycott was robustly defended. The women argued, and hoped to show, that they could not be ruled without consent. Refusal to complete the official form may have resulted in a fine or imprisonment, but such punishments would still have failed to achieve their objective. The census information would still be withheld. The women also told the Prime Minister that they would have called off the action as late as the day before the count had he pledged facilities for women's votes. As the Ilford suffragette Ethel Haslam put it: "Two courses were open to the government; either to quietly accept defeat or to turn all the police courts in the country into pulpits, from which woman suffrage would be preached. They have chosen defeat." 19.

The 12th census of Great Britain involved 9000 enumerators in Scotland. Papers were left at properties the week before the count. The same form distributed to Edinburgh tenements went to the new king at Buckingham Palace. The statutory penalty for non-compliance was £5. Hundreds of posters declaring 'No Votes, No Census' were pasted on public buildings, schools, shopfronts, tramcars and lampposts.

In Edinburgh, large numbers of women were put up in private houses of friends, who placed 'No Vote, No Census' notices on their doors and refused to open them to enumerators. The Café Vegetaria on Nicolson Street was

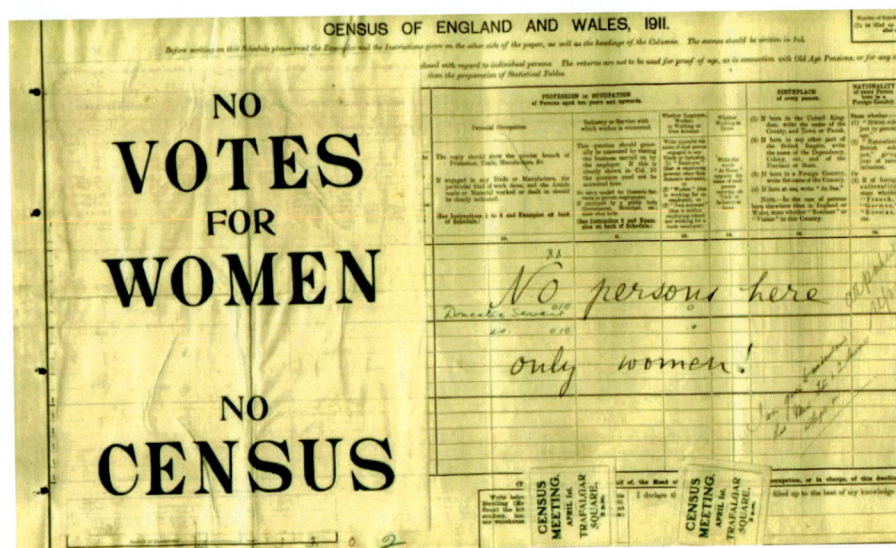

This 1911 census form was returned with a large 'No Votes for Women, No Census' label pasted into the page for household details. Stamps advertising a Trafalgar Square meeting are stuck along the bottom of the form, which also shows the message "No persons here, only women!" (Courtesy of findmypast.co.uk)

hired by Lucy Burns of Edinburgh WSPU and became the rendezvous for dozens of resisters. They were advised to "bring a pillow and a rug," and part of the evening was devoted to impersonations of Herbert Asquith and Winston Churchill. The size of the restaurant, which extended to three floors, allowed the accommodation of "over 100" evaders. It was reported, however, that the enumerators "were not asleep" and took measures to have the women counted as they entered and left the building. Two detectives were also posted outside. To counter the surveillance, Arabella Scott went in and out of the building "so the Census people could not count how many were there." *Votes for Women* noted that the Scottish members had carried out their protest "most enthusiastically," and that the Edinburgh evaders seemed to have "enjoyed themselves exceedingly." Meanwhile, the unusual spectacle of an Edinburgh café brilliantly illuminated at midnight on a Sunday drew

hundreds of sightseers – though one paper noted solemnly that "the Sabbath calm was not greatly disturbed." [20].

Once the dust had settled, the Edinburgh Registrar R. D. Robertson wrote to the Registrar General for Scotland to report the women's refusal to supply information: "Being aware that there was likely to be a large gathering of people in the Café Vegetaria, Nicolson Street, I instructed the Enumerator to deliver a large schedule there. The manageress informed him on his call that she would not be responsible in the matter, the place having been sublet for the weekend to Miss Burns of the Women's Social and Political Union. On Monday he called for the Schedule and received it with the words 'No Vote etc' written across the face and signed by the said Miss Burns. I have seen the said lady but can obtain no satisfaction."

The Registrar General, James Macdougall, asked for details of the women known to have been present in the café to be collated with statistics supplied by the police. He also thought the manageress should have been held responsible, "and should be so informed." [21].

The Women's Freedom League took no part in the Café Vegetaria protest, but volunteers filled their homes with members, or took to attics, barns and haylofts to avoid Edinburgh's 520 enumerators. All undertook not to return to their homes until after midday on the Monday. President Sarah Munro promised a house full of suffragettes and wrote "No votes – no information" on her schedule. A bill-sticking crusade was also a WFL ploy and among places 'defaced' with 'No Votes, No Census' posters was the government complex in Waterloo Place. Three members of the League were arrested, but released without charge.

The total population count for the city was 339,239, an increase of only 2780 compared with 1901. The *Edinburgh Evening News* mused, "Of course, it is possible all the suffragettes may not have been recorded, and this will no doubt please the militants if they think that the returns have been made unreliable by their action." The public's reaction was less charitable. Theodore Napier of West Castle Road wrote angrily to the *Edinburgh*

Evening Dispatch recommending "a good whipping" for all those involved. 22.

Today, the availability of the 1911 census allows historians to examine evidence of this unique civil disobedience. Although the true scale of the protests will never be known, the returns show the women's boycott was observed in all parts of the country. The form filled in by Kate Gillie, for example, dedicates its protest to the "loving memory of Mrs Clarke and Miss Henria Williams who lost their lives for the cause." Gillie was referring to Emmeline Pankhurst's sister Mary Clarke, who had died on Christmas Day as the result of alleged police brutality on Black Friday, and the death of Henria Williams on January 2, similarly mistreated. Although known to have a weak heart, Williams had been "terribly knocked about" on that fateful November afternoon and had returned to Caxton Hall "gasping for breath, with face and lips blackened by suffocation." Silent suffragettes kept a vigil at St Pancras as her coffin was gently placed on the midnight train north to Glasgow, where she had lived until her mid-twenties. Her burial in Cathcart Cemetery was watched over by Glasgow WSPU. Black Friday had occurred the previous November and on her census form Kate Gillie cites Winston Churchill's reluctance to investigate the police conduct as a cause, adding, "If I am intelligent enough to fill in this census form, I can surely make an 'X' on a ballot form." And she defiantly signed off by declaring her home, "a house full of evaders." 23.

When another attempt was made to revive the Conciliation Bill in early May 1911, the women's movement threw its combined weight behind it. A series of meetings in Edinburgh culminated on May 4 in a major demonstration in the city centre by five societies, the ENSWS, WSPU, WFL, Men's League and Universities' Union. The Women's Freedom League took up a stance at the west end of Princes Street, where three members, Sarah Munro, Alexia Jack and Elizabeth Finlayson Gauld, spoke from a lorry decked in the League's green, gold and white. The platform at South Castle Street was occupied by members of the Scottish University Women's Suffrage Union. Its president, Frances Simson, Arabella Scott, Elizabeth Ireland and Dr Alice Hutchison

Eunice Murray, an accomplished writer and a regular contributor to The Vote, the newspaper of the Women's Freedom League. (Courtesy of DC Thomson, Dundee)

spoke there. The incoming Edinburgh National Society president, Katherine Louden, led ENSWS speakers in the middle of Princes Street. At the WSPU platform in St David Street the principal speakers were Muriel Scott, Lucy Burns and Morag Burn Murdoch. Meanwhile, in London, the movement marked the coronation of King George V in June with an impressive 50,000 turn-out for the Women's Pageant, a colourful protest march along the Embankment which involved 1000 banners and 75 bands. [24].

Standing in for the Prime Minister on August 16, David Lloyd George stated that facilities might be given to any Suffrage Bill which could secure a second reading. In other words, the future of such a bill would depend solely on the luck of the members' ballot. This outraged campaigners and Lord Lytton, chairman of the Conciliation Committee, wrote urgently to the Prime Minister to demand that he kept his promise to advance the Conciliation Bill, which was supported by the women's suffrage societies and had been twice passed by enormous majorities. For once, Asquith's reply was reassuring: "I have no hesitation in saying that the promises made by and on behalf of the government in regard to giving facilities for the Conciliation Bill will be strictly adhered to, both in letter and in spirit." [25].

That week, Prime Minister Asquith received a letter signed by 124 Members of Parliament setting out reasons for *not* allowing votes for women. It claimed, once again, that there was no evidence that women wanted the franchise. It forcibly suggested a majority of women did not. It urged caution on the government in allowing the Conciliation Bill further progress and asked the Prime Minister not to commit himself to it. Eunice Murray, the most erudite Women's Freedom Leaguer, offered this riposte ... "May I point out that the anxiety of the Suffragists to have the Bill made law is that they are weary of asking for justice. They are weary of laying their case before the people. These 124 members say that the majority of men and women in the United Kingdom are opposed to women's suffrage. This year on the streets of London, seven miles of women walked five abreast asking for the vote and for the passing of the Conciliation Bill. Beside them paraded 12 sandwichmen

bearing the legend 'Women don't want the Vote. Let them prove it.' It looks to me as though they did." [26].

On 7 November 1911, out of the blue, Prime Minister Asquith announced that a Manhood Suffrage Bill would be introduced in the next session to enlarge the male vote, with the possibility of a women's suffrage amendment being added to it, should Parliament so desire. As a consequence, no further time would be given to the Conciliation Bill in the present session. It was an extraordinary statement and completely unexpected. The entire women's movement was shocked and incredulous. Everyone had pinned hopes on the bill. Christabel Pankhurst recalled feeling "icily calm" as her Women's Social and Political Union announced "uncompromising hostility" to the idea of women's votes being dependant on parliamentary amendments.

On November 21, an angry body of suffragettes marched from the Tenth Women's Parliament at Caxton Hall and confronted hundreds of police positioned to protect the House of Commons and Parliament Square. It led to a violent confrontation. Within the first hour 20 women were forcibly escorted to Cannon Row. Others who replaced them were flung back into the crowds. While this first wave of activists was moving within range of the Commons, a shower of stones flew through the air in other parts of central London. Reports of broken windows in Kensington, Brompton, the Strand and Charing Cross soon testified to the choreographed use of missiles by different squads of militants. Not only government buildings were targeted this time, but shop windows, men's clubs, newspaper offices and department stores. By 9 pm, hundreds of windows in central London had been shattered by pairs of women with stones and toffee hammers. By 10 pm, more than 150 women had been arrested, among them Emmeline Pethick-Lawrence, co-leader of the WSPU, Victor Duval, leader of the Men's Political Union — and the pioneering hunger striker Marion Wallace-Dunlop, the Scottish artist's fifth arrest. But Constance Lytton passed down Whitehall later that night and was thrilled to see that "every window smiled." [27].

By morning, the shocked country learned that 220 women and three men were in custody. The majority of the women gave London addresses, but many had volunteered from other areas. Edinburgh WSPU had sent a seven-strong contingent – all aware that they were being asked to deliberately break the law.

The Misses Elizabeth and Agnes Thomson of Hartington Place had laboured for 18 years as missionaries in India. They told Arabella Scott they had joined Edinburgh WSPU after hearing Emmeline Pankhurst give a remarkable speech in the city. Both had been hurt on Black Friday. Jessie Methven, of Great King Street, had acted as honorary secretary of the older National Society, working under Priscilla McLaren, before joining the WSPU. Edith Hudson had given up her nursing career in the Scottish capital to act as a paid employee of the WSPU. She had been imprisoned after the 'Leith Riot' in 1909 and arrested on Black Friday. Alice Maud Shipley of Warrender Park Road, Mrs Bessie Davis and Mrs Marion Grieve also travelled. Mrs Grieve, of Coillesdene House, Joppa was known as one of five pioneering female climbers who had reached the summit of Mont Blanc in 1874. She was also rumoured to pick up stones on Portobello beach and place them in her handbag to take to demonstrations. Shipley, then aged 32, had worked as a maid in Dumfries before moving to Edinburgh. She was one of the few working women involved in the London raids. Bessie Davis gave Edinburgh as her home address, but nothing more is known of her other than her entry on the *Suffragette Roll of Honour*, compiled in the 1950s. 28.

The first case at Bow Street police court on November 24 was heard by Mr Marsham and included two defendants from Edinburgh, Edith Hudson and Jessie Methven (as well as Emily Fussell from Aberdeen WSPU). They were charged with breaking windows in Horse Guards Parade. A police inspector said he saw the defendants smash three windows at the Foreign Office. On passing through Downing Street on the way to the police station, Hudson had said to him, 'Oh, do let me have a shot at No 10,' and she was found with a stone in her hand. Her offer was declined. Hudson and Methven were each fined 10 shillings and ordered to pay 18 shillings' damage, or to go to prison for 10 days. They opted for prison.

Edinburgh sisters Agnes and Elizabeth Thomson were also convicted of window-smashing. Elizabeth recalled, "We walked about in Westminster near the House of Commons until the hour of seven struck. Then we proceeded to throw stones at some Government windows in Great Smith Street. We were promptly seized by a policeman and marched into Cannon Row police station. The crowd cheered us as we crossed Whitehall." The sisters refused to pay their five-shilling fines and chose five days' imprisonment. Elizabeth Thomson told the magistrate that she had been waiting for 40 years for a women's suffrage bill to be passed and "found that constitutionalist ways were no use." Alice Maud Shipley was similarly charged and she, too, was handed five days. Mrs Bessie Davis was sentenced to seven shillings or seven days for trying to break through a cordon of police opposite St Margaret's Church. A police witness said Davis had sat down on the pavement, and he claimed that she had struck him. Davis countered by telling the court that he was twisting her arm, and it had "been very much hurt." Joppa's Marion Grieve was discharged and escaped a conviction. She would be less fortunate next time. 29.

So, by November's end, six of the Edinburgh seven were behind bars in Holloway. As news of the jailings spread, the non-militant NUWSS issued a forceful condemnation of the WSPU action, arguing that it had damaged the cause more than it had damaged Westminster's windows: "The National Union appeals most strongly to all Suffragists to remember that such outbreaks injure women far more than anyone else, and that they are organised by one society only of the many existing Women's Suffrage Societies." A letter to *The Scotsman* from the Edinburgh National Society also condemned the violence – "emphatically." Such criticism must have hurt and frustrated suffragettes from all backgrounds and walks of life, many of whom had the conviction and courage to act in a manner that would have been completely out of character at any other time, and from which, ordinarily, they would have recoiled. 30.

Afterwards, Elizabeth Thomson provided details of the prison experience she had shared with her sister Agnes. She said that after throwing a stone at the windows of the Local Government Board offices, without hitting the target,

THE LADY HOOLIGANS.

TITLED DEFENDANT BREAKS WINDOWS.

THE ATTACK ON AN HOTEL.

STONE WHICH JUST MISSED A BISHOP.
(BY OUR PRIVATE WIRE.)

The hearing of the charges arising out of the rioting by suffragettes on Tuesday evening was continued at Bow Street Police Court to-day, by Mr. Marsham. The court was again crowded, the spectators for the most part being lady friends of the prisoners.

The first case heard to-day was one in which Edith Hudson, Edinburgh, Emily Fussell, Bristol, Evelyn Constance Lummis, Cambridge, and Jessie Methven, Edinburgh, were charged with being concerned in stone throwing and window smashing in the Horse Guards Parade.

The Yorkshire Post labelled Edith Hudson and Jessie Methven 'The Lady Hooligans' in its report of their appearance at Bow Street police court.

she was arrested and "dragged off." When the House of Commons rose at two o'clock in the morning she and Agnes were bailed. They waited for the court appearance for four days before being sentenced to five days' imprisonment. "We were driven to prison in a Black Maria. We were conducted to a cell and locked up after having our watches, money and jewellery taken from us.

I was taken to the [prison] Infirmary in consideration of my age and my sister followed and was given the next bed to me." Before the sisters returned to Edinburgh, they called on Jessie Methven who had been moved from Holloway to a nursing home in Albany Street. "She had been ill with erysipelas [a bacterial skin infection] in her cell and was not well enough to go home with us." [31].

At a late-November meeting at the WSPU's Melville Place headquarters, Lucy Burns expressed satisfaction that "an emphatic protest" had been made by their Edinburgh sisters. She reminded members of "the brutality with which their friends were treated by the police in London when making a peaceful protest a year ago," and mentioned that one of their members had been so maltreated that she had not yet recovered – a reference to the worsening condition of Cecilia Haig after her Black Friday sexual humiliation and mauling.

Sadly, Cecilia Haig would survive for just a month more. [32].

References

1. The Scotsman, 24 January 1910; Edinburgh Evening News, 12 February 1910.
2. Sarah Pedersen, The Scottish Suffragettes and the Press (2017), p129; Mary Richardson, Laugh A Defiance (1953), p12; Elizabeth Crawford, The Women's Suffrage Movement (1999), p439.
3. Edinburgh Evening News, 25 March 1910.
4. The Vote, 21 May 1910. The former WFL headquarters at 33 Forrest Road is now a post office.
5. The Vote, 5 August 1910; Glasgow Herald, 25 July 1910.
6. Midge Mackenzie, Shoulder to Shoulder (1975), p167; Daily Record, 19 November 1910; Diane Atkinson, Rise Up Women! (2019), pp224-5.
7. Elizabeth Crawford (1999), p432; The Times, 23 November 1910: Atkinson (2019), p228. The Bank of Scotland Flora Murray £100 note had her image on the reverse side in the foreground, with female stretcher-bearers at Endell Street Hospital behind. She also appeared in the banknote's security hologram.
8. The Globe, 23 November 1910; Votes for Women, 5 December 1910.
9. Sylvia Pankhurst, The History of the Women's Suffrage Movement (1931) p343; Atkinson (2019), p283.
10. Memoirs of Elizabeth Thomson (c1914), pp106-108.
11. 'Report of the Treatment of Women's Deputation, Conciliation Committee, 1911', quoted in Diane Atkinson, Votes for Women (1998), p30; Also titled on the original, 'The Treatment of the Women's Deputations of Nov 18th, 22nd and 23rd 1910 By The Police'.

12. *Votes for Women, 1 July 1910; Common Cause, 21 July 1910; Edinburgh Evening News, 16 November 1910.*

13. *Edinburgh Evening News, 14 December 1910; Evening Telegraph, 20 December 1910; Mid-Lothian Journal, 23 December 1910.*

14. *Leah Leneman, A Guid Cause (1991), p99; Claire Eustice, et al, A Suffrage Reader (2000), p192; Laura Mayhall, The Militant Suffrage Movement (2003), pp103-104; Crawford (1999), p752. Teresa Billington-Greig explained her rejection of militancy in The Militant Suffragette Movement, which she published in 1911. By 1913 she was living in High Possil, Glasgow.*

15. *Ethel Moorhead, Incendiaries (1925), p264; Courier, 20 January 1911.*

16. *Common Cause, 30 March 1911; The Vote, 8 April 1911.*

17. *The Scotsman, 14 October 1910.*

18. *Leneman (1991), p101; The Vote, 25 February 1911; The Scotsman, 20 March 1911; Edinburgh Evening News, 21 March 1911; Edinburgh Evening Dispatch 1 & 3 April 1911.*

19. *Tower Hamlets Independent, 29 April 1911.*

20. *Arabella Scott, My Murky Past (Frances Wheelhouse typescript); Edinburgh Evening Dispatch, 3 April 1911.*

21. *NRS 685-4, J. P. Macdougall to Edinburgh Registrar, 6 April 1911.*

22. *Votes for Women, 7 April 1911; The Vote, 15 April 1911; Scotsman, 3 April 1911; Edinburgh Evening News, 3 & 22 April 1911; Arabella Scott, My Murky Past.*

23. *www.findmypast.co.uk/blog/discoveries/suffragettes-in-the-1911-census*

24. *The Scotsman, 5 May 1911. Dr Alice Hutchison of the ENSWS spent six and a half months in the Balkans during the Great War – six weeks with the Women's Sick and Wounded Convoy Corps, and the remainder with the Bulgarian Red Cross.*

25. *Northern Whig, 25 August 1911.*

26. *Votes for Women, 2 September 1911.*

27. *Atkinson (2019), p272.*

28. *The Scotsman, 23 November 1911.*

29. *Memoirs of Elizabeth Thomson (c1914), p110; London Evening News, 24 November 1911.*

30. *Common Cause, 30 November 1911; The Scotsman, 18 December 1911.*

31. *Memoirs of Elizabeth Thomson (c1914), pp111-112.*

32. *The Scotsman, 24 November 1911.*

Four-times jailed Mary Allen, who was soon to move to Edinburgh as WSPU Organiser. (Courtesy of the Mary Evans Picture Library)

PETITION
TO THE PRIME MINISTER.
THE UNDERSIGNED PRAY THAT THE
NMENT WILL   BILL
VOTES TO

EIGHT:
HAVING A SMASHING TIME! 1912

"I barricaded my cell, but directly the door was opened I escaped and on to the wire netting. After much struggling and resistance I was got back into my cell and held down firmly on the ground by wardresses and a young man assistant, and then and there, without any feeling of pulse or time to recover my breath, a tube was forced up my nostril. It seemed to stick at the larynx and directly the fluid was poured down coughing and choking set up most violently, the milk all pouring out of my mouth …"

Edinburgh suffragette Edith Hudson, describing forcible feeding, March 1912.

The truce had survived for nearly two years, but it was over. Militancy was now the only way forward for the Women's Social and Political Union. The Women's Freedom League held back from violence, but increasingly took noisy (and courageous) protests to the government's door. The National Union of Women's Suffrage Societies continued, with effort, to remain constitutional and peaceful. As 1912 began, the WSPU office was at 8 Melville Place in Queensferry Street, an address also used by the Men's Political Union. The WFL Suffrage Shop and offices were at 33 Forrest Road, south of George IV Bridge. It was on the cusp, however, of moving its shop to 90 Lothian Road. The old Edinburgh National Society remained at 40 Shandwick Place, the premises it had occupied from 1909. The Scottish Federation of Women's Suffrage Societies, a new umbrella group for the 60-odd Scottish constitutionalist societies, occupied an office at 2 St Andrew's Square. It was headed by the former ENSWS president Sarah Mair and the administration was placed in the hands of Edith Kirby.

On March 2, and against all expectations, the second reading of the Conciliation Bill fell by 222 votes to 208, a Commons defeat of 14. The previous year's majority had been 167. It was a remarkable change in the attitude of

the House and the blame fell squarely on Mrs Pankhurst's militants. The *Daily Graphic* was in a queue of big-selling publications to wade into her tactics: "The window-smashing campaign was the last straw. Just as their sympathisers at once fell away by thousands in the country, so they fell away heavily in the Commons...at last they have done their worst to the cause they pretend to champion." Such criticism reflected a view expressed regularly that the WSPU's destructive strategy was making the women's cause "march backwards." Voting patterns appeared to bear this out. On each of the previous four occasions, a women's suffrage bill had secured majorities of 179, 35, 109 and 167. The results had shown a tide running strongly in favour of votes. Had the Conciliation Bill passed its second reading, the government had pledged to give it further facilities to allow it to become law. Now, even if the government proceeded with its promised Reform Bill, it was probable that a women's suffrage amendment would be rejected. (In fact, in January 1913 the Speaker ruled out such an amendment.) The campaign was stalled.

Now more voteless than ever, the women's frustration and anger boiled over. On the evening of 4 March 1912, mass window-smashing raids took place across the West End of London in attacks painstakingly planned and

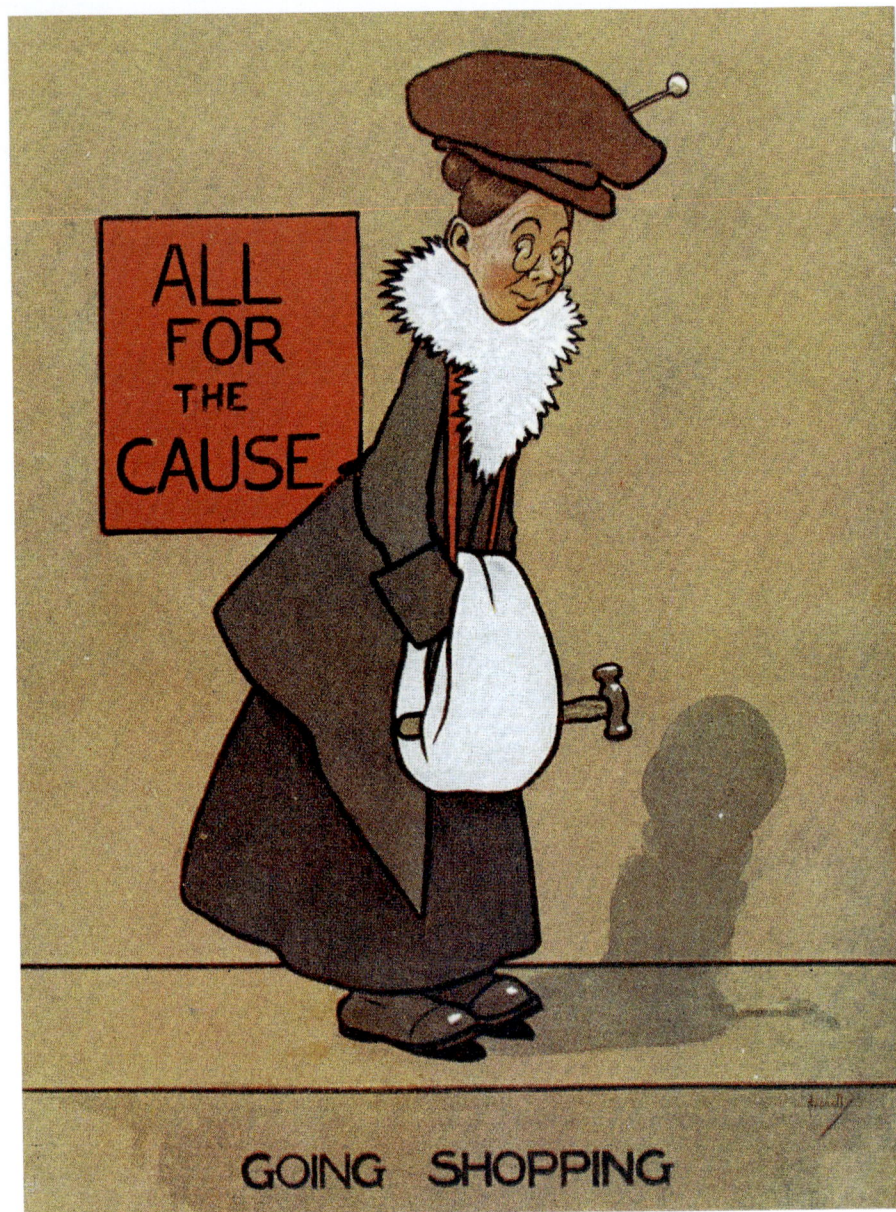

Postcard publishers were quick to parody the London raids.

carried out by 150 women supplied with hammers at the WSPU headquarters at Clement's Inn. Scotland had Kensington 'to do' and over 20 women travelled south for the task. Leith's Lilias Mitchell recalled how the thought of breaking windows had made her "shake from head to foot." Nevertheless, when she reached Kensington High Street and saw her Scottish comrades being collared by the police, she stood before Barker's window and "feeling now quite sick, I banged a window with my hammer. People stared and I stared, and then I banged another window, breaking it thoroughly." After her conviction, Mitchell told the magistrate how she would "afterwards be proud that I had taken part in the raid." 1.

The *Kensington News* reported that 30 large windows belonging to around 20 firms were broken. Fifteen short-handled hammers were confiscated by the police. The whole affair, said the paper, was deliberately planned and carried out – "the going about of their foolish work in a most methodical manner." The *Daily Mail* captured the extraordinary scenes: "People started as a window shattered by their side; suddenly there was another crash in front of them; on either side of the street, behind – everywhere." 2.

Ten women were brought up at the West London police court on March 7, charged with the Kensington raids. With one exception the defendants gave addresses in Scotland – five were from Edinburgh. One of their co-accused, Janie Allan, called them "the Scotch Batch"...

- Edith Hudson, aged 40, gave the Edinburgh WSPU office in Melville Place as her address. Former matron Hudson was convicted of breaking two windows – one at John Barker & Co, the other at the Gas Light & Coke Company shop – valued at £30, and was given six months' imprisonment, an extraordinarily harsh sentence enhanced by convictions for window smashing the previous November and after the 'Leith Riot' in 1909. She immediately declared a hunger strike and was forcibly fed through a nasal tube for several days. Lilias Mitchell recalled how Hudson had "fought like a tiger and knocked down all six wardresses – and told the doctor what she thought of him!"

- Lilias Mitchell of Leith gave the Aberdeen WSPU office address at 7 Bon Accord Street, having been moved north a month earlier by the Pankhursts. She was found guilty of breaking four windows at John Barker & Co in Kensington High Street valued at £48. Mitchell (27), whose family owned a timber business in Edinburgh, received a sentence of four months' hard labour. She, too, adopted a hunger strike and was artificially fed for four days.

- Florence McFarlane (44), a former Edinburgh nursing home matron, and now a salaried WSPU organiser, was convicted of breaking the windows of Sanders & Co, jewellers, in Kensington High Street valued at £25, a figure reduced to £13 at her trial. A policeman told the court he had seen her strike the window with a hammer, smashing the glass. She then dropped the hammer and "went quietly." The window had been full of diamond jewellery. McFarlane was prevented from making a political statement, but told the court she had spent "17 years of my life binding up wounds." When asked by the magistrate if she would give an undertaking to abstain from breaking the law, she replied, "If you give me six months or six years, I shall accept it." She received four months and was forcibly fed. She was released on June 28 in a seriously weakened state.

- Ethel Moorhead (35) of Queen Street, Edinburgh was accused of breaking a window occupied by Young & Co, wine merchants, valued at £40, and another next door valued at £20 at Thomas Cook & Sons. Remarkably, Moorhead was found not guilty owing to a witness muddying the evidence [Moorhead thought on purpose] and despite being arrested with her pockets full of stones and the testimony of a top London barrister who said he saw her smashing one of the windows! Writing in the third person as 'Mrs Ormond', one of her suffragette pseudonyms, Moorhead alluded to her role and arrest in the autobiographical *Incendiaries*. Arriving in London,

Florence McFarlane recuperating in London after being forcibly fed at Holloway in 1912. (Courtesy of Wikimedia Commons)

she was told she was part of "a big window smashing" which was to take place the following evening. But when the volunteers were at breakfast, "a Scotch scout rushed in with orders to be ready for the smash at eleven that morning in broad daylight." Some volunteers had to hurry out to buy hammers – but ironmongers were by then reluctant to sell them to women. Moorhead continued her story in the

Incendiaries (*Work in progress*)

by ETHEL MOORHEAD

In the night they were monoliths of black granite stalking along to crush a pagan temple. Now they were mad she, Night, would wrap her soft mists around them and shove them along safely—They were her masters—She functioned for them—She had twelve hours allotted for eternity to work her spells for them, so that in her moods they would do what they had to do—She knew their madness—had not some fool called her the complement of day? Now they were mad she would wrap her soft mists around them and push them along safely. They had a madness now… They were blocks of granite stalking through the night to crush a pagan temple…

They were madder than the others knew. The others worshipped in the temple and were sane. The protestant pastor was sane, so were the props of the protestant church who took the collection (all men) and the well-balanced fathers, brothers, husbands, brother-in-laws, judges, lawyers, doctors, architects, bank managers, bank clerks, farmers, waiters, gardeners, railway porters, scavengers, trustees all dictators to the *mad women*. Now they were mad. They had had sanity for centuries, the centuries of their sanity couldn't be counted. They were the Jew-begotten legend of a rib of man.

In the night they were monoliths of black granite stalking along to crush a pagan temple…

In their great madness their dictators were but puny puppets. Their well-balanced fathers, brothers, and husbands had bid them goodbye when they had become insane. There was a house of puppets like unto the great House of Beelzebub undivided against itself that punished them. Its prince was a Home Secretary and

Ethel Moorhead's autobiographical Incendiaries in the extremely rare second issue of This Quarter magazine (1925).

third person…"Mrs Ormond found herself in front of her windows just in time for the stroke of eleven. She was scared, how would she do it? Mrs Ormond was trembling so she didn't know how she could drag out the hammer concealed up her sleeve. She got it out and gripped it tight so that it wouldn't fall out of her shaking hand, and then her bang woke her up like an earthquake. A man in a frock coat and silk hat caught Mrs Ormond's hand at her fourth window…"

- Elizabeth Finlayson Gauld (59), matron of a children's home, gave the Edinburgh WSPU as her address. She was charged with breaking two windows valued at £30 and £20 at the Wholesale Fur Company in Kensington High Street. When the raids were reported, "an elderly woman, dressed in costly furs" (appropriately, given her target) was said to have cut her hand while hitting a window. This was Mrs Gauld, and after treatment she appeared in court with her right hand and arm bandaged. Gauld, sometimes reported as Gould, was released after giving an undertaking not to take part in further militancy, as she was the guardian of 42 orphaned girls in the Scottish capital. This did not, however, prevent a busy campaigning role on her return.

A further two Edinburgh women appeared before Mr Curtis Bennett at Bow Street police court on March 6…

- Elizabeth Thomson of Hartington Place was fined 40 shillings or one month for stone throwing in an area of government buildings. With her sister Agnes, she had already spent a week in Holloway the previous November. Sixty-five at the time of her second arrest, she was confined to Holloway's 'B' Ward and recalled standing on a chair to wave a handkerchief to the London militant Daisy Solomon as she exercised. After a period of solitary confinement, Thomson was allowed to go to chapel and given needlework to do. She did not adopt a hunger strike. When she was released on April 4 her sister

Agnes was waiting for her at Holloway's gates. She was taken to a restaurant where her sister "gave me a right good breakfast."

- Agnes Macdonald (31) of Edinburgh WSPU appeared in front of the overworked Mr Bennett on March 9 alongside the novelist Annie S. Swan, Nancy John and Janet Barrowman of Glasgow WSPU. All were charged with breaking windows at government buildings. Bennett sentenced the Scots to two months' hard labour. Agnes Macdonald grew up in Dublin Street. She donated small amounts to WSPU funds and described her prison experience at an Edinburgh meeting in May 1912. In October that year she chaired an outdoor meeting in St David Street at which Arabella Scott spoke. As the Melville Place branch Press Secretary, she sent letters to the Edinburgh papers defending hunger striking, but denying involvement with attacks on letter-boxes in the city. Nonetheless, she refused to condemn the tactic. [3.]

By the end of the second week of March, more than 200 window-smashers were in Holloway, facing each other's cells across the two grim wings of the old castle. Some of the other convicted women had strong connections to Edinburgh:

- Florence Haig, in mourning for the death of her sister Cecilia, was sent to prison for four months for breaking the windows of D. H. Evans in Oxford Street. Halfway through her sentence the former Edinburgh WSPU militant adopted a hunger strike and was released early without being force-fed. Haig, 56, a cousin of Douglas Haig, who would become Field Marshal Haig in 1915, was working from her studio in London at this time. She had enjoyed Holloway's comforts twice in 1908 – six weeks for the Pantechnicon Raid and three months for storming the House of Commons. She was secretary of Chelsea WSPU at this time.

Janie Allan, who provided finance to Scotland's leading militant and non-militant suffrage societies.

- Frances Parker (32), formerly organiser of Edinburgh WSPU, provided the Glasgow WSPU address at 502 Sauchiehall Street. She was convicted of breaking a window at the London and North-Western Railway Company's building in Kensington. She told the court, "I have noticed that men at Swansea, when they were held up for rioting, got a fortnight's imprisonment, and the ringleader of them

The front cover of Holloway Jingles.

only got six weeks." Parker was given four months for her £15 worth of damage. Ethel Moorhead recalled seeing Parker in Kensington High Street "pulling stones out of a bag and hurling them at Fuller's sweet shop." Moorhead had shouted, 'Bravo!'

- Janie Allan (44), the WSPU's principal financier in Scotland, was found guilty of breaking five windows at Fleming Reid & Co, Scotch hosiers, two windows at the Saxone Shoe company, another at McCombie Bros, tailors, and one at the Butterick Publishing Company. The total value was £130. The police witness stated that he saw the defendant walk quickly along the pavement smashing one window after another, and before he could reach her she had broken five windows. He had found a small hammer concealed in the fur muff covering her hands. Miss Allan, the wealthy heir of the Allan Shipping Line, received a sentence of four months, barricaded her prison door in Holloway and kept crowbar-wielding officials at bay for 45 minutes. Back home, a petition calling for her release attracted the names of 10,500 Glaswegians. 4.

Scotland is also associated with the 1912 raids through the publication of *Holloway Jingles*, a booklet of verse compiled in the prison and collected by Nancy John. A few months after being smuggled out of Holloway by Janet Barrowman it was published by the Glasgow branch of the Women's Social and Political Union and sold for a shilling. Its cover shows a sketch of Holloway cells, and it was stitched in the WSPU colours of purple, green and white. *Holloway Jingles* includes a tribute to Janie Allan from Maggie McPhun titled *To A Fellow Prisoner*, a poem by Dr Alice Ker, a niece of Flora and Louisa Stevenson, and a contribution from Emily Wilding Davison. Perhaps the most poignant lines were penned by Kathleen Emerson in *The Women in Prison*:

Oh Holloway, grim Holloway,
With grey forbidding towers,

Stern are thy walls, but sterner still,
Is woman's free, unconquered will,
And though today and yesterday
Brought long and lonely hours,
Those hours spent in captivity,
Are stepping-stones to liberty. 5.

Later, Home Secretary Reginald McKenna put a value of £6000 on the 270 windows broken in the West End raids. In Scotland, however, the *Forward* newspaper devoted its front page to an article commending the women's action and condemning the government's "cack-handed policies and vicious savagery." There was also criticism of the harsh sentencing. Kitty Marshall was given 10 days for shouting just one word – though it was 'Charge!' 6.

There were consequences to the London raids. Three days later, on March 5, the large street-front window of the WSPU office at 8 Melville Place was smashed. The police reported that two hammers were found among the debris. The oddity was that the alleged perpetrators were not students or youths, as might be expected, but two well-dressed women who were seen to leave the scene immediately and make off in a car "at speed." *The Edinburgh Evening News* was confident that the "carefully planned" action was a retaliatory message to the WSPU from "their more moderate and reasonably minded sisters" who, the paper said, disapproved of "the extraordinary window-smashing scenes in London." No arrests were made, and Edinburgh WSPU made no public comment. On March 14, the front window of the Women's Freedom League headquarters in Forrest Road was smashed in a 'copycat' attack. Again, no arrest was made. Another incident recalled the London raids. At Bo'ness police court on March 5, a "scantily clad" old woman named Agnes Malloy or Brown, and stated to be a vagrant, was sent to prison for 20 days for maliciously breaking a window at the police barracks in the town. With the weather turning cold, she had imitated the suffragettes to get locked up.

Lilias Mitchell, the Leither who endured forcible feeding in Holloway. (Courtesy of HistoryLinks Archive)

The raids were defended at a WSPU meeting in the Edinburgh Café on March 7. Jessie Methven took the chair and members heard Morag Burn Murdoch condemning the length of sentences on the London window-breakers. She claimed that the authorities were now imposing prison terms six times the maximum for the crimes allegedly committed. At an evening gathering at Melville Place, Mary Lees said the London raids would "remind

Mr Asquith and others that women were not going to give in." To cheers, Lisa Chapman said that they had been gaining members "every day" since the raids. She described the protests as "magnificent" and "inevitable." Resolutions protesting against the "hard sentences and cruel treatment" were passed at both meetings. 7.

Prisoners returning to Edinburgh were welcomed as heroines. Homecoming celebrations were arranged, and sometimes sixpence or a shilling was charged to boost branch funds. There were lurid tales of Holloway's privations, but inspiring speeches, too. As the stories of imprisoned suffragettes reached their friends in Scotland, Annie Murray, secretary of Bo'ness WSPU, expressed her outrage at the treatment they had endured. She quoted from a letter she had received from a fellow prisoner of Edith Hudson, the Edinburgh militant who was serving a six-month sentence: "The writer of the letter says: 'I went to Miss Hudson's cell the first day of the forcible feeding and found her lying on a mattress on the floor, face downwards. Her blouse was torn to bits. She said to me, "I thought they had done for me that time. I felt as if I were drowning. They (the doctors) seem to have put the nasal tube in the wrong place." She choked and choked, so that the tube was brought up partly, and hung in a loop outside her mouth. The doctor evidently thought that the choking was part of her fight, and pushed the tube back again. She thinks the food was sent into the windpipe and lung'." This harrowing account was corroborated by another Edinburgh prisoner, Lilias Mitchell, who also wrote to Ann Murray: "I heard her [Hudson] choking horribly during the operation, and the coughing continued during the rest of the day. About eight hours afterwards I saw her. She was in a state of utter exhaustion and hardly able to speak above a whisper." 8.

On July 9, Lilias Mitchell issued a statement in which she said it was thought likely that she herself might die in prison: "I feel all right again, but am still absurdly shaky. I have been so since the first hunger strike. I was fed once after five days. A week or two after, my hands were trembling so bad I had to get strychnine from the doctor. This second hunger strike I missed all the suffering the others have endured so magnificently, as I was released after four days. They would not feed me, as in all probability I should have departed this life with awkward suddenness. Miss [Edith] Hudson was just below me, and Mrs [Alice] Green quite near. They both struggled simply heroically, but, knowing what they were suffering, it nearly killed me to hear them."

Edith Hudson also left a distressing account of the feeding procedure she 'stomached' in Holloway: "I barricaded my cell, but directly the door was opened I escaped and on to the wire netting. After much struggling and resistance I was got back into my cell and held down firmly on the ground by wardresses and a young man assistant, and then and there, without any feeling of pulse or time to recover my breath, a tube was forced up my nostril. It seemed to stick at the larynx and directly the fluid was poured down, coughing and choking set up most violently, the milk all pouring out of my mouth. The doctor put his finger into my mouth to try to press the tube back and the operation left me struggling for breath." 9.

Hudson's awful treatment – though not her heroic struggle – was referred to in Parliament by Lord Edward Cecil on June 27. When the Home Secretary Reginald McKenna robustly defended the procedure, acts of militancy multiplied across the country. In rural Oxfordshire, Helen Craggs was found in the garden of Lewis Harcourt, the Colonial Secretary, carrying all the materials necessary for arson. She was arrested and charged with attempting to maliciously set fire to the minister's house. It was the first time a WSPU activist had attempted an act of serious damage to a property. Craggs was sentenced to nine months, adopted a hunger strike, was forcibly fed and, after 11 days, was released. In Dublin, Mary Leigh and Gladys Evans tried to burn down the Theatre Royal. Leigh was further charged with throwing a hatchet during a demonstration. Protest meetings were staged across Scotland against the five-year sentence handed down to both women. On Leith Links the WSPU attracted large crowds to listen to former prisoner Arabella Scott. The Women's Freedom League also attended, with Nina Boyle and Alexia Jack among its platform speakers. Boyle, too, had been jailed by then. Over 600 postcards were sent from Edinburgh to the Prime Minister demanding the release of the hunger-striking Dublin prisoners. When Leigh was finally liberated on licence she weighed just five stones. 10.

In the north-east the protests were taken a step further when the Prime Minister and Home Secretary Reginald McKenna were ambushed at the Royal Dornoch Golf Club. They had reached the tenth green when two women appeared. Asquith was asked, "Why are you forcibly feeding our women?" McKenna was reported to have pushed one of the women and made a grab for the other. With the Prime Minister watching, a struggle ensued. According to *Votes for Women*, McKenna threatened to throw one of the women into a burn. Her retort was, "If I go in, you go too." At that point a detective arrived and held the pair. They were removed from the links and the ministers resumed their game. The *Glasgow Herald* named them as Miss Mitchell – Edinburgh's Lilias Mitchell – and a Miss Howie. This may have been Elsie Howey, a trouble-prone WSPU militant from the south who had previously assaulted Herbert Asquith on a golf course. Howey, a Regent Street window-smasher, had studied at St Andrews University and had previously got into scrapes with the two 'Florences' of Edinburgh WSPU, Haig and Macaulay. Lilias Mitchell recalled the adventure being "tremendous fun." No charges were brought – the Prime Minister not daring to appear in court. Some creative militancy took place the same month when the flags on Balmoral Golf Course were replaced with those in the purple, white and green of the WSPU. The royal family was in residence, but the perpetrators – including Lilias Mitchell again – had eluded its protection officers. An inquiry began. 11.

Another Edinburgh militant was later implicated when two women were alleged to have assaulted the Prime Minister while he was with his daughter Violet on Lossiemouth Golf Course. Flora Ellen Smith gave the city's WSPU office as her address when she appeared with Dundee's Winnie Wallace at Elgin Sheriff Court. The pair pled not guilty to a charge of breach of the peace, and a trial was pencilled in for the following month. When asked to stand, the women refused, saying they could hear just as well sitting down. When asked a second time Flora Smith said, "Oh! We had better stand up to please them."

SUFFRAGETTES IN COURT.

TRIAL FIXED FOR FRIDAY NEXT.

The two Suffragettes, Winnie Wallace, of Nethergate, Dundee, and Flora Helen Smith, of Frederick Street, Edinburgh, who were arrested at Lossiemouth on Thursday night on the charge of assaulting Mr Asquith, were brought before Hon.

The Lossiemouth incident shocked people in the north.

155

Once again, a trial never happened. Wallace and Smith were said to be bitterly disappointed. They had cited Mr Asquith as a witness and, had the case proceeded, the WSPU would have had an extraordinary opportunity to promote their claims from the witness box, not to mention adding considerably to the government's discomfort by insisting on an appearance in court of the Prime Minister himself. Instead, they spent just three hours in Inverness Prison before being bailed by a female friend and released. Violet Asquith later recalled the Lossiemouth 'meeting': "I suddenly looked up and saw my father being savaged by two women. They were trying to tear his clothes off." 12.

At a less hurried pace, the Scottish Churches League for Woman Suffrage was formed in Edinburgh in May 1912 after a meeting in which one of the mainstays of the Edinburgh National Society, the Rev Dr Robert Drummond of Chalmers Street Church, said he felt the church should no longer remain silent. Among the questions posed from the floor was the League's attitude towards militancy. One woman suggested no other society should be criticised for their work or actions, which brought applause. Indeed, the Rev Dr W. Morison referred to "these noble women who have struggled courageously" and said he admired "violence in fighting for the right." This attracted further applause. The Edinburgh-based Scottish Churches League for Woman Suffrage duly became a powerful group of ministers and faith leaders, both men and women, who ploughed existing networks to sow support for the cause. The deeply religious Lady Frances Balfour was appointed president with Dr Drummond as vice-president.

The thrice-jailed Lucy Burns was back in the news in mid-May 1912. Edinburgh's WSPU organiser appeared before Bailie Richardson at the city's police court. She gave the office in Melville Place as her address and her name as 'Louisa Burns.' The court heard that she had been arrested on May 3 and subsequently charged with obstructing the throughfare on the corner of Castle Terrace and Lothian Road by standing on a chair and causing a crowd to assemble, to the annoyance of one Phineas Bell Brander of 12 Castle Terrace. Burns pleaded not guilty and conducted her own defence in a courtroom packed with the branch membership.

The police witness said he saw a woman – not Lucy Burns – standing on a chair in Castle Terrace addressing a crowd. He said he told her that she was not allowed to stand there, because people in the neighbourhood had complained about meetings obstructing the traffic. Lucy Burns had asked him to produce the relevant bylaw. He could not do so. When he returned 15 minutes later Burns was addressing the crowd, which had increased in size. She said she would finish her speech and then leave. He returned with another policeman at 9.20pm and Burns was still addressing the crowd, which had grown to around 200. The complainer, the solicitor Phineas Brander, told the court that the whole thoroughfare was blocked. He saw a

policeman talking to a young lady and assumed he was asking her to leave. Mr Brander added that had no personal feelings against the women, a comment which brought peals of laughter from the public benches.

Somewhat unusually, witnesses were allowed for the defence. Mrs Currall of Edinburgh WSPU was the first to speak. She said she had been at Castle Terrace selling *Votes for Women*. She had used the stance numerous times without objection from the public or the police. She said there had been no danger to anyone and that she was "very surprised" when Burns was stopped from speaking. Muriel Scott was also called. She told the court that it was a quiet audience. She heard Burns offer to change her 'pitch,' but at no time heard her refuse to leave. Despite these accounts, Bailie Richardson found Burns guilty of obstruction. He said he did not consider the case serious enough for handing down the usual fine with a custodial alternative. Instead, he discharged her without proceeding to conviction. Lucy Burns was free to go – a fortunate outcome in a busy summer of convictions and ever-harsher sentencing. [13]

With hopes of votes dashed by the introduction of the Manhood Bill on June 17, militancy was ramped up – Lucy Burns telling an Edinburgh WSPU meeting in George Street that the Union was "never stronger than at the present moment, never more devoted or united, never better equipped financially and never more able to rely on the self-sacrifice of its members." [14]

On June 28, the plate-glass windows of three Edinburgh post offices – Marchmont Road, Frederick Street and Hope Street – were smashed in a coordinated attack. The police secured two missiles: a small stone and the head of an axe wrapped in a copy of *Votes for Women*. Found alongside was a note with the message, "To protest against the forcible feeding of women prisoners." Then, at the start of August, Edinburgh suffragettes were blamed for cutting the telephone lines connecting the public call boxes in the Waverley and Caledonian railway stations. Notices were pasted inside the boxes – "No votes, no peace. War to the end." No arrests were made at either incident.

Such protests aroused passionate opinions and responses. An anonymous newspaper contribution titled *Suffragettes and Their Methods: Some Plain Speaking by A Working Woman* set out the argument that Edinburgh's militants had recklessly damaged a cause so carefully cultivated by the Victorian suffragists: "Then it was that the vulgar, senseless orgies of the militants undid so much of the work that patience and tact and skill had accomplished." She claimed the WSPU's oft-stated response that British men had won the vote through violent political protest could not be justified by the Pankhursts and their "well-dressed hooligans" who knew "nothing of life's stress and struggle," and who had lived "idle, luxurious lives."

'Working Woman's' unflinching views drew a response from another unnamed contributor, 'Early Suffragist.' This was obviously someone who had been around the local movement for a number of years – perhaps the veteran Jessie Methven. 'Early Suffragist' claimed there was little divergence between the old and new campaigner. "Working Woman is evidently unaware that the founders of the militant policy, Mrs Pankhurst and Miss Christabel Pankhurst, along with large numbers of their followers, were members of the early suffrage societies." She recalled the late Priscilla McLaren's sympathy with militant methods and how the Edinburgh pioneer had been "deeply moved" when Christabel Pankhurst and Annie Kenney were arrested in Manchester in 1905... "but Mrs McLaren, with her clear insight and wide outlook, defended them." There was no dividing line, she argued, between the suffragists in the movement before militancy began and "the suffragettes active now." 15.

In July, knots of passers-by gathered to gawp at two posters pasted to the inside of the front windows of a house in Leith Walk. One had the printed words, 'No Votes, No Tax.' A smaller handbill called for 'Votes for Women.' The *Edinburgh Evening News* noted that it was Dr Grace Cadell's property and reminded readers that the Leith GP was a prominent suffragette among those "apprehended in London recently." By mid-1912, however, Cadell had transferred from the WSPU to the Women's Freedom League

Dr Grace Cadell. (Courtesy of Wikimedia Commons)

The women on either side of the Dutch bureau 'bought in' by supporters are possibly Morag Burn Murdoch (left) and Dr Grace Cadell.

– passing Elizabeth Finlayson Gauld, who crossed in the opposite direction, from the WFL in Forrest Road to the more militant Edinburgh WSPU in Melville Place.

In the first week of October, sheriff officers visited 145 Leith Walk and took away several items of furniture in lieu of unpaid tax of £2. 3s 4d. The seized goods were put up for auction at the Mercat Cross on October 11. The sale was witnessed by a large crowd, as well as by several women waving suffragist flags and distributing copies of *The Vote*. After keen bidding a Dutch bureau was 'bought in' for £4. 5s by one of Dr Cadell's friends. As this sum exceeded the amount of tax due, the sale was over in less than a minute. Dr Cadell would repeat her tax boycott the following year, her many friends once again rushing to buy the auctioned goods to return to her. 16.

What of the constitutionalists in the second half of 1912? The focus of the old-time Edinburgh National Society – now also known as the Edinburgh NUWSS branch – was the Midlothian by-election, where it supported Provost Brown, the Labour candidate. This was in line with a new NUWSS ruling following a Labour Party conference decision to support votes for women. The NUWSS thereafter pledged to support Labour candidates, which placed it at odds not only with the WSPU and WFL, but also with a multitude of women Liberals, many of whom were the mainstay of Scotland's non-militant societies.

The ENSWS opened committee rooms in Dalkeith and West Calder and bands of workers set out from Edinburgh each morning to campaign in surrounding villages. The meetings were co-ordinated by Lindsey Jardine of Craigroyston. The main speakers were Lisa Gordon and Mary Low. Annot Robinson, then with the Women's Labour League in Manchester, joined the campaign. As Annot Wilkie of Dundee WSPU she had taken part in the Pantechnicon Raid – the barnstorming Trojan Horse-style attack on the House of Commons in 1908. Running the Women's Freedom League campaign in Midlothian was Nina Boyle, a fiery journalist turned activist who was later made head of the League's political and militant department. Boyle took a leading role in campaigns and demonstrations. During the course of the women's struggle, she was arrested on five occasions and imprisoned three times – one of many Leaguers quite prepared to take part in militant action.

Once again, however, the old Edinburgh society managed to fall out with its militant sisters. After a noisy protest at a Liberal Party meeting in the constituency, the ENSWS felt moved to declare that "they thoroughly disagree with and disapprove of the interruption, and that the interrupter is not connected with their Society." It reminded the public that the ENSWS represented the largest suffrage society in the kingdom and that its activities were "thoroughly" based on constitutional lines. Other comments were less nuanced. Maude Royden, of the Hawick Women's Suffrage Society, called the militants "a few excited, hysterical women, who had nothing to do in the world, and had not been lucky enough to catch a husband." 17.

Ethel Moorhead had moved to Edinburgh following the death of her father and lived at 12 Queen Street. In 1910, while living in Dundee, she threw an egg at Winston Churchill, the incoming Home Secretary. The following year she evaded the census, gathering WSPU members at her home in the city. Later that year, her silver candelabra was sold in lieu of taxes she had refused to pay. She had been a self-confessed Kensington window-smasher, but at trial was bizarrely released. Now, in 1912, she was on another mission. On the last weekend of August, Scotland awoke to the shock news that an attack had been made on a powerful symbol of Scottish identity, the Wallace Monument at Stirling. In broad daylight, a woman had walked calmly towards the glass case in which the William Wallace sword was displayed and smashed it with a stone. She was held and taken by police to Stirling. Another woman who lingered outside was not apprehended. The accused gave her name as 'Edith Johnstone'. She was charged with malicious damage. A message was found in the broken case: "Your liberties were won by the sword. Release the women who are fighting for their liberties. Stop the forcible feeding." Once again, the compositors on *The Scotsman* reached into the uppercase drawer to pull out the seven large letters spelling "OUTRAGE." Edith Johnstone, of course, was Ethel Moorhead and no doubt she was in cahoots with her conspiratorial friend, Frances Parker.

Moorhead was described in court as a "stylishly-dressed middle-aged lady." She was 43. She denied breaking the glass cabinet containing the sword. She was informed by the magistrate that she would be tried the following Tuesday. She objected to this, stating that it would be very inconvenient for her to appear on Tuesday and that she probably would not turn up: "I have appeared today, and I shall not appear again." She withheld her address, and the Tuesday trial was abandoned when she failed to attend.

A warrant was issued for her arrest and Moorhead, still answering to her nom-de-plume, was apprehended the following Friday at her home in Edinburgh. She appeared at Stirling Sheriff Court on 7 September 1912 after a night in the cells that she found not to her liking. This drew a frustrated response from Stirling's Chief Constable that her complaints were made for the sole purpose of causing trouble and that, "she was more comfortable here than she had any right to be."

Thousands gathered at Edinburgh's Mercat Cross to witness the sale of suffragette goods after the city's women refused to pay their taxes.

In court Moorhead said that she approved of the action of the woman who broke the display case. She also agreed with the protest written on the paper found in the damaged cabinet. But it did not follow, she said, that because she was a suffragette whenever she went into a museum she would smash something. Unconcerned by the incriminating nature of the statement, she added, "Your liberties were won with the sword, our liberties are being won with stones and hammers." The sheriff was unmoved. Declaring her guilty (as she was the only person in the room when the case was smashed), he imposed a fine of £2, or seven days in prison. At this, Moorhead replied, "I shall take the imprisonment, Sir."

Moorhead was taken to serve her sentence in Perth, where she defied all authority, broke windows and refused to conform to prison rules. The serious side to her incarceration was the decision by the prison authorities to allow artificial feeding after being informed by the prison's medical officer that it "may be appropriate." This was confirmed in a letter from the Scottish Office on September 11. Moorhead's short sentence of seven days, and her acceptance of "a special diet" – probably something like bread, milk and eggs – ensured forcible feeding was not required. Meanwhile, the custodians of the Wallace Monument said they planned to sue 'Johnstone' – but nothing came of it. Probably the prospect of taking on Ethel Moorhead in court sent them home to think again. [18].

It was not unusual for suffragettes to admit their guilt – or drop hints to that effect. When, in October 1912, the Edinburgh Central Conservative MP Charles Price suggested that militants from outside Edinburgh had disrupted his meeting, and that he had recognised them as coming from London, he was put right by "one of those who protested." She said she was a resident of Edinburgh and had been to London only twice in her life – "once when a child of five years old and again in 1909, when I experienced His Majesty's hospitality in Holloway. I do not remember having met Mr Price on either of these occasions, and, as the other interrupters all belong to Edinburgh, I fail to see how he has any foundation for his statement." The telling-off was from Muriel Scott. She and her sister Arabella had been sentenced to three weeks in 1909 "for walking up Downing Street." [19].

Ethel Moorhead was not done with her protests. Towards the end of 1912 Fanny Parker and the Dundee missionary-turned-militant May Grant found themselves in Aberdeen concealed in an entrance pay booth in readiness to gatecrash a Lloyd George meeting. They were discovered by police prior to the Chancellor's arrival: "Before they had time to smooth their dishevelled hair, they were caught hold of by the ankles, dragged out, and from the way they were handled, compelled to use some violence." There followed the usual procedure – arrest, search, charge, bailed or held on remand and finally a day in court. At their appearance, Parker refused to reveal her age or address. Grant gave her name as Marion Pollock, a corruption of her full name May Pollock Grant, but did not divulge any other details. Parker drew the magistrate's attention to the fact that, actually, no law had been broken. That cut no ice and the pair were convicted of breach of the peace and

sentenced to a £1 fine or five days' imprisonment. Meanwhile, 'Mary Humphreys,' better known as Ethel Moorhead, was given £2 or 10 days by the same Aberdeen judge for throwing a stone which connected with a car she thought contained the Chancellor. She refused to leave the dock and had to be forcibly removed in the ensuing fracas, amid cries of 'Shame!' from supporters. All told, the day's events were of sufficient magnitude for one paper to lead its coverage, 'Suffragettes Run Riot at Aberdeen.'

The women elected to accept the custodial sentence and were taken to Craiginches Prison in Aberdeen to be fitted out in regulation prison attire. Edinburgh militant Arabella Scott obligingly provided a description: "A large ugly skirt and blouse that could have fitted anyone. The material was a type of jute, pale green in colour and stamped all over with broad prison arrows. The skirt was ankle length. The shape and size of the underwear was unbelievable. Then a large disc, the size of a saucer, was buttoned on our blouses on the left side. These identity discs bore our ward and cell number. My identification was DX2/23 and my sister's [Muriel] was DX2/24. We were then given a white cap, an apron, dreadful woollen stockings and shoes, which came from a big basket. We were ordered to find a pair which fit." As for prison food, Lila Clunas recalled, "We sometimes took it with our eyes shut." [20].

'Pollock', Parker and 'Humphreys' immediately adopted a hunger strike. Moorhead lived up to her reputation, writing under her alias 'Mary Humphreys' to the Prison Commissioners to complain of being held overnight in "police drunk cells with no sleeping accommodation and no female warders." Worse, she accused the police of breaking the law. She said the cell lights were left on and "male warders wandered in and out at will." She claimed that if the women succumbed to fatigue and fell asleep, they were roughly awakened with a shake. Such conditions broke numerous prison rules, she said. May Grant corroborated her complaints, describing their treatment in Aberdeen as "scandalous." But Moorhead and Grant's accounts can be viewed against the report by the Aberdeen medical officer, which stated that the trio had been cosseted with "extra pillows and hot water bottles." [21].

160

No artificial feeding was attempted on the Aberdeen prisoners and they were released after a few days and after two of them had their fines paid without their knowledge or permission. Craiginches was probably glad to be rid of them. They had broken every window within reach, refused to return to their cells after exercise, and one of them – no prizes for guessing – threw shards of glass at anyone who approached and had to be taken "kicking, fighting and struggling desperately" from her cell. 22.

The Edinburgh to London long-distance women's walk in October 1912 was the year's most significant visual demonstration of the fight for votes. It was organised by Florence de Fonblanque and her sister Maud Arncliffe Sennett of the Women's Freedom League, with additional support from Mrs Pankhurst's WSPU and the National Union of Women's Suffrage Societies, with the aim to fire the public's imagination and promote the campaign. The walk was intended to cover 400 miles from the Scottish capital and to take 35 days. From a raised platform in Charlotte Square speeches were made by Edinburgh WFL secretary Alexia Jack, Anna Munro, who was then the League's organising secretary in Scotland, and by the twice imprisoned WFL national president Charlotte Despard. Ethel Moorhead of Edinburgh WSPU also addressed the marchers and crowd. It was a further example of the co-operative spirit in the Scottish movement, as well as a sign of Moorhead's growing status.

Huge crowds gathered to see off the marchers. Participants who hoped to complete the entire route were dressed in brown coats and dresses and wore green cockades in their hats. Scarves were in the suffragist tricolours. A large banner with the words 'From Edinburgh to London for Woman Suffrage', was carried at the front, followed by about 200 women, four abreast. Along the way a 'monster petition' for votes would be gathered and presented on arrival to Prime Minister Asquith. The rear was brought up by the 'Petition Van', drawn by a mare called Butterfly owned by Mrs de Fonblanque, and from which literature was distributed and signatures gathered. The petition consisted of a roll of linen 779 yards in length,

Few pictures of Ethel Moorhead survive. This newspaper image shows her selling suffrage papers.

The start of the 1912 Edinburgh to London march attracted huge crowds.

every yard stamped with 'We the undersigned, pray the Government to bring in a bill for Woman Suffrage this session.'

Spectators lined the route out of the city. *The Scotsman* called it the biggest crowd ever seen in the capital. Designated 'The Women's March', the initial group walked for around six hours per day, with the first stop at Portobello, where 100 marchers took tea in the Marine Café. Over 50 women then continued to Musselburgh. Supporters laden with drinks and food awaited the marchers along the route, allowing open-air meetings to take place. Most participants walked small sections, with other suffragists joining for part of the walk as it made its way south. Agnes 'Nannie' Brown from Edinburgh was one of only six women to march the entire 400-mile route. Brown, the daughter of an Edinburgh fruiterer, had been active in the Women's Freedom League for a couple of years. 23.

On arrival in London, the marchers were given a heroines' welcome by thousands of well-wishers. They were cheered every step by detachments of women from the WFL, WSPU and NUWSS, the Women Writers' Suffrage League, the Catholic Women's Suffrage Society, the Suffrage Atelier, the Church League, the Actresses League and the London Society for Women's Suffrage. There was considerable support from men's groups, including the Men's Political Union, the Men's League for Women's Suffrage and the Men's Federation for Women's Suffrage. The procession was led by bands into Trafalgar Square via Tottenham Court Road and Charing Cross Road. A demonstration followed in Hyde Park, where Anna Munro and Elizabeth Finlayson Gauld addressed the crowds.

Nannie Brown recalled many of the halts being devoted to gathering signatures to present to the Prime Minister, but she was proud that the marchers had kept to their timetable, even after walks of 14 to 18 miles per day: "It was no easy matter to turn out after the evening meal to conduct an open-air meeting, which usually lasted about two hours; yet each meeting was held at exactly the advertised hour, and we marched into London on the date, and at the exact hour, previously arranged." 24.

October is also remembered for another acrimonious split in the WSPU hierarchy. The Pethick-Lawrences – Emmeline and her husband Frederick – who had been founding members, financiers and 'managing directors' of the organisation, announced that they disagreed with Emmeline and Christabel Pankhurst's hard-line policy, and had left the Union. According to Mrs Pethick-Lawrence, Christabel returned from her exile in Paris to tell them that she had "no further use for them." The manner of the expulsion not only upset the wider movement, but revealed Christabel's ruthlessness. The Pethick-Lawrences continued to publish *Votes for Women*, while the Pankhursts brought out a new WSPU weekly newspaper, *The Suffragette*. Coincidentally, Edinburgh WSPU at this time put on a lantern show at the Oddfellows' Hall charting the militant campaign from 1906 to 1912. The lantern slides are thought not to have survived. Meanwhile, the branch started a Legal Defence Fund, no doubt in anticipation of protests to come. Lucy Burns remained its salaried organiser, although she was at this time visiting her home town of

The Edinburgh to London marchers staged impromptu meetings at stopping points on the route south. (Courtesy of the Mary Evans Picture Library)

New York. Her trip to the USA may have been the result of further strife within the WSPU, Christabel Pankhurst writing to the Glasgow militant Janie Allan in 1914: "Miss Lucy Burns was virtually driven away from Edinburgh, so unhappy was she because of a few members. The ostensible reason for the trouble was the stand she made with regard to a certain Miss Gorrie..." Isobel Gorrie was the WSPU's organiser for its scattered membership, or its 'travelling' organiser. It was a paid role within Edinburgh WSPU and it seems she was a popular choice for the position. She had been a member of the branch since its formation. It is unknown if or why she and Lucy Burns had a problem or argument, although it perhaps speaks volumes that Belle Gorrie, a local woman, took over as Edinburgh WSPU organiser when Burns returned to the United States later in 1912. 25.

On 6 October 1912, the attorney general Sir Rufus Isaacs arrived in Edinburgh to speak to a Liberal Party gathering in the Synod Hall. Isaacs had led the prosecution in the famous 'conspiracy' trial involving Emmeline Pankhurst and the Pethick-Lawrences, resulting in controversial sentences of nine months for each of them. Ethel Moorhead was in the audience, but when she launched into the usual interruption, she was pounced upon and dragged out. Eight other women shared the same fate. Some were physically assaulted before being ejected, "their clothes were torn, hats dragged off, and men brutally kicked those women again and again." A man who protested "That's not like Scotland, Sir" was also removed.

Moorhead wrote to the *Edinburgh Evening Dispatch* to describe the 'special treatment' she had received: "I am one of the suffragettes who interrupted Sir Rufus Isaacs last night. A maniac sat beside me – evidently placed there to exercise brutality on my being recognised as a suffragist. When I rose to make the remarks, he was ready and dealt me a blow in the ribs which sent me flying, as intended, into the hands of his confreres – the stewards. During former interruptions, he had made himself conspicuous by frenzied yells of, 'Throw her out; throw her over the seat,' etc, inciting other men to violence. Men and women in my neighbourhood remonstrated with

him for his hysterical excesses." An eyewitness to the incident, the Edinburgh window-smasher Agnes Macdonald, claimed that what had remained with her was "the brutal joy of the men in witnessing the 'chucking out'." 26.

No sooner had Ethel Moorhead regained her composure than she was back in the news – and back in court. In October 1912 she appeared on a charge of assaulting Peter Ross, a maths teacher at Broughton High School. Moorhead had strolled into the school, entered Ross's classroom and struck him on the face with a whip – a reprisal, she said, for her brutal treatment at the Isaacs meeting in the Synod Hall earlier that month. Ross, of Eyre Crescent, Edinburgh, was apparently the "maniac" who had assaulted her and screamed for her removal. Moorhead's blow was slight, and Ross was not hurt. Nevertheless, the police were called and she was arrested. She then broke seven panes of glass with her shoes at the High Street police station. In court she gave the Edinburgh WSPU office as her address and pled guilty to both charges. Then an extraordinary intervention was made. An unidentified woman rose and said, "Excuse me, she intends to plead not guilty." With confusion in court, the case was adjourned.

When the bespectacled Moorhead returned to Edinburgh Police Court the following Saturday, she was met by spontaneous applause, partly, claimed one newspaper, because "she was fashionably dressed in a short coat of black furs and wore a veil." As expected, she was convicted. Her fine of £1 was paid for her and she did not go to prison on this occasion.

In the third week of November 1912, unsealed envelopes containing bottles of liquid were dropped into letter boxes in Melville Street, Ainslie Place, Shandwick Place, Nelson Street, North Castle Street, India Street and Howe Street. There were no corks in the bottles and their unspecified contents spilled out and damaged many letters and packets. Suffragists were blamed for a flagrant attack on the Post Office, a vital public institution. Then, just before Christmas, an Edinburgh postman doing his rounds in Polwarth Crescent opened a pillar-box to find an unsealed envelope containing a phial of what he thought was paraffin. The phial was open and the liquid had oozed out, damaging a number of letters. Militants were also blamed for depositing corkless bottles of corrosive fluids in two pillar-boxes at Leith. 'Votes for Women' messages were stuck to them. 27.

Another incident occurred on 8 February 1913 when a piece of heavy electric cable was thrown from an upstairs gallery at the Royal Scottish Museum, smashing a glass display case below containing specimens of seals brought back from the 1902 Scottish Antarctic Expedition. Attached to the cable was a luggage label bearing the message: 'To the Liberal Government, Votes for Women.' The perpetrator escaped unnoticed. The building was immediately evacuated. Fortunately, the occupants of the case suffered no damage. The museum and other public buildings had previously received a police warning to be on their guard against outbreaks of suffragette violence. Extra precautions were introduced, and attendants were instructed to inspect umbrellas, fur muffs and overcoats carried over the arm, and any parcels which might conceal a missile.

Edinburgh post-boxes continued to be targeted. On February 19, bottles containing ink and paraffin were deposited in over a dozen boxes. On the same day a container containing inflammable liquid was dropped into a box at Leith. It burst into flames, but the fire was extinguished before any damage was caused. At the start of March, a box in Marchmont Road was found ablaze. The police who attended stuffed a wet cloth into its aperture to choke the fire, but a number of letters and postcards were burned. In the first week of April the contents of the Arboretum Road box were soaked in cod liver oil. The same night Lothian Road was targeted, a message left behind reading, "Stop torturing Mrs Pankhurst. Beasts!" In May, further damage to letters occurred in Edinburgh. A postman clearing a box in Princes Street, at the corner of Hanover Street, found an uncorked bottle containing an oily liquid wrapped in a copy of *The Suffragette*. About 20 letters were damaged. 28.

The practice of pouring ink, corrosive chemicals or incendiaries into letter boxes, which became the militants' favoured policy from 1912, hurt the women's cause as it had the potential to impact on the everyday lives of

"AUTOMATIC SUFFRAGETTE EXTERMINATING PILLAR-BOX"
(PATENT NOT APPLIED FOR).

Letter-box raids were deeply unpopular with the public, who were happy to snap up postcards like this – where the tables are turned on an unsuspecting suffragette.

"Beg pardon - I thought you were a letter-box," says this apologetic
- and short-sighted - suffragette.

ordinary people. A letter which did not reach its intended destination had all sorts of ramifications, more so in a period when other forms of communication were limited. The rationale behind the indiscriminate burning, destruction or disruption of posted mail also proved deeply unpopular among many suffrage sympathisers, so much so that Christabel Pankhurst later rowed back from the tactic by claiming that charred paper had been put into some letter boxes "to give an impression of militancy." [29].

The General Post Office, at a loss to understand why it had been so targeted, eventually took precautions and offered incentives for information on those behind the attacks – though it could do as much to prevent them as it could to explain them. As the raids became co-ordinated, widespread and relatively sophisticated, Winston Churchill was forced to write urgently to his wife Clementine warning her to be "very careful not to open suspicious parcels arriving by post without precautions...these harpies are quite capable of trying to burn us out." [30].

Muriel Scott defended the tactic. She accepted that some important letters, or cheques, might be destroyed, and acknowledged the private anger and public condemnation. On the other hand, "lives were being destroyed owing to the conditions under which women had to live." And Scott warned that the WSPU "had only just begun this campaign of destroying letters." If they could bring the Post Office to a standstill, they would have Prime Minister Asquith "wringing his hands and weeping and passing a measure giving votes for women."

But her sister Arabella was less taken with the letter-box protests. She recalled going on one nighttime raid that ended with roles reversed ...

"I was pouring in some prescribed treacle when a big hefty woman came along – and slapped me across the face." [31].

References

1. Leah Leneman, A Guid Cause (1991), pp110 & 266.
2. Kensington News, 8 March 1912; Diane Atkinson, Rise Up Women! (2019), p293.
3. Leneman (1991), p112; Memoirs of Elizabeth Thomson (nd c1914), p115; Dundee Courier, 28 March 1912; Votes for Women, 15 March 1912. Following a raid on WSPU headquarters at Clement's Inn in May 1913, detectives revealed in court a book found on the premises which listed women who had been convicted of crimes on property. Among the names read out in court were Agnes Macdonald and Edith Hudson of Edinburgh WSPU. Both women are on the Suffragette Roll of Honour. My thanks to Edinburgh Central Libraries for access to the Agnes Macdonald Collection.
4. Atkinson (2019), p294, Leneman (1991), p112; Elizabeth Crawford, The Women's Suffrage Movement (1999), p257; Elspeth King, in Esther Breitenbach, et al, Out of Bounds (1992), p137 & p143; Helen Crawfurd, unpublished autobiography (nd).
5. Holloway Jingles, WSPU Glasgow (nd, 1912).
6. Forward, 16 March 1912.
7. Edinburgh Evening News, 5 March 1912; The Scotsman, 8 March 1912.
8. Linlithgow Gazette, 5 July 1912.
9. Lilias Mitchell released this statement to the WSPU on 9 July 1912; London Standard, 10 July 1912.
10. Midge Mackenzie, Shoulder to Shoulder (1975), p197; Atkinson (2019), p342.
11. Votes for Women, 13 September 1912; Leneman (1991), p116.
12. NRS, HH16/45, correspondence relating to Flora Ellen Smith; Atkinson (2019), p438. 'Winnie Wallace' may have been an alias. The official records do not mention this as a possibility, however.
13. Edinburgh Evening News, 15 & 18 May 1912.
14. The Scotsman, 29 June 1912.
15. Idem, 13 July 1912.
16. Edinburgh Evening News, 22 July 1912.
17. Edinburgh Evening News, 5 September 1912; Hawick News, 13 December 1912.
18. NRS, HH16/40, letter, Stirling Chief Constable to D. Crombie, secretary to Prison Commissioners, 26 September 1912; NRS, HH16/40, letter, John Lamb, Scottish Office to Prison Commissioners, 11 September 1912; Dundee Courier, 9 September 1912 & 20 October 1909.
19. Edinburgh Evening News, 7 October 1912.
20. Arabella Scott, My Murky Past (Frances Wheelhouse typescript); Dundee Advertiser, 7 December 1912.
21. 'Mary Humphreys' letter to The Scotsman, 16 December 1912; 'Marion Pollock' letter to The Scotsman, 19 December 1912; NRS, HH16/41, letter, 'Mary Humphreys' to Prison Commissioners, 19 December 1912; NRS, HH16/41, minutes between Governor of HM Prison Aberdeen and Prison Commissioners, 3-4 December 1912.
22. Idem, NRS, HH16/41.
23. Mid-Lothian Journal, 18 October 1912; Alnwick Mercury, 26 October 1912; Crawford (1999), p236.
24. The Suffragette, 15 November 1912; Leah Leneman, The Scottish Suffragettes (2000), p65.
25. Crawford (1999), p88 & p538; Atkinson (2019), p344 & p348. On her return to New York in 1912, Lucy Burns and fellow militant Alice Paul formed The National Women's Party.
26. Edinburgh Evening Dispatch, 7 October 1912.
27. Votes for Women, 22 November 1912; Northern Whig, 6 December 1912.
28. The Scotsman, 3 March 1913; Edinburgh Evening News, 17 May 1913.
29. Ethel Moorhead, Incendiaries (1925), p264.
30. Atkinson (2019), p370.
31. Arabella Scott, My Murky Past; Southern Reporter, 5 December 1912.

Ethel Moorhead (centre) and Dr Dorothea Smith on trial at Glasgow High Court on the charge of fire-raising. Both were sentenced to eight months in prison.

NINE:
NO SURRENDER! 1913

"I am out on licence till 7th June. This is the document. I am going to send it to the Home Secretary by the early post with my compliments. I calculate that to serve my nine months' sentence I will have to go into prison sixty-five times and hunger-strike five days on each occasion."

Edinburgh militant Arabella Scott after being released on licence from Calton Prison under the notorious 'Cat and Mouse Act', May 1913.

As 1912 gave way to a new year, the National Union of Women's Suffrage Societies claimed support from big city councils such as Edinburgh, Glasgow, Birmingham, Leeds, Liverpool, Manchester, Newcastle and Sheffield; 82 town councils, including Dundee and Inverness, and more than 40 urban district councils. By the start of 1913, over 80 Women's Liberal Associations and 78 trade councils and trade unions had passed resolutions in favour of women's votes. Around 160 local authorities had signed off favourable resolutions or forwarded petitions to Parliament. Among significant bodies to pledge support were the Labour Party, the Independent Labour Party, the British Women's Temperance Association, the Federation of University Women, the Women's Co-operative Guild, the Women's Labour League and the National Union of Women Workers. 1.

The movement appeared to be heading in the desired direction – but a surprise awaited one of the generals of that advance. A major political meeting in Edinburgh in February 1913 welcomed women's champion Keir Hardie to the Synod Hall. It quickly became evident, however, that Hardie would not be allowed to forget that suffragists held the Labour Party jointly responsible for the government's anti-suffrage blockade, as it was propping up the minority Liberal administration. Christabel Pankhurst claimed Labour was trying to have its cake and eat it: "They cannot be friends of the Government and friends of women, too...they share the Government's guilt."

In the course of his Edinburgh speech Hardie claimed women had been badly treated by the government. At this a suffragette interrupted to lay equal share of the blame on the Labour Party, but she was told to sit down. Proceeding, Hardie was again interrupted, this time by a woman in the gallery who shouted, "You are as great a traitor as Lloyd George." She refused to stop speaking and was put out by stewards. Another suffragist rose and was similarly ejected. Her removal elicited a remark from Hardie that the interruptions had come from women who had "never earned an honest penny in their lives." This was immediately challenged by another woman, who told him the person ejected "had been a hard-worked teacher." At the close of the meeting Hardie apologised and withdrew his statement. 2.

It seems bizarre that Keir Hardie, the Scottish founder of the Labour Party, and with a remarkable record of supporting women's votes over 30 years, found himself heckled by Edinburgh's suffragettes and called "a traitor." Hardie was a close friend of the Pankhursts, especially Sylvia, and he had continued to support the WSPU even as militancy accelerated. He had led the famous Woman's Sunday march in Hyde Park; he had organised support in Parliament; he had condemned the treatment of suffragette prisoners and, indeed, he had just launched the Free Speech Defence Committee in response to a new ban on large outdoor meetings. In spite of that, in the complex context of the Edwardian struggle for votes, Hardie was seen as a

J. Keir Hardie – shouted down as "a traitor" by a suffragette at an Edinburgh meeting.

representative of a party which was too often in cahoots with the government. Remarkably, he was also 'hissed' and 'booed' by constitutionalists in the NUWSS, many of whom were Liberal Party devotees. At times he must have wondered where he went wrong.

In late January 1913 a party of women from Edinburgh joined a demonstration of 'Working Women' for a pre-arranged meeting with Lloyd George in London. They were nine in number – three representing Newhaven fishwives, four from the Women's Co-operative Guild and Mrs Forbes and Miss McLeod of the Women's Social and Political Union. Prior to their departure the women gathered at the WSPU office in Frederick Street and were joined by another 50 supporters in a march to Waverley Station. In London, the Edinburgh contingent joined 300 delegates, including factory hands, seamstresses, mill workers, nurses, teachers, one shop assistant and one domestic servant. With no explanation, Lloyd George wrote at the last minute to the deputation leader Flora Drummond to say he could not meet the women, and to put any issues in writing. Grossly insulted, Drummond replied expressing amazement at his letter. She reminded him that he had agreed to meet the deputation and said the women would "visit" him in the House of Commons that night. The subsequent melee scuppered any chance of a meeting. Within days, a WSPU epistle warned, "We are determined to make Mr Lloyd George's life a misery." 3.

Fresh from her window-smashing adventure in London, Marion Grieve of Joppa now opted for another form of protest. When a tax bill for £9. 15s arrived in April 1913, she sent it back unpaid. This brought sheriff officers to Coillesdene House to seize various goods. On May 30, her property was sold at Douglas & Smart's saleroom in Portobello. A table and four chairs were bought back for £14 by Mrs Grieve's friends and, as usual, with the amount required reached, the sale was terminated. Having issued an appeal to support Mrs Grieve "in large numbers," a body of women walked from Coillesdene House to the Windsor Street auction rooms carrying placards emblazoned with 'Tax without Representation is Tyranny' and 'No Vote,

No Tax'. Elizabeth Finlayson Gauld, a recent WSPU recruit from the WFL, and Morag Burn Murdoch, the Edinburgh branch president, addressed a large crowd outside the premises. 4.

In April 1913 four women and one man were accused of attempting to burn down the grandstand at Kelso racecourse. At Jedburgh Court they faced a charge of wilful fire raising before Sheriff Chisholm and a jury of 15 men. Standing before them were Arabella Scott, Marchmont Road, Edith Hudson, Middleby Street, the sisters Agnes and Elizabeth Thomson of Hartington Place and Donald McEwan, an elderly gardener of Downfield Place, all Edinburgh.

The five defendants faced a mountain of incriminatory evidence. When police raided the Marchmont Road home of Arabella and Muriel Scott, they found a notebook detailing the purchase of firelighters and oil from an Edinburgh merchant. The shopkeeper, Alexander Lowe, identified one of them in court as the purchaser. The boy who delivered the firelighters and oil remembered the delivery address, that of the Thomson sisters. A detective was sent to watch the house in Hartington Place occupied by the Misses Thomsons. A taxi drove up, picked up passengers and left. Charles Gray, the cab driver, told the court he was engaged by Donald McEwan to drive a party to Kelso. He described the journey and said that when they were near Kelso racecourse, two women took parcels from the vehicle and climbed inside the rails.

Two Roxburghshire police constables took up the story. They said they had been watching Kelso racecourse. They saw the taxi arriving. Then they saw a light in the grandstand and proceeded to arrest Arabella Scott and Edith Hudson. Candles had been lit and sarking boards had been placed over a benzine lamp. In court the constables identified articles they had discovered at the stand, including quantities of firelighters, rags saturated with paraffin and tins of petrol. They also claimed to have found a small flag and a copy of *The Suffragette* in front of the building.

With overwhelming evidence amassed by this extraordinary surveillance effort, it is scarcely surprising that Arabella Scott, in defence, spoke only to

Arabella Scott. The much-imprisoned Edinburgh militant wears a WSPU brooch. (Courtesy of the late Frances Wheelhouse)

The Suffragette," June 13, 1913.
Registered at the G.P.O. as a Newspaper

The Suffragette

Edited by Christabel Pankhurst.

The Official Organ of the
Women's Social and Political Union

No. 35—Vol. 1.   FRIDAY, JUNE 13, 1913.   Price 1d. Weekly (Post Free 1½d.)

IN HONOUR AND IN LOVING, REVERENT MEMORY
OF
EMILY WILDING DAVISON.
SHE DIED FOR WOMEN.

"Greater love hath no man than this, that he lay down his life for his friends."

Miss Davison, who made a protest at the Derby against the denial of Votes to Women, was knocked down by the King's horse and sustained terrible injuries of which she died on Sunday, June 8th, 1913.

The WSPU issued a commemorative edition of The Suffragette to mark the death of Emily Wilding Davison in 1913.

justify the women's suffrage movement. Edith Hudson addressed the jury along similar lines and both said that it should have been Prime Minister Asquith in the dock. Their speeches were greeted with applause from the gallery. After the Sheriff's summing-up, the jury retired and deliberated for half-an-hour. They found the charge against 67-year-old Agnes Thomson not proven. The others were found guilty, but the jurists recommended 65-year-old Elizabeth Thomson to the leniency of the court. The Sheriff pronounced sentence: Arabella Scott, Edith Hudson and Donald McEwan each received nine months' imprisonment. Elizabeth Thomson was given three months. The courtroom erupted in fury. Arabella Scott shouted, "We shall not serve these sentences. We won't do it!" Supporters in the gallery called out, "Never surrender," and, to the jury, "Shame!" [5].

A mass protest was quickly organised at the foot of the Mound. Hundreds of supporters heard an impassioned plea for her sister's release by Muriel Scott, as well as speeches from May Grant and Morag Burn Murdoch of the WSPU. Janie Allan, writing in *Forward*, pointed out how the nine-month sentences compared with the punishments given to male sexual predators in 1911-1912: "For defilement and indecent assault on girls under 16 and on little children, 18 got nine months, 144 were sentenced to six months, and 106 to three months, while quite a number escaped with the trifling sentence of one month, and, in some cases, 14 days." Following further harsh sentences, the Women's Freedom League announced that it would protest against convictions made on police evidence alone. It pointed out that the police were allowed to remain in the courtroom during a case to listen to other evidence – which they would then be asked to corroborate! [6].

The Kelso quartet were taken to Calton Prison in Edinburgh, where Scott and Hudson declared a hunger strike, refusing to take food of any kind. There was no attempt to forcibly feed them, and within four days they were released under The Prisoners' (Temporary Release) Act, rechristened the Cat and Mouse Act, controversial legislation introduced by Home Secretary Reginald McKenna whereby hunger-striking women were released on licence until fit enough to be returned to custody. Liberated women had to remain at a pre-agreed address for the period of time given on the licence, at which point they were liable to be re-arrested if their health had recovered. Arabella Scott was quite ill, and she was taken under the care of Marion Grieve in Joppa.

Interviewed at Mrs Grieve's home, Scott described her hunger strike: "I was let out, I think, because my heart was weak. Forcible feeding was not reverted to. At first we were simply asked if we wanted food, which we refused. Then the food was put in the cell and left there. We were refused newspapers, letters or visits from friends. We fought against that tyranny in Holloway. I am out on licence till 7th June. This is the document [licence]. I am going to send it to the Home Secretary by the early post with my compliments. I calculate that to serve my nine months' sentence I will have to go into prison sixty-five times and hunger-strike five days on each occasion."

Meanwhile Edith Hudson was taken under licence to the Leith Walk home of Dr Grace Cadell. She declined to make any statement. Dr Cadell, however, said her patient's pulse was very weak and that she had been confined to bed. She had taken only water in prison. Donald McEwan, meanwhile, did not adopt a hunger strike and the Scottish Prison Commissioners, somewhat sympathetic to his lonely incarceration, confirmed his early release later in the year: "As this old man has now served nearly five months of his sentence while the three women who were the real culprits have only served a few days, the Commissioners think that the Secretary for Scotland might now be disposed to consider remitting the remainder of his sentence." 7.

On June 12, having failed to present herself at Calton Prison on the expiry of her licence, Arabella Scott was rearrested at her home in Marchmont Road. Agnes Thomson and Edith Hudson, whose licence had also expired, had gone to ground. After a few days in hiding, the Thomson sisters sailed from Granton to the safety of Sweden. By this time, suffragettes had learned how to outwit the Cat and Mouse Act with disguises and false trails. Dorothy Chalmers Smith, arrested with Ethel Moorhead in the act of setting fire to a house in Glasgow, was kept under strict watch. But police patrols outside Dr Smith's

property had to be withdrawn when it became known that "the bird had flown" – dressed as her mother! The surveillance, reported an exasperated *Herald*, had cost Glasgow ratepayers £10 per week. Ethel Moorhead also avoided recapture. She recalled in *Incendiaries* that she disguised herself in a red wig called 'Rufus', presumably after Sir Rufus Isaacs, from whose meeting in Edinburgh she had been brutally ejected. She also paid tribute to Fanny Parker for protecting her from the 'cats' by organising disguises and safe houses. Arabella Scott captured the essence of the cats (police) chasing the mice (suffragettes) and how there was little possibility of a meek return to the cells... "Each time I was let out they would give me a slip of paper to say I was to report back to gaol at 6 o'clock on a certain morning by the date stamped thereon. Usually the licence for temporary release was about ten days to a fortnight. Can you imagine me knocking on the Calton Prison gates at 6 o'clock in the morning asking to be put back inside?" 8.

Meanwhile, the summer of 1913 brought the serious side of the struggle into sharp focus when Emily Wilding Davison shocked the nation by stepping in front of the King's horse Anmer during the Epsom Derby. Davison sustained a fractured skull and died in hospital on June 8, a suffragette guard of honour around her bed. The coroner recorded death by misadventure. No single act did more to emphasise women's sense of injustice and to demonstrate their determination to carry the struggle to victory regardless of personal cost.

Suffragettes from all over Britain – wearing white dresses, sashes and carrying lilies in the colours of the movement – carried Davison's coffin in a remarkable procession half-a-mile in length. Over 1500 wreaths were sent. Emmeline Pankhurst, weak from hunger strikes, was arrested and taken away as she was about to lead the massed ranks of mourners. Her carriage was driven empty at the front of the procession as a protest, and the authorities were afterwards criticised for their lack of compassion and decency.

The reaction in Scotland was one of shock. A dignified service was held in Dundee on June 11 – the only memorial event outside London. Once again, the divisions present throughout the rest of the country were discarded,

The Press was in no doubt that suffragettes had tried to blow up Edinburgh's landmark observatory.

as members of the NUWSS and WFL, wearing black mourning clothes, stood shoulder to shoulder with the WSPU as an orderly crowd watched on respectfully. Frances Parker said the service was to honour Davison's "heroic self-sacrifice." May Grant added that she had risked her life "willingly and nobly, knowing that she might lose it." Ethel Moorhead described her friend's sacrifice as a "brave one" and that she had intended no disrespect to the king. [9].

Emily Wilding Davison's loss was felt deeply, and suffragists blamed the government. Within days of the funeral, militancy was resumed with intensity... not least in the vicinity of the Scottish capital:

- On May 16, a "home-made bomb" was found in the Duke of Buccleuch's private chapel at Dalkeith. Suffragettes were blamed, but there was no claim of responsibility or arrests. No damage was caused.
- On May 22, an explosion shook the Royal Observatory on Blackford Hill. Reports stated that it, too, was caused by "a bomb." Its fuse wire was said to be 40 feet long and it had been "fired" by means of a burning candle. Little damage was caused. The Press, however, was united in laying the blame on "the suffragettes." The *London Evening Standard* commented: "The quantity of gunpowder used must have been considerable, as fragments of the earthen jar which contained it were embedded in the walls and woodwork, and the glass of two windows was blown out and carried a considerable distance." Another paper claimed a bag, biscuits and suffragette literature had been left behind. HM Government's Office of Works, in a memorandum on May 25, confirmed that "the outrage is considered by the police to be the work of the suffragettes," and urged the authorities to protect the landmark building. No claim of responsibility was made.
- On June 10, Stair Park House in Tranent, a large East Lothian mansion owned by Mrs Durie of Albany Street, Edinburgh, was destroyed by fire. The house had been unoccupied for over a year. It was reported widely

that the incident was the work of suffragettes and that the Tranent folk were "indignant." 10.

It has long been stated that such burnings and bombings weakened Mrs Pankhurst's militant organisation through a desertion of members and because of the anger and hostility such violence and fire-raising attracted. Several historians have argued that militancy was actually counterproductive after 1912. That perception is contradicted by what was happening in Scotland. At the height of the attacks, between April and June 1913, the WSPU offices in Scotland's four biggest cities reported increases in membership, Glasgow by a remarkable intake of 108 new women. Edinburgh WSPU, meanwhile, bucked the trend in the south by opening a larger headquarters at 27 Frederick Street and closing its long-established Melville Place office. In one week in May 1913 its volunteers sold a record "fifty dozen" copies of *Votes for Women*.

The collective momentum of suffrage groups in Scotland as militancy escalated in 1913 defies modern notions of rancour. Neither did the loyalty and obedience demanded by the Pankhursts drive many women out of the WSPU north of the border, although movement between the organisations occurred from time to time.

Editors, meanwhile, knew the commercial value of attributing every "outrage" and "dastardly attack" to suffragettes. Acts of militancy were sensationalised and given prominent headlines and columns of space. Although the publicity-conscious WSPU neither admitted nor denied involvement in destructive acts and kept the authorities guessing, it is sensible to believe that many of the 'outrages' had little to do with the women's campaign. It is also probable that some fires blamed on militants were purposefully set by owners or their agents in order to claim insurance money on unwanted properties. That was the view of several suffragists, including Helen Crawfurd. There were occasions, too, when 'copycat' militancy was exposed. Such was the case in Glasgow in March 1913 when two boys "emulated the example of suffragettes" (as one paper put it) to set fire to Mossbank Industrial School. The boys thereafter appeared

The huge fire which destroyed Kelly House in Wemyss Bay in 1913 was firmly attributed to the suffragettes.

before the Glasgow Juvenile Delinquency Board, where it was claimed they had been "carried away" by the exploits of the suffragettes. They were 'carried away' to a reform school.

From 1913, all suffragists encountered more aggressive audiences, and all known suffragettes were liable to arrest at the drop of a hat. With every bombing and burning, the public's anger grew and it took exceptional courage for women to hold outdoor meetings. Edinburgh's Florence McFarlane, a survivor of Black Friday and a London window-smasher, recalled a meeting in which, "one man gave me a blow on the chest with his elbow and, to my amazement, a woman turned upon me and pommelled me with her fists as if she was beating mud from a doormat." Consider the courage of WSPU militant May Grant, who was forcibly removed from meetings held by Prime Minister Herbert Asquith, Chancellor David Lloyd George, Home Secretary Winston Churchill, Labour Party leader Keir Hardie, Prime Minister-in-waiting Ramsay MacDonald and Irish nationalist T. P. O'Connor. Little wonder that some experienced footsoldiers packed their clothes with corrugated paper for protection. 11.

One newspaper noted a hardening of attitudes in the Scottish capital: " A decided change has come over the temper of the crowds attending the open-air meetings in Edinburgh. Instead of being accorded a patient hearing as on former occasions, the speakers find, that since outrages on public properties have become part of the suffragist campaign, this courtesy is denied to them." Its words were reflected across the city in a summer of retribution … 12.

- On June 14, a WSPU meeting at Leith was broken up by youths. Twice the women's platform was overturned and they were forced to retreat, escorted by the police and followed by a threatening mob.
- On June 16, a party of women from the Church Guild was attacked on Arthur's Seat after being 'mistaken' for suffragettes by a crowd of youths.
- On June 17, around 200 boisterous students besieged the new WSPU centre in Frederick Street. The police prevented any trouble. Some of the students then made their way to the Women's Freedom League shop in Lothian Road, where once again the presence of a police detachment prevented damage, although the green, white and gold flag outside was torn from its mountings. The culprit was arrested, and later released without charge.
- On June 27, Jean Lambie and the French suffragist Madame Liptay, two members of Edinburgh WSPU, were mobbed and pelted with turf in Inverleith Park after being recognised by some of the crowd. Several policemen went to the women's assistance, and they were taken by car to the safety of Frederick Street. One 15-year-old boy was arrested and later liberated. 13.

The constitutionalist societies used different arguments and methods. When the Anti-Suffrage League claimed it had 50,000 members across the country and 'spoke' for women in Britain, the NUWSS quickly responded to demonstrate the strength of its supportive networks. By 1913, there were 40 women's suffrage societies – the largest being the NUWSS with over 400 branches and a membership steadily rising towards 50,000. The Women's Freedom League and the militant Women's Social and Political Union were the other mainstream societies, but they were joined by suffrage organisations formed by writers, artists, graduates, church and men's groups. The National Union of Women Workers with 40,000 members; the Liberal Federation's 140,000; the National British Women's Association's 155,000; the Scottish Women's Temperance Association's 110,000 and the Women's Cooperative Guild's 28,000 members, were the largest of dozens of groups which offered support, many of them overwhelmingly in favour of women's votes. 14.

Meanwhile, the men of Scotland were preparing for their most significant contribution to the cause. Over 50 of them, mostly from Edinburgh and Glasgow, travelled to London to seek an audience with the Prime Minister and to put a stop to the Cat and Mouse Act. Three times the deputation wrote in advance to Herbert Asquith claiming their right to an interview with him, and three times the Prime Minister replied that he would not receive them. Nevertheless, the men telegrammed Asquith to say they were coming. They also set out their speeches in advance in a 16-page pamphlet for distribution in London, *Scotchmen at Downing Street: Speeches by the Delegates*, which was sold at a penny a copy.

The 'Scottish Men's Deputation to Downing Street' carried significant clout. It included ex-Lord Provosts, bailies and councillors, barristers and solicitors, ministers and teachers. The Edinburgh contingent included the Pitt Street businessman Alexander Orr. It was Orr, from Fettes Row, who had come up with the idea for a deputation in a conversation with Maud Arncliffe Sennett, who had met her husband while playing Helen in the *Lady of the Lake* in Edinburgh in the 1890s. By the turn of the century she was at the centre of the British suffrage movement and had organised the famous women's 'Mud March' in London in 1907. Arncliffe Sennett and Alexander Orr had met at Emily Wilding Davison's funeral and had discussed cross-border ideas. Further planning for the journey south was delegated to Nannie Brown, who had completed the Edinburgh-London 'Women's March'. 15.

On July 18, the men of Scotland marched in dignified procession along Whitehall to Downing Street. On arrival they were greeted with cheers from massed ranks of suffragettes and onlookers. Alas, the Prime Minister was not at home, having 'escaped' in a taxi as the men turned the corner into the street. In protest, they 'showered' their visiting cards through the No 10 letter box and used Mr Asquith's doorstep as a speaking platform. Later, the Home Secretary Reginald McKenna pointedly refused to meet them, and Scottish Secretary Thomas McKinnon Wood (at first) was suspiciously absent from his Whitehall desk. A stormy meeting was held in the House of Commons with a small number of Scottish MPs who consented to see the men, some of whom reportedly made fun of the Cat and Mouse Act. *The Scotsman* noted, "The meeting was in private, but it is understood that it was by no means of a pacific nature." The following day the rebuffed deputation joined the Men's League and the Actresses' Franchise League at an authorised demonstration in Hyde Park, where the men received a sympathetic and orderly hearing.

On their return, the leaders of the delegation telegrammed Asquith to say they considered themselves "grossly insulted." Scotland, they felt, had been snubbed. Their hosts, the English-based suffragists, praised their efforts and called for the Prime Minister's resignation. In fact, Alexander Orr, the delegation's secretary, had prepared an elegant speech for the Premier which, alas, remained unsaid. It ended, "I therefore approach you as a Scotsman born and bred, fired with as great a sense of justice as ever dominated my countrymen who fell at Bannockburn or fought as Covenanters, to ask of you your aid to pass this measure of simple justice to the long-suffering women of my country." A practical outcome of the deputation was the formation of a Scottish Men's Federation for Women's Suffrage, initially with branches in Edinburgh and Glasgow. Alexander Orr was named treasurer of the new body. 16.

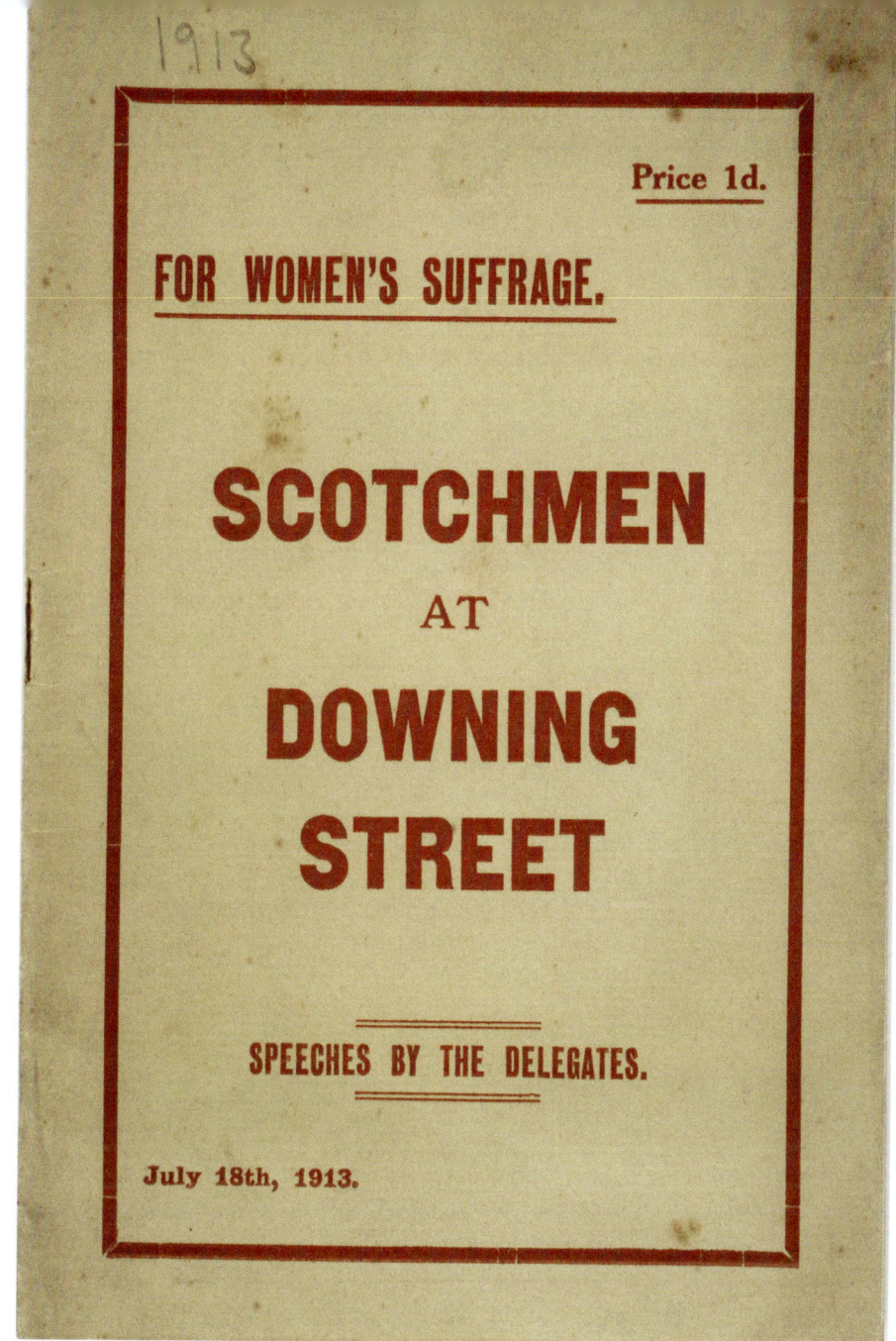

The cover of the pamphlet produced by the Scottish men's deputation to Downing Street in 1913. (Courtesy of London Museum)

THE VOTE
July 25, 1913.
ONE PENNY.

INSURANCE ACT PROTEST.

THE VOTE

THE ORGAN OF THE WOMEN'S FREEDOM LEAGUE.

Vol. VIII. No. 196.   Registered at the General Post Office as a Newspaper.   FRIDAY, JULY 25, 1913.

Edited by C. DESPARD.

OBJECTS: To secure for Women the Parliamentary vote as it is or may be granted to men; to use the power thus obtained to establish equality of rights and opportunities between the sexes, and to promote the social and industrial well-being of the community.

THE SCOTTISH SUFFRAGE DEPUTATION ARRIVING AT THE PRIME MINISTER'S HOUSE, 10, DOWNING STREET, LONDON, JULY 19, 1913.

The Women's Freedom League official newspaper featured the delegation on its cover.

Ironically, when the WSPU staged a massive demonstration in London just a week later – the famous gathering at which Emmeline Pankhurst addressed 20,000 from a plinth in Trafalgar Square – the women's attempt to see Mr Asquith in Downing Street resulted in a riot and 24 arrests. The men's visit, of course, was fruitless and futile, but it had passed off without even a hint of police intervention. The contrast in how male sympathisers and suffragettes were treated by Scotland Yard was not lost on Edinburgh's Muriel Scott: "Although the Premier refused to see them and ran away as usual, they were allowed to ring his bell, allowed to enter, and, more wonderful still, allowed to address a meeting from his doorstep without being hauled up to Bow Street and whirled away in a Black Maria to Pentonville or Wormwood Scrubs. For attempting to do what these men have done, women were sentenced to terms from 14 days to three months' 'hard'. My sister [Arabella] and I each received a sentence of 21 days in the Second Division for merely walking up Downing Street..." [17].

Militancy resumed in Edinburgh in August 1913 with alleged attacks on two city properties. Morelands, a house in Grange Loan owned by an Edinburgh stockbroker named Bowhill, was severely damaged by fire. As was then custom among Scotland's wealthier business classes, Bowhill had shut up his town house during August while he holidayed in the North of Scotland. The *Edinburgh Evening News* was convinced suffragettes were to blame and laid out the evidence before its readers: "It appears that an entrance had been gained to the grounds from the house adjoining, the suffragettes having climbed over the wall separating the two properties." It reported the finding of candle ends and a "lady's umbrella." It added that two copies of *The Suffragette* had been discovered, and that cans of paraffin had been placed near the staircase, "where the fire seems to have originated."

On the same day, another fire attributed to suffragettes was discovered at Fettes College. The blaze affected the Fifth and Sixth Form classrooms on the first floor. Edinburgh Fire Brigade managed to extinguish the flames but not before the doors and windows of both rooms were damaged and portions of the walls burned. The Press accused the militants of entering the school via a window, and 'evidence' of the deed included sheets of brown paper smeared with soft soap which "showed that a now familiar process of treating window panes had been resorted to." It added, "the intruders then proceeded up the stairs to the first landing." Contemporary photographs show debris on the floors of the Fettes classrooms and damage to windows and doors. 18.

Grace Cadell was back in the news in the summer of 1913 after refusing to pay £10 of tax. When the bill arrived from Customs & Excise in Waterloo Place, Dr Cadell sent it back in an unstamped envelope, leaving the tax inspector to pick up the tab for the twopence 'postage due' on it. That was asking for trouble. On June 2, sheriff officers showed up at 145 Leith Walk. Several items of furniture were removed, including a chest of drawers, armchair, barometer, umbrella stand, mantel clock and pictures, all of which eclipsed in value the amount due. Remarkably, Dr Cadell was called to appear at two different courts on the same day. Not even Ethel Moorhead managed that!

At the Midlothian County Justice of the Peace court the 58-year-old doctor faced two counts of contravention of the Revenue Act for taxes relating to her property in Leith Walk. The clerk read a letter from Dr Cadell stating that as she was not a "person" in the eyes of the law it was impossible for her to appear "personally." Firstly, the witness for Customs and Excise stated that Dr Cadell kept two carriages, and only held a licence for one. She had been told about the contravention and had refused to take out a second licence. A fine of £2, with the option of 10 days' imprisonment, was imposed. She was secondly accused of not taking out a licence for the armorial device painted on one of the carriages. A fine of £3. 3s was imposed, which included the licence, with the option of 10 days' imprisonment. Both counts appear petty, but no comment on the nature of the offences was made at the time.

Later the same day, Dr Cadell was prosecuted at Edinburgh Sheriff Court for failing to pay insurance contributions in respect of her domestic staff. This case was adjourned to September 25. When called on that day she was quickly found guilty and sentenced to pay a modified 'penalty' of £10. No option of a custodial sentence was mentioned.

The only known photograph of the damage in the Fettes classrooms.

By the following month, however, Dr Cadell had still not paid her fines or been apprehended for non-payment. She told an open-air meeting at the Mound that she was not behind bars because the court was so far unable to answer her question as to how she could appear 'personally' when she was not a 'person' in law [following the legal ruling in the Scottish women graduates appeal]. There is no further mention of the two cases, and no reports that goods belonging to the Leith doctor were auctioned on this occasion. Perhaps the outcry across the country when Kate Harvey was sent to Holloway for failing to pay a few pounds in tax persuaded the Edinburgh fiscal to quietly drop the case. That was not the end of the matter, however. The following month, October 1913, Dr Cadell was fined

Suffragettes were said to have gained access to Fettes College from this ground floor window.

a further £10 for not stamping her National Insurance cards. This time she paid her fine in copper coins weighing half a hundredweight – all carefully wrapped in suffragette newspapers! 19.

As 1913 drew to a close, the Edinburgh National Society attracted an audience of 1000 to the Music Hall to hear an address by Millicent Fawcett. As they listened to the NUWSS president, the capital's students made another attack on the WSPU's rooms in retaliation for a women's protest at Lord Haldane's rectoral address at the university. Around 100 young men marched to 27 Frederick Street where four windows were broken. The retribution continued in Lothian Road where the large window of the Women's Freedom League shop at No 90 was similarly dealt with. Two students were arrested following the second incident, but subsequently acquitted after a number of associates corroborated their pleas of innocence (despite incriminating police evidence). Riding their legal luck, the accused said they wished it to be known that the Lothian Road attack was carried out under "the misapprehension" that the WFL was a militant body, and that they intended to make good the damage done to those premises. 20.

Over several days the WSPU canvassed doctors across Edinburgh for signatures to a petition against forcible feeding. When a lack of support became obvious, handbills began appearing on GP practice doors with the wording, "Join the humane of your profession! Refuse to co-operate with the Government or give any sanction whatever to the cat-and-mouse torture and forcible feeding!" Meanwhile, one suffragette attracted headlines at a meeting of the Labour Party in Edinburgh by chaining herself to her seat. As Keir Hardie began speaking, so did she! It was reported that she screamed in pain as she was unchained, while many in the audience cheered and clapped. Other women were brutally ejected, leading to complaints in the Press about the strong-arm tactics of the Labour stewards and an aggressive group of Young Scots, who had previously clashed with the suffragists. Given his record of support, Hardie took badly to the WSPU's criticism. He claimed in his Edinburgh speech that only he and the Blackburn MP Philip Snowden, the former Independent Labour Party chairman, supported militancy in the Commons, but the women "seemed determined" to drive them both away. 21.

On Christmas Eve 1913, the morning service at St Giles' Cathedral and the evening service in St John's Episcopal Church in Princes Street were interrupted. Around a dozen women took part in the cathedral incident. All rose to chant a prayer for Emmeline Pankhurst and other prisoners who were undergoing 'torture'. As a result, nine of them were arrested. Two gave addresses in Glasgow, a third lived in Dundee, while the remaining six gave the address of the WSPU office in Frederick Street. The women were bailed after being charged rather sloppily with "annoying the congregation in the service." Unsurprisingly, nothing came of the matter and the case against the unnamed women was abandoned. At the service in St John's, only three women chanted the intercession for the leaders. They left the church while the service was still in progress.

Although considered disrespectful by some women and sacrilege by others, the WSPU orchestrated church protests across Britain in support of imprisoned volunteers. In Glasgow, for example, leaflets were distributed to the congregations of around 50 churches, and 30 women took part in a protest at Glasgow Cathedral. Another 'indignation' meeting took place outside the building where a crowd of 2000 listened respectfully to speakers on four platforms, including Muriel Scott and Elizabeth Finlayson Gauld of Edinburgh WSPU. There was no disorder, nor were the women disturbed. In Aberdeen the chant "rang through the whole church." In Dundee, Enid Rennie offered up a prayer for Mrs Pankhurst and the other prisoners, but carried out her task "with prayerful reverence." [22].

Thomas McKinnon Wood then came face to face with Edinburgh suffragettes at the opening of a school in the city. The Secretary for Scotland had just finished his speech when a woman made her way to the platform and threw a packet of flour at him. It did not strike his face, but the contents covered his coat and trousers. The woman was seized and prevented from throwing a second missile. She was removed from the hall while loudly asking why he had tortured women. In the same week, diners at Patrick Thompson's new restaurant on North Bridge were interrupted by a woman who began to harangue the clientele "quite regardless of the fact that not a word of her

Alice Crompton, Scottish organiser of the non-militant NUWSS, is seen scaling a fence to enable her to interrupt Prime Minister Asquith's speech at Ladybank in Fife.

The Scottish executive committee of the NUWSS met in Edinburgh in 1913. The Scottish organiser Helen Fraser is seen second from the right at the front, with the Edinburgh National Society secretary Elsie Inglis fourth from the right. (Courtesy of The Women's Library at LSE)

speech was heard amidst the volley of sarcastic remarks, the shuffling of feet and the tinkling of cutlery and crockery." Another woman distributed copies of *The Suffragette* around the tables. [23].

It was coming home to Edinburgh's 350,000 population that votes for women was impacting on every aspect of their lives – in the street, at work, at meetings and events, where they dined and where they went to pray. There was no escape from the campaign – for the people, or for their beleaguered government.

References

1. *Dundee Courier, 5 December 1912; Westminster Gazette, Wednesday 22 January 1913; The Scotsman, 15 February 1913.*
2. *The Suffragette, 7 & 14 February 1913.*
3. *Edinburgh Evening Dispatch, 22 January 1913; Press & Journal, 10 February 1913.*
4. *The Suffragette, 18 April 1913; The Scotsman, 31 May 1913.*
5. *Southern Reporter, 22 May 1913; Arabella Scott, My Murky Past (Frances Wheelhouse typescript).*
6. *Forward, 13 May 1913; Laura Mayhall, The Militant Suffrage Movement (2003), p112.*
7. *NRS, HH16/40, noted on a Scottish Prison Commission list of prisoners.*
8. *The Guardian, 21 November 1913; Ethel Moorhead, Incendiaries (1925).*
9. *Dundee Advertiser, 11 & 12 June 1913.*
10. *NRS MW5/109, Ministry of Public Buildings & Works, Office of Works Memorandum 'Royal Observatory Bomb Outrage by Suffragettes', 24 May 1913; Evening Standard, 22 May 1913; Strathern Herald, 14 June 1913.*
11. *Norman Watson, Dundee Suffragettes (2018), pp 110-117.*
12. *Leah Leneman, A Guid Cause (1991), p139.*
13. *Edinburgh Evening News, 16, 18 & 28 June 1913.*
14. *Arabella Scott, My Murky Past.*
15. *Elizabeth Crawford, The Women's Suffrage Movement (1999), p625.*
16. *The Scotsman, 19 July 1913.*
17. *The Vote, 25 July 1913; Glasgow Herald, 19 & 22 July 1913.*
18. *Edinburgh Evening News, 22 August 1913. The Fettes College images are from a contemporary photographic album (private collection).*
19. *The Vote, 19 September 1913; Leneman (1991), p68; The Scotsman, 22 September 1913.*
20. *The Scotsman, 15 & 21 November 1912.*
21. *The Scotsman, 3 November 1913; Press & Journal, 24 November 1913; The Suffragette, 19 December 1913.*
22. *The Scotsman, 23 February 1914.*
23. *Edinburgh Evening News, 9 February 1914.*

Calton Prison, which opened in 1817 and was once the site of Edinburgh executions.

TEN:
'THE SUFFRAGETTE PRISON' 1914

"The bulk of the people up and down the country are in favour of votes for women, but they don't like militancy. We want you to hate it, to loathe it, and rise up and put a stop to it…so that the average man in the street will say, 'For Heaven's sake give the women what they want, and let's have peace'."

Flora Drummond explaining to an Edinburgh audience why women like her were prepared to go to prison again and again, March 1914. 1.

In February 1914, Scotland awoke to the shocking news that Ethel Moorhead was being fed by force in Calton Prison, Edinburgh – the first prisoner in Scotland to undergo the 'treatment' for hunger striking. Moorhead's 'crime' dated back to July 1913, when, as 'Margaret Morrison', she had been arrested with Dr Dorothea Chalmers Smith while allegedly attempting to set fire to a house in Glasgow.

Held on remand at Duke Street Prison, Moorhead smashed a window and knocked off the governor's hat. Trial was set for Glasgow High Court in October 1913, by which time the police had realised that 'Morrison' was actually Ethel Moorhead. When both accused said they would defend themselves, which brought cheers from supporters in the public gallery, the judge, Lord Salvesen, suggested they might be better with legal help. "We usually find they make a muddle of it," responded Moorhead casually.

Moorhead continued with her interruptions, refused to plead, harangued witnesses and was eventually removed from the court – though not before she had thrown her shoes at the judge. In her absence, both women were found guilty. When the sentence of eight months' imprisonment was handed down on each of them, "a scene of indescribable disorder and confusion" occurred. It seemed the whole court was on its feet shouting, "Shame! Shame!" – as a bag of apples was flung at the bench.

Admitted to Duke Street Prison on October 16, the women declared a hunger strike. After refusing food for five days they were released under the Cat and Mouse Act. Both went into hiding, with Moorhead taken into the care of Fanny Parker.

Ethel Moorhead was re-arrested early in 1914 after a tip-off to Edinburgh police that two 'suffragettes' had been seen in Peebles. The next morning a local policeman went to the hotel where the women were staying and recognised Moorhead. She was immediately re-arrested. The assumption was that the duo were planning a firebomb attack on Traquair House, where two women had been seen acting suspiciously the day before. By February, Moorhead was in Calton Prison in Edinburgh facing the 'artificial feeding' that suffragettes in England had endured for four years. On February 19, the Calton governor telegrammed the Secretary of State for Scotland for authorisation to forcibly feed the Queen Street militant. Permission was granted the following day by telegram – despite intercessions by Janie Allan and Elizabeth Finlayson Gauld at a meeting with the Prison Commission's senior doctor, James Devon. 2.

On February 21, Moorhead became the first suffragette in Scotland to be fed by force. The medical officer reported that day that Prisoner No 540 had been artificially fed "by a small sized catheter by the mouth." The food consisted of

Ethel Moorhead's treatment led to a permanent WSPU presence outside Calton Prison's gates.

two eggs and a half pint of milk. He added that she had felt no pain. The procedure was initially administered by staff from Morningside Asylum. When the asylum's board of governors objected, the operation was placed in the hands of Dr H. Ferguson Watson, the medical officer from Peterhead Prison. Watson continued the procedure for five days, during which time Moorhead endured eight forcible feedings. Dr Devon accepted full responsibility and dismissed the possibility of being targeted by militants for doing so: "My personal view is that the risk is very slight, and I have been far too frequently threatened by lunatics to worry about this lot." On the evening of February 25, Ethel Moorhead was released under licence, wrapped in

blankets, and was taken home in an ambulance by Dr Grace Cadell and a nurse. She had contracted double pneumonia. 3.

Women were shocked. *The Suffragette's* front page proclaimed, 'Scotland Dishonoured and Disgraced.' Many suffragists had believed the Scottish authorities would not adopt the procedure used south of the border. Janie Allan wrote in *Forward*, "It has been fondly believed that this barbarity was to be left to England." Emily Wilding Davison, on being released from Aberdeen Prison the year before, had praised the decision not to feed her by force: "The truth is that bonnie Scotland will not adopt the barbarity of forcible feeding!" Teresa Billington-Grieg had also applauded the perceived policy difference, calling it a "great triumph" for Scotland. The reality was otherwise. The Scottish Office and Prison Commissioners had been keen to adopt forcible feeding as early as the 1909 jailings in Dundee but were effectively prevented from doing so by the courage of the city's medical practitioners. And when it was revealed that the procedure had been used on Moorhead, there was disbelief and distress across Scotland. From Edinburgh came condemnatory letters from Elizabeth Finlayson Gauld and Dr Cadell, the former bluntly questioning the prison medical supremo James Devon: "A woman came into your hands. She was in normal health and vigour. In one short week she is carried out. How?" 4.

During Moorhead's incarceration women took it in turns to stage a permanent 'sentry' outside the Calton's gates, walking slowly back and forth holding flags in the Union's colours. A megaphone was used to shout encouragement to the prisoner. On the day of her release, 80 members of Edinburgh WSPU gathered in Charlotte Square before marching behind suffragette piper Bessie Watson in solemn procession along Princes Street and down Leith Walk towards the home of Dr Cadell, where she had been taken to recover.

The prison authorities claimed that Ethel Moorhead had brought pneumonia upon herself by removing her clothes and breaking a cell window. This was contradicted by Dr Cadell, who stated that food getting into her lungs had caused her illness. Moorhead attempted to set the record straight, saying that she had been clumsily forcibly fed by "two young doctors" who "looked like medical students." On another day, a doctor had carried out the forcible feeding unaided. She was so ill by this time that two nurses sat up with her all night – a vase of sweet peas from Arabella Scott next to her bed. She was asked if she would like to send for any relatives, and she later claimed a priest had been called to administer the Last Sacrament to her. On February 23, she had been asked to make her will. [5]

There was widespread anger – not to mention a high-level inquiry – once Moorhead's account of her treatment was made public on March 5. It was no coincidence when, hours after her release, the historic Church of St Mary, Whitekirk, 25 miles east of Edinburgh, and one of Scotland's great medieval treasures, was destroyed in a fire probably started by her friend Fanny Parker. As the news broke, the criticism was unrelenting. The *Evening Dispatch* called the blaze a "dastardly crime" and a "new line in villainy." As hundreds arrived to visit Whitekirk's smouldering ruins, *The Scotsman* described it as "obviously the work of the suffragettes" and told readers that "the roofless and scorched walls stand as melancholy proof of the success of the outrage." From St Andrew's Square the Scottish Federation of Women's Suffrage Societies wrote urgently to the same paper to condemn the attack. Muriel Grant Wilson, organiser of its 64 branches, recorded the federation's "strong disapproval of, and deep regret at, the destruction of Whitekirk Church, one of our most notable national monuments." Lady Betty Balfour, sister of Lady Constance Lytton of the WSPU, voiced her "sorrow and indignation," and said that it was "not humanly conceivable" that any cause could be advanced by such an act. [6]

Despite a £100 reward for information, no arrests were made. The authorities, however, had been warned to expect a backlash once Moorhead's condition was known. The WSPU's ever-generous financier Janie Allan wrote to Thomas McKinnon Wood, the Secretary for Scotland, in effect admitting liability for the fire: "The burning of Whitekirk was the direct result of the forcible feeding of Ethel Moorhead in Calton Prison... Whitekirk would have been standing

The ruins of Whitekirk Church. Edinburgh WSPU did not deny involvement in the fire that led to its destruction.

today had forcible feeding not been introduced to Scottish prisons." In the women's eyes it was a necessary lesson in equality – a barbaric medieval torture introduced, a precious medieval church forfeited. Allan added an undisguised threat regarding the imminent arrival of the king and queen in Scotland. She told McKinnon Wood that the royal visit would "present many opportunities in protests of a memorable and disastrous nature" and it seemed to her a pity "to enter on a course calculated to entail such serious consequences." [7]

The anger over Ethel Moorhead's treatment continued. In Edinburgh, a window was smashed at the Scottish Prison Commissioners' office in Rutland Square. Wrapped around the missile was a paper with the words, "Defiance! To protest against the brutality and cowardice of the Prison Commissioners, who are forcibly feeding a woman who is giving her life to free her fellow women." In mid-March, James Devon, the Commission's senior doctor, was struck several times with a horsewhip by Jean Lambie of Edinburgh WSPU

Another contemporary postcard showing the damage to the historic church.

as he approached the entrance to Duke Street Prison in Glasgow. Lambie was bundled into the building, but the doctor refused to charge her. Devon boasted after the incident: "She said I was afraid to appear in court. I told her I was not afraid, but was too busy to waste time in prosecuting a daft woman." 8.

On March 9, Thomas McKinnon Wood defended the forcible feeding taking place in Edinburgh. Called to make a Commons' statement, the Glasgow MP said Moorhead was undergoing a sentence of eight months for breaking into a house with intent to set fire to it, and that she was suspected of being concerned in other fires which had taken place since her previous release. Under these circumstances, he said, it was, "evidently undesirable to liberate her and she was forcibly fed." He denied the treatment had caused her illness. He insisted her condition was brought about "by her own action." 9.

Wood was suggesting that the decision to forcibly feed Scotland's best-known suffragette was based on offences of which she was only suspected. The Scottish Secretary's basis for such a decision centred on the police view that the Edinburgh militant had been responsible for the firing of three

Perthshire mansions on February 4 – conspicuously the day Lloyd George was due to speak in Glasgow.

One of the houses, Aberuchill Castle, two miles west of Comrie, was the property of the English cotton merchant George Dewhurst. The House of Ross, a large mansion nearby, was owned by Douglas Maclagan, an Edinburgh stockbroker whose home in the capital was in Eton Terrace. A shortage of water resulted in its total loss. Allt-an-Fhionn, near Crieff, was the country home of Mrs Stirling Boyd, vice-president of the Edinburgh branch of the Anti-Suffrage League. Only its outhouses escaped demolition. This prompted Marjory Mackenzie of the League to write to *The Scotsman* condemning the "dastardly incendiarism" and calling its alleged perpetrators "miserable, hysterical, hired mercenaries." Letters also peppered *The Scotsman* deriding the old Edinburgh National Society for not denouncing the arsonists. This drew further contributions pointing out that the ENSWS had repudiated the tactics of the WSPU so often that it hardly required repeating. In fact, police in Perth had issued a warrant for Moorhead's arrest in connection with the fires without, it seems, having any evidence whatsoever that she was in the area at the time. 10.

Moorhead was described in prison files as "five feet six inches tall, very dark hair, brown eyes, wears pince-nez, oblong face, receding chin, slim build, stooping shoulders." She was released from prison under the Cat and Mouse Act on a 12-day licence and sought sanctuary with Dr Grace Cadell in Leith Walk, where she slowly recovered. On February 26, the Chief Constable of Leith wrote to David Crombie of the Prison Commissioners to tell him that "a special watch" was being kept on the property "day and night." She was due to return to Calton after her licence expired. She did not, having escaped from Dr Cadell's home using a disguise and "false curls" provided by Fanny Parker. She was never caught again. Piling irony upon irony, a new Perth street has been named in Ethel Moorhead's honour on the site of a young offenders' institution – and overlooking the surviving prison block where four of the five Scottish suffragettes fed by force underwent the procedure. 11.

As matters transpired, the veterans of the Edinburgh National Society had no intention of muddying the clear blue water between themselves and the militants. They spoke from a position of progress, with the ENSWS membership now in excess of 1000 and an additional 1500 supporters enrolled as 'friends'. Such numbers provide an indication of the level of non-militant support at a time when the Edinburgh WSPU and WFL could muster perhaps 100-200 activists in the city, though no membership details survive. This was not lost on Sarah Mair, who roused the ENSWS yearly gathering in February 1914 with a resolution leaving no-one in any doubt of the society's view: "That this annual meeting, while expressing deep dissatisfaction with the Government on the question of Women's Suffrage, desires to state in the most emphatic terms its reprobation of the action of the Women's Social and Political Union in advocating militant methods, which the meeting believes to be altogether unjustifiable and doing incalculable harm to the Suffrage cause." 12.

Women such as S. E. S. Mair who had spent their adult lives campaigning for equality, found militancy deeply upsetting and counter-productive. Dr Elsie Inglis, another with long years of service with the ENSWS, shared Mair's view, writing to *The Scotsman* on February 14: "Nothing does more harm than these wicked and indefensible acts...after every outburst I get letters from our secretaries from one end of Scotland to the other saying the same thing, viz, that people will not come to our meetings...and that the spirit of antagonism aroused makes it almost impossible to carry on the work. Your readers ought to know that practically the whole of the suffrage movement in this country is constitutional. There are 48 separate societies and only two are militant. The National Union alone numbers 51,000 subscribed members." The letter went unchallenged, probably out of respect for Inglis' pioneering role in medical education and training.

The ENSWS was not alone in denouncing militancy. At the Scottish Women's Liberal Federation annual meeting in Edinburgh in early March 1914, Isabella McKinnon Wood, wife of the Secretary for Scotland, proposed a motion recording the "indignant repudiation of the violent and criminal acts

Christabel and Emmeline Pankhurst, who laid down the WSPU's policy and direction, shown on a contemporary 'retouched' Press photograph.

Flora Drummond, pictured in Edinburgh as the WSPU 'General'. The image was later issued locally as a postcard.

committed in professed support of women's suffrage as wrong in themselves and injurious to the cause." And yet a counter-motion reaffirmed the organisation's support for female enfranchisement and urged the government to adopt women's suffrage as part of its parliamentary programme. It was carried by 110 to 86. The grassroots of the Liberal Party remained largely supportive of the women's cause, if not their methods. 13.

Members of such organisations found themselves drawn to the United Suffragists, a new group which emerged from London in early 1914. It drew its membership from constitutionalists who wanted to do a bit more, and from militants who believed things had gone too far. There were many, too, who despaired of the Pankhurst leadership, which by this time was fragmenting. Adela was about to be banished by her mother and elder sister Christabel to Australia. (She was duly seen off by her friend, the Edinburgh suffragette Helen Archdale.) Sylvia had launched the East London Federation of Suffragettes, after which her mother and elder sister threw her out of the WSPU. Christabel herself, as well as Annie Kenney, were in and out of hiding. At times it seemed as if the entire organisation was being carried by Mrs Pankhurst alone, despite her frailties. The United Suffragists was open to both men and women and had the backing of Emmeline and Frederick Pethick-Lawrence and several leading suffragists, including Evelina Haverfield, Maud Arncliffe Sennett, Beatrice Harraden and Dr Louisa Garrett Anderson. It also found work for Mary Phillips. It opened a small office in Edinburgh at 50 Frederick Street.

On March 9, Emmeline Pankhurst was at the centre of an extraordinary disturbance as 4000 gathered in Glasgow to hear an address by the weakened WSPU leader. Mrs Pankhurst was then at large on licence. She thumbed her nose at the authorities by agreeing to be the principal speaker in Glasgow, which led everyone to expect an attempt to re-arrest her. The authorities did not disappoint. The evening before, she wrote to her friend Ethel Smyth from the 'Scotch Manse' that was sheltering her: "Here I am, in time for the Glasgow meeting tomorrow...there is now a Scotch bodyguard, and they are eager for the fray." And when Mrs Pankhurst quietly took her place on the platform she was given a tremendous ovation, thousands of women rising and cheering. The police were determined to stop her speaking – and the WSPU was spoiling for a fight. "The Bodyguard, dressed in white, sat on the stage innocently nursing their Indian clubs beneath their skirts."

Dozens were injured as the group of specially-trained women battled hand-to-hand with 150 policemen. In one of the most violent incidents of the British campaign, women were thrown to the floor and struck with batons. Flowerpots and chairs were cast as missiles and hands were left bloodied by strands of barbed wire concealed beneath the platform fringe. At the height of the battle Janie Allan fired blank shots from a pistol. Inspector Walker of Glasgow Police recorded that the Scotch Bodyguard "fought like tigers." But another eyewitness, Leonard Gow, described the baton-wielding police laying out "in all directions, hitting and felling women," and said the scene "must have made the blood of every true man boil with indignation and shame." 14.

As the fracas continued, Emmeline Pankhurst was overpowered and dragged away by detectives, weakened, badly shaken and under arrest. Women stormed out of the hall in a furious rage. Nearby windows were smashed, and as a group of suffragists neared the police station in George Square, missiles were procured and launched at its windows. Mrs Pankhurst was held overnight in the same office, where she refused to take food or drink. From Glasgow she was taken to Coatbridge Station, where it had been arranged to stop the Aberdeen to London express. There, Mrs Pankhurst and the Scotland Yard officers boarded the train without fuss.

Emmeline Pankhurst's 'capture' led to an outpouring of militant action across the country. A timber-yard was destroyed at Bristol, Farington Hall mansion in Dundee was burned to the ground, as was a pavilion at Birmingham. Properties were fired in the Midlands, and two serious farm fires occurred at Nottingham. Birmingham Cathedral had to close for several weeks, owing to large, threatening messages in white paint. The Home Secretary's house was attacked in the night and 18 of its windows broken. Six women were arrested,

one giving her name in court as 'Boadicea'. The most striking protest, on the morning following the arrest, was Mary Richardson's hatchet attack on Velásquez's Rokeby Venus at the National Gallery. Her action caused a sensation. Questions were asked in the Commons and leading London galleries were hurriedly closed as panic set in across the art world.

Pankhurst's arrest also led to a great 'indignation' meeting in Edinburgh's Synod Hall. Over 1800 angry women heard fighting speeches by Flora Drummond and Barbara Wylie, who had attended the 'Battle of Glasgow' the previous night. Loud cries of 'Shame' punctuated the air as they described the scenes and the hand-to-hand fighting. Drummond explained why women like her were prepared to go to prison again and again: "The bulk of the people up and down the country are in favour of votes for women, but they don't like militancy. We want you to hate it, to loathe it, and rise up and put a stop to it by getting votes for women. We are not an entertaining society; but we are a society to make things intolerable, so that the average man in the street will say, 'For Heaven's sake give the women what they want, and let's have peace'." 15.

Elsewhere in the city, a number of churches became the target of demonstrations and disruptions. On March 3, a carved screen in front of the chancel at St John's Episcopal Church in Princes Street was defaced by a knife or chisel, and portions cut away. Suffragettes were blamed. The church was put under watch and its historic centre roped off. On March 15, the morning service at the Tron Kirk was interrupted by half a dozen women. Four rose in one part of the church, two in another and began chanting, "God save Emmeline Pankhurst and Mary Richardson." The incident was allowed to pass.

Edinburgh suffragists also directed their attention to the services at St Giles. On March 22, women stood to chant for Emmeline Pankhurst's release just before the sermon. They were requested to leave, but remained seated. Unknown to them, several plain-clothes police officers were in the cathedral's congregation, forewarned of the possibility of a protest. Seven women were

Maude Edwards, in white, in a photograph probably taken by a police surveillance camera as she left Perth Prison. (Courtesy of National Records Scotland)

arrested. On March 26, the women appeared at Edinburgh City police court on a charge of breach of the peace. They were named as Onah Ni Ceailaig, Marion Downie, Alexei Turner, Emma Stanley, Marjorie Macfarlane, Janet Wallace and Caroline Brown. It is not known if these were their real names. All pleaded not guilty, but at this appearance, they lodged an objection to the relevancy of the charge on the grounds that it raised a question of civil and ecclesiastical rights, and should have been dealt with by the Church Courts, and that the offence, if proved, constituted only a breach of the Scots Statute of 1587 against disorder in church, and not an offence in common law.

The objection was thrown out and on April 1 the seven women appeared again at the central police court. Before the case was called, the courtroom had to be closed to the public due to the public benches being filled by "well-dressed women" – and the 30 police officers scattered among them. The charges stated that the women conducted themselves in a disorderly manner, chanted or shouted, interrupted the Rev Edwin Davidson and the Rev Gordon Stott, disturbed the congregation and thus committed a breach of the peace. The Session Clerk gave evidence that the accused, at the close of the intercessory prayer, chanted 'God Save Emily Pankhurst'. The court also heard from Jean Lambie of Edinburgh WSPU. She denied that any offence had taken place and said that the morning service had proceeded as normal.

All seven women were found guilty. The magistrate, Baillie Richardson, imposed a penalty of £5 caution for the women's good behaviour for six months, with the alternative of 10 days' imprisonment. That night, the Women's Social and Political Union met in the Oddfellows' Hall to protest against the outcome. Another WSPU meeting in the Queen's Hall, attended by 400 women, brought laughter as Flora Drummond wondered aloud if the St Giles' clergyman had objected to the competition. The women lodged an appeal against their convictions and were allowed their liberty. The appeal was due before the High Court of Justiciary in September, but no more was said of the matter as the country then faced a greater challenge: war in Europe. 16.

Acts of militant protest continued throughout the summer of 1914. On May 21, an attempt was made to damage Rosehall United Free Church in Edinburgh. Newspaper reports claimed an explosion was caused by a "bomb" made from a piece of hollow iron filled with gunpowder and placed against the wall of the building. Glass in one window was smashed. "The work is believed to be that of Suffragettes," concluded the *Press and Journal*. Then, two days later, attacks on works of art, which had been a feature of militant activity in London, were adopted in Edinburgh for the first time when Sir John Lavery's portrait of King George V in the Royal Scottish Academy was targeted by a woman. She was seen to approach the half-length portrait and strike two heavy blows on the canvas. She was then seized by several people and did not resist.

News of the "outrage" spread quickly, and a large crowd gathered outside the RSA's landmark columns in Princes Street. The 'culprit' was escorted to the central police station in the High Street. Beyond stating that her name was Maude Edwards, she declined to say anything more, other than exaggerating her age by claiming she was 75. She was described as around 25 to 28. Later in the day she was released on bail. Back at the Royal Scottish Academy, the large gallery was closed while the damaged picture was removed. The painting had been protected by glass, which had been smashed. There was a ragged four-inch gash on the king's left breast, below his medals and decorations. There was also a mark on his blue sash, the result apparently of the second blow.

Maude Edwards appeared at Edinburgh Sheriff Court amid extraordinary scenes. The court was already filled to capacity, but it was significant that men were accommodated on one side of the room, and women on the other. The 'wisdom' of the move was demonstrated when cheering, clapping and stamping of feet began as soon as Edwards appeared. As the noisy welcome continued, Sheriff-Principal Maconochie ordered the women out of the court. Forty policemen materialised for the task, and the women did them the honour of putting up a struggle. It took four officers to remove Grace Cadell. Three cheers rang out for the accused as the women were bundled out.

Edwards gave her address as the WSPU office at 27 Frederick Street. The charge stated that she had "wilfully and maliciously struck and cut with a hatchet and damaged a portrait of King George by John Lavery RSA." When asked to answer the indictment, Edwards shouted, "I will not be tried. I am not going to listen to you or anyone whatever." The sheriff responded, "I take this as a plea of not guilty."

From that moment, Edwards began a running commentary in a loud voice, and nothing would induce her to be quiet. When the 15 jury men had filed in and were seated, she bawled, "What are you up there for? We don't care a scrap for you. You are all sworn liars." She shouted down the Procurator Fiscal and made it impossible for the jury to hear answers from witnesses. One newspaper was mesmerised: "She never ceased shouting and it mattered not whether she was talking common-sense or nonsense – it was mostly the latter." The judge found he could hear nothing and had to move his chair nearer the witness stand. It was also impossible for the Press to follow the case, so journalists amused themselves by listening to what Edwards was saying and were often convulsed with laughter.

Edwards had no defence witnesses and the jury, without retiring, rushed to return a guilty verdict. Maconochie ended the comedy by sentencing her to three months, to which she responded that she would not care if she was sentenced to 50 years. She was removed from the court, still shouting, and taken out of the building by the back door, leading out to the Cowgate. Maude Edwards had had her day in court. Now she faced the degrading, painful and strength-sapping procedure of forcible feeding. 17.

On June 15, in one of the last acts of militancy before the outbreak of war, suffragettes were accused of damaging four greens on the 18-hole Braids Hills Golf Course in Edinburgh, and two on its 9-hole course. *The Scotsman* reported that the greens were "hacked apparently by a trowel," and directed blame towards local militants: "A pair of ladies' gloves was found. Suffragette literature was scattered about the course." The alleged attack was described at a Town Council meeting the following day as "a poor return for the

Perth Prison – where four suffragettes were forcibly fed.

sympathetic attitude of the Council to the suffrage movement." There was no response from Frederick Street.

A few days later Edinburgh Fire Brigade was called to a blaze at a large woodyard occupied by Walkinshaw & Co, the Annandale Street timber merchants. The Central, Stockbridge and London Road stations turned out. A search was said to have discovered three bottles containing oil and a piece of oil-saturated cloth. A bag was also found, apparently having been dropped while its owner was making a hurried exit. It was presumed to have been used to carry the bottles for a premeditated attack. Two suffrage

leaflets were found with a copy of *The Suffragette* nearby. This amounted to incontrovertible evidence that the "outrage" was the work of the militants, reported the *Edinburgh Evening News*. No arrests were made and there were no claims of responsibility. [18]

The summer of 1914, however, was dominated by the Scottish Secretary's decision to begin the forcible feeding of four hunger-striking prisoners at Perth Prison. The Scottish authorities in 1909 had won considerable praise for resisting Home Office pressure to force-feed hunger strikers, despite official records showing their apparent willingness to do so. By the summer of 1914 only one woman – Ethel Moorhead – had faced the ordeal. But in June that year, at the height of the burnings and bombings, and embarrassed by the failings of the Cat and Mouse Act, HM Prison Perth was selected as the new centre for the controversial procedure.

The Napoleonic penitentiary – still a frontline prison – was to be the location of all but one of the artificial feedings carried out in Scotland. Why Perth was chosen was a question asked in the House of Commons. The Secretary for Scotland's chilling answer served only to heighten concerns: "We have doctors there who are thoroughly skilled in the matter of forcible feeding." In fact, it was entirely due to the presence of Dr Ferguson Watson, by then medical officer at the Criminal Lunatic Asylum in Perth, and the only Scottish prison physician willing to carry out the controversial procedure. It was Watson who had eventually overseen Ethel Moorhead's earlier force feeding in Edinburgh, supported by a government which continued to believe the 'treatment' fulfilled a dual purpose: it acted as a deterrent, as well as a clever remedy to prevent women dying.

Edinburgh teacher Arabella Scott, who had been sentenced to nine months for planning to burn down the Kelso racecourse stand in 1913, was the first. At the end of that year she had been returned on licence to Calton Jail to continue her sentence. And while her co-accused Edith Hudson and Elizabeth Thomson had simply 'vanished,' and Donald McEwan had been released, so began a spell of months when, after being released under the Cat and Mouse

Act a few times, and then re-arrested a few times, and imprisoned a few times more – and being protected in Edinburgh by a WSPU bodyguard of 30 young members – Arabella Scott was eventually transferred to Perth Prison on 20 June 1914, where she had the unenviable distinction of being the first prisoner there to be fed by force.

Scott's treatment was instructed via a note from the Under-Secretary of State for Scotland to the Prison Commissioners: "It may be desirable to begin forcible feeding without delay...my own view is that this is a case for forcible feeding." Confirmation to the Secretary of State that Arabella Scott had been "artificially fed by the mouth" on June 21, was provided by the Prison Commissioners the following day. In fact, she had been fed three times during her first 24 hours in Perth. [19.]

She later recalled the harrowing details of the procedure... "The doctor greased the tube and inserted the gag. Then I would close my eyes and pray that I should have no feelings of resentment or anger towards those who caused me pain. I always dreaded the insertion of the tube, which was accompanied by dry retching and choking sensations. Often, as the tube was withdrawn, I ejected a considerable quantity of the stuff. On the removal of the gag, my head was seized, my jaws and lips held tightly together. Sometimes voluntarily, sometimes involuntarily, the food would be returned into my mouth and, unable to escape, would burst through my nose. Then my nose would be pinched and I was ordered to swallow it again. I wouldn't, and struggled for breath. Then they would say, 'We will let you breathe when we see you going purple.' From time to time, by a sudden wrench, I would free my head for a second or two and bring up a quantity of the food, which would pour over my face and eyes and hair." [20.]

Ethel Moorhead, who knew the horrors of forcible feeding, pleaded with the governor of Perth Prison on her friend's behalf: "I have heard that Arabella Scott has been sent to Perth Prison. I am in many ways thankful that she is in your care, for I know you will not countenance such practices. But should you not have the moral courage to oppose and prevent forcible feeding, then

I beg of you to have the courage always to be present during the operation and to satisfy yourself that it is carried out with the least possible cruelty." [21.]

The Secretary for Scotland later told the House of Commons that Scott had been "artificially fed by the mouth." She had offered some resistance, but had never been strapped down. He added that her state of health on release was good. She had gained a few pounds in weight, he told MPs. Arabella Scott contradicted this. Writing to the *Perthshire Advertiser* she said her agony was prolonged in Perth in an attempt by the authorities to force her to give an undertaking to break her allegiance to the WSPU. This she had refused to do.

Scott spent long periods in isolation and visitors were not allowed. Her mother and sister Muriel in Edinburgh were repeatedly denied access by the Prison Commissioners. A request to visit by the WSPU's Dr Grace Cadell was declined and Dr Dorothea Smith of Glasgow, one of 79 women doctors from a total of 118 who had written to *The Times* calling forcible feeding 'unwise and inhumane,' also protested at the treatment which was believed to be under way in Perth. Letters Arabella Scott wrote to her sister Muriel, a teacher at Dr Bell's School in Great Junction Street, Leith, and mother Harriet in Liberton, are marked 'Undelivered' in prison files, by order of the Commissioners. One she wrote to Muriel poignantly tries to reassure her family... "I am confined to bed, not allowed to write. Tell mother not to worry too much..." It was never sent. Muriel's moving appeals to the prison continued, one telegram in June 1914 pleading, "Please may I see my sister..." [22.]

When Scott tried to tell her mother she was confined to bed, she was not exaggerating her situation: "All my clothes were taken off and eight wardresses shoved me on to a bed. They put a sheet over me and held me down by the ankles, by the knees, by the hips and by the shoulders. Two doctors and eight wardresses did their damnable task in my stripped and naked condition, partly covered by a sheet." [23.]

Pleas for information on her daughter's location by Scott's widowed mother to the Prison Commissioners were ignored until, on July 22, Harriet Scott complained that, "If my daughter had been a murderer I would have known

Leith teacher Muriel Scott, who pleaded for information on her sister, Arabella, and led huge protests outside the gates of Perth Prison. (Courtesy of the late Frances Wheelhouse)

her whereabouts. I, her mother, demand to know where you are hiding her." Only then was she told her daughter was held at Perth.

Arabella Scott resisted forcible feeding every inch of the way. Her state of mind during the procedure can only be imagined. She was described in medical reports as "highly excited" and "emotional," but at other times "depressed" and "dour." On one occasion Dr Watson wrote to the Prison Commissioners: "In front of several witnesses and myself she said that she would shoot me when she got out." [24].

Scott was released on July 26 feeling more militant than ever. "To try to force a person to yield her opinions under such pain is torture and nothing else. The only effect it has on me is to strengthen my principles." On the recommendation of the Dundee WSPU organiser Olive Walton, she was taken to recover at a private house in the Kinnoull area of Perth. [25].

Arabella Scott endured five harrowing weeks of force feeding in Perth, while her sister Muriel, a former prisoner herself, led thousands of sympathisers in slow, dignified processions to the prison gates in solemn demonstrations of support.

Histories of the women's movement generally accept that the London suffragette Olive Wharry had the dubious honour of the longest period of forcible feeding – 32 days in total. This was also the view of Sylvia Pankhurst in her memoir. Arabella Scott endured artificial feeding by stomach tube from 9pm on June 21 to the day of her release, July 26 – certainly 35 and possibly 36 days. The Edinburgh teacher had sustained the longest period of hunger strike and forcible feeding of any woman in British history. Arabella Scott remained proudly 'a suffragette' until her death at the age of 94.

The second prisoner taken to Perth for artificial feeding was 'Frances Gordon', an alias for the suffragette Frances/Florence Graves, who had been sentenced in Glasgow at the end of June to one year's imprisonment for breaking into Springhall, near Rutherglen, with intent to set fire to the property. The prisoner "fully admitted it," the judge was told, while he ducked missiles thrown at him from the public gallery. In Gordon's case, the Secretary for Scotland said in reply to questions in the House that it had been necessary to "exercise some restraint" while force feeding was carried out because, in his words, Gordon had been drugged and was vomiting when she arrived in prison, and this had prevented her retaining food. 'Frances Gordon' also wrote to the Press saying that the politician's statement was completely devoid of truth and that she was in perfect health when she was admitted to prison.

Gordon, described in prison files as a little woman aged about 40, was fed through the rectum 10 times over four days in Perth before being released on July 3 under licence into the care of Dr Mabel Jones, who described her as looking like a famine victim: "Her skin brown, her face bones standing out, her eyes half-shut, her voice a whisper, her hands quite cold, her pulse a thread..." To this, McKinnon Wood responded that Gordon was "absolutely fine" when she left Perth prison. He added that she had stepped into a cab, caught the train to Glasgow and "had enjoyed the scenery." The following week two suffragettes attacked him as he left his London home.

When news of the feeding into Gordon's bowels was revealed to a hushed House of Commons, a storm of protest broke across the country. Typical of the condemnation was an editorial in the *Daily Herald* of July 11: "The horrible story, told in our columns and in Suffrage journals, of the iniquitous treatment dealt out to Miss Gordon has roused very considerable indignation everywhere, and unless an end is put to this infamous conduct of the prison officials, the records of the present British administration of prisons will be the blackest of any country in the world. Torture is torture, whether it is inflicted by means of the thumb-screw or the rack, but there is no torture quite so bad as that inflicted on people for their supposed good."
Frances Gordon's scandalous treatment and ruined health, made public by Dr Jones, unquestionably helped to turn the tide of sympathy in favour of the women in Perth, where a street is now named 'Frances Gordon Road'. 26.

The third woman forcibly fed at Perth prison was Maude Edwards, serving her three-month sentence for slashing the portrait of the king in the Royal Scottish Academy. After trial in Edinburgh she had been moved to Perth on July 3. Although Edwards carried a doctor's certificate stating she had a heart condition, Dr Watson took it upon himself to declare her fit for forcible feeding. On July 10, she successfully applied to be "liberated under licence" under the Cat and Mouse Act as the medical officer had told her that "excitement is injurious to my health." After an undertaking to refrain from militancy, Edwards was released on July 14 having endured six days of forced feeding by mouth tube. A striking contemporary photograph shows her being escorted from prison by two friends. She has been dressed all in white, with a suffragette sash, and carries flowers. Yet it is also a sobering reminder of what these women were willing to put themselves through. 27.

The woman arrested for trying to burn down Robert Burns' historic birthplace in Alloway on July 8 gave her name as Janet Arthur. But she was better known as Frances Parker, the hard-working, vocal and popular former organiser of Edinburgh and Glasgow WSPU – and the militant twice run out of Perth the previous year following a cricket pavilion fire. A night watchman had been placed at the Ayrshire cottage precisely to deter suffragettes. He apprehended one woman on the premises, but was unable to stop another running off into the early morning darkness. Ethel Moorhead recalled in *Incendiaries*, "On one dangerous militant duty and adventure when she [Parker] and her comrade were surprised and about to be arrested she allowed herself to be taken that her comrade might escape." Moorhead, once again, was Parker's accomplice. Moorhead also recalled an escapade with her friend in early July 1914 which the London historian Elizabeth Crawford has recently linked to an attempt to set fire to Carmichael Parish Church (now Cairngryffe Parish Church) in Lanarkshire.

Parker had already served terms in Holloway and Aberdeen when she became the fourth and final suffragette to be forcibly fed in Perth. Arabella Scott, in an adjacent cell, was by then on her third week of the procedure. Parker had adopted a hunger and thirst strike in Ayr prison on July 8 while police inquiries were being carried out and was moved to Perth on July 13 – still without facing a trial. Despite Janie Allan warning the authorities that Parker was Lord Kitchener's niece and that her death in custody would create

Frances Parker, as 'Janet Arthur', is escorted from Ayr Sheriff Court in July 1914. (Courtesy of National Records Scotland)

a national outcry, Dr Ferguson Watson began her forcible feeding the following morning, and repeated the treatment via a nasal tube seven times over the next four days. "Six wardresses held me down and one of them reached forward and slapped my face, with, I suppose, the approval of the doctor, as he said nothing. The assistant doctor held my head in a most painful grip. Dr Watson then tried to force my teeth open with the steel gag and said that if he broke a tooth it would be my own fault. As he was unable to open my mouth he called for the nasal tube. He tried to force it up one side, but with all his strength could not force a passage. He succeeded in forcing it down the other nostril, and left it hanging there while he went out of the room. As it was extremely painful, I asked the assistant to remove it, but he only laughed."

Continuing to react badly to food poured into her by stomach tube, Parker then faced the ignominy, pain and shock of being twice fed by the rectum. She was released from this humiliating, painful ordeal on July 16, the prison medical officer reporting that her condition was "satisfactory." In fact, she was in a state of collapse. A later examination showed that the woman who would shortly lead one of Britain's greatest wartime movements and be decorated twice, had swelling in her genitals and had been forcibly fed in what she called a "grosser and more indecent way" – an attempt to access her vaginal passage. She recalled, "The way this was done was so unnecessarily painful that I screamed with agony."

Janie Allan was so concerned that she telegrammed the Perth Prison Governor on July 14: "Much obliged if you will inform me if Miss Arthur is still alive." The reply from the prison commissioners was a terse "Arthur is still alive." Frances Parker was released under licence and taken wrapped in blankets to an Edinburgh nursing home, from which she promptly escaped.

The war to come would see her become Deputy Controller of the WAAC in Boulogne, commandant-in-chief of the Woman Signallers Corps, win the military OBE and be twice Mentioned in Despatches for bravery. Yet Fanny Parker had been in Perth prison for 10 days and forcibly fed for three days by nasal and stomach tubes, by the rectum and once by an attempt via the vagina – incredibly, all without being convicted of any crime. 28.

As the country became aware of the procedures being carried out there, hundreds of suffragists descended on Perth and kept up protests by day and dignified but noisy vigils outside the prison gates at night. Every bed in the town was reportedly taken up. Fifty extra police from Glasgow and more troops were drafted in as a precaution. The prison governor reported to Perth's Chief Constable that between 2000 and 3000 women were outside the gates, but that there had been no trouble. The *Perthshire Advertiser* concluded on July 18, "The city may really be said to be in the hands of the militants. Not only are they maintaining a close siege of the prison, but they are to be heard and seen at practically every turning in the streets." The paper noted that the prison had been famous in the past as a military prison, a convict prison, a lunacy prison, and now young women had "glorified it and immortalised it as a Suffragette Prison."

By this time, mid-1914, a dozen unoccupied private properties in Scotland had been fired, allegedly by suffragettes. One magnificent gothic church – Whitekirk – had suffered a similar fate. Two sports facilities had been burned to the ground. Three Scottish railway stations and timber yards had been engulfed by flames and there had been explosions at Dudhope Castle, Dundee, Glasgow Botanic Garden and Edinburgh's Royal Observatory. Postmen had been injured, church services interrupted and artworks damaged. There had even been an audacious attempt to cut off Glasgow's water supply.

Into all this confusion and public alarm came the unsuspecting king and queen on official visits to Edinburgh, Glasgow, Dundee and Perth in July 1914. Predictably, elaborate security precautions were taken for the entire Scottish tour. Known suffragettes were watched and conspicuously followed at close quarters. Rooftops were searched and public buildings guarded. After a decade of protest, the collective trepidation and authorities gripped by fear were possibly the greatest compliments that could have been paid to the women's campaign.

The royal couple arrived in Edinburgh by train on July 6, to be taken by car to Holyrood Palace. Two women took up a position at the east end of

A contemporary postcard showing the huge crowd in Princes Street waiting to welcome the royal couple.

Rutland Street, immediately opposite the exit from the station. Some handbills fluttered down to the road, and as the royal carriage passed over them, the king reportedly looked to where detectives were detaining the women. The suffragists were surrounded by a hostile crowd, and about two dozen policemen formed a protective cordon around them. They gave the names of Lock and Owen, which were likely false. No charges were brought against them. Then, when the king and queen were making their way from Holyrood to a service at St Giles' Cathedral, a message about forcible feeding wrapped around a rubber ball was thrown into their carriage. It landed on the queen's lap, and she brushed it aside. Olive Walton of Dundee WSPU was taken into custody, but liberated after the royal party had left the cathedral.

As the royal tour progressed, suffragettes were blamed for a small explosion at Rosslyn Chapel. A window suffered slight damage, and the building remained open to visitors. Suffragette newspapers were found nearby, but no arrests were made. The chapel had closed temporarily the previous March after 'threats' from militants. 29.

EDINBURGH NATIONAL SOCIETY
FOR WOMEN'S SUFFRAGE
(N. U. W. S. S.)

Fiftieth Report

AT LAST!

Presented at the Annual Meeting held at 40 Shandwick Place,
April 5th, 1918

The Edinburgh National Society for Women's Suffrage issued a special report on its 50th birthday in 1918 – the year that some women won the right to the parliamentary vote.

The Suffragette, the newspaper of the WSPU, was by then in trouble. Its London office had been closed by police, its papers confiscated and its editorial staff arrested following attempts by the Home Office to suppress the title and intimidate its stockists. The switch of *The Suffragette* to a Manchester printer led to a further arrest, and an undertaking not to print the paper there. At that point it was suggested to print the newspaper in Scotland, as the rushed English restrictions did not apply north of the border. Both Helen Crawfurd and Annie Kenney recalled that it was sent to Tom Johnston's printing house in Glasgow, which produced *The Forward*. There is also a possibility, however, that it was published for a time in Edinburgh. On August 3, the *Edinburgh Evening News* reported "an unusual court case" in the city at which "a firm of Edinburgh printers" was fined £10 for printing *The Suffragette* without fixing the printer's imprint on the copies produced – the 'Printed and Published by...' line which every newspaper must carry by law. That week's issue of *The Suffragette* recommended that those who had difficulty obtaining a copy could write to the publishers at 65 Frederick Street – a further indication that the Scottish capital may have been responsible for a time for the WSPU paper's output. [30].

On July 8, just weeks from war, an extraordinary development brought the emergence in the Scottish capital of a completely new women's suffrage organisation. It was called the Edinburgh Franchise Club – and its guiding principle appears to have been to welcome anyone who was not a militant! Its leading lights were familiar to the campaign – Rosaline Masson of the Conservative and Unionist Women's Franchise Association, Sarah Siddons Mair of the Edinburgh National Society and Frances Simson of the Scottish University Women's Suffrage Union. Lady Betty Balfour presided over its opening meeting at 9 Melville Street on 4 November 1914. Given that all militancy had been abandoned by the WSPU and WFL at the start of the war in August, it was surprising that membership remained restricted to men and women who were "in favour of the extension of the franchise to women, but who are not militant in their methods working for it." By January, membership of the Edinburgh Franchise Club was stated to be 300. [31].

As matters transpired, the women's campaign stopped almost completely when the First World War broke out. On August 4, the first day of the conflict, Emmeline Pankhurst pledged the entire membership of the WSPU to the national effort, bringing to an end the brilliantly-orchestrated, if controversial, WSPU campaign. On the same day, Millicent Fawcett of the NUWSS announced the suspension of all political work and urged her 50,000 members to support the government: "Let us show ourselves worthy of citizenship, whether our claim to it be recognised or not." And she added, "Women, your country needs you." Only the Women's Freedom League kept its organisation intact and, while suspending militancy completely, continued its political campaign for votes. The government, meantime, had announced an amnesty for all suffragette prisoners, allowing women to be released from jails across the country. 32.

As the war began, *The Scotsman* reported that the old Edinburgh National Society for Women's Suffrage had "over 3000 adherents in the Edinburgh area." There were a great many pacificists among constitutionalist suffragists and several decided to leave the movement rather than support war work. Chrystal Macmillan, for example, resigned from the NUWSS executive to become secretary of the International Committee of Women for Permanent Peace. But the veteran campaigner Sarah Elizabeth Siddons Mair pledged the ENSWS to the war effort and its members threw themselves into the new challenge. By the end of August it had taken a shop at 106 George Street to be used as a Registration Bureau for classifying and distributing voluntary work. A register was kept of offers of help and workers were allocated to different relief agencies. The George Street bureau also accepted gifts for soldiers at the Front, books and magazines for the Navy, and comforts for the Belgian refugees who had begun to arrive in Scotland.

The ENSWS also worked with the Labour Exchange and various voluntary associations, such as the Red Cross and the Soldiers' and Sailors' Families Association. Large numbers of members began visiting the dependents of servicemen. Cooked food was distributed to the needy and classes for first aid and elementary nursing were started. Several ENSWS members had by then joined Dr Elsie Inglis' remarkable medical operation, soon to be known as the Scottish Women's Hospitals for Foreign Service, which provided female doctors, nurses and drivers on the Front. Its first unit served in Serbia; its second in France.

The WSPU also suspended all militant action, even though, just a week before the outbreak of hostilities, Muriel Scott was busily trying to form a WSPU branch in Perth and was looking for premises for it. In London, Emmeline Pankhurst urged members to wholeheartedly support the government and later changed the WSPU's name to The Women's Party. Its newspaper, *The Suffragette*, was retitled *Britannia*. Christabel returned from exile in Paris and travelled to America to try to persuade the United States to join the war. Flora Drummond toured Britain to promote recruitment and rouse the fighting spirit of the nation. The dramatic change in direction ill-suited many volunteers and Jean Lambie, of Edinburgh WSPU, became organising secretary of a breakaway organisation, The Suffragettes of the W.S.P.U., who aimed "entirely to disassociate themselves from the line Mrs Pankhurst has taken up since the outbreak of war." Instead, Lambie continued campaigning for votes. 33.

The four WSPU branches in Scotland – including the Frederick Street headquarters of Edinburgh WSPU – diverted their energies to war work. Former Edinburgh organiser Frances Parker became deputy controller of the Women's Army Auxiliary Corps in Boulogne. Her replacement at Frederick Street, Mary Allen, helped to establish the Women's Police Volunteers. Ethel Moorhead worked for the Women's Freedom League's National Service Organisation, which was formed in 1915 to put women workers in touch with employers.

Anti-suffragists also gave up their campaign. The Edinburgh League for Opposing Woman Suffrage opened an office at 10 Queensferry Street and from August 8 this was loaned to the Red Cross to be used as a clothing depot for The Soldiers' and Sailors' Families Association. The services of the League's staff were also placed at the disposal of the city's war effort.

Of the major British societies, only the Women's Freedom League continued the campaign for votes – and resumed its offer of speakers throughout Scotland. The League, however, also established the Women's Suffrage National Aid Corps in the first month of the war, which helped women who found themselves in financial difficulties through the conflict. Eunice Murray served on its national executive. The Edinburgh Suffrage Shop in Lothian Road was turned into a workroom for the war effort.

While engaged with these efforts, and continuing with their suspension of militant activity, the Women's Freedom League determinedly ensured that the suffrage flag still flew proudly above Edinburgh – and did so until votes were finally won.

References

1. The Suffragette, 20 March 1914; The Scotsman, 11 March 1914.
2. The Suffragette, 6 March 1914; NRS, HH16/40, Letter D. Crombie to the Under Secretary for Scotland, 21 February 1914; Report by Dr Sir Thomas Fraser, medical adviser to the Prison Commission for Scotland, 25 February 1914.
3. NRS, HH16/40, Dr James Devon's memorandum to Prison Commissioners, 26 February 1914; Dundee Evening Telegraph, 20 February 1914.
4. Leah Leneman, A Guid Cause (1991), p178; Sarah Pedersen, The Scottish Suffragettes and the Press (2017), p145; NRS, HH16/40, letter, Elizabeth Finlayson Gauld to Dr James Devon, 14 March 1914.
5. The Suffragette, 6 March 1914; NRS, HH6/40.
6. The Scotsman, 6 April 1914; Edinburgh Evening Dispatch, 26 February 1914.
7. NRS, HH55/336, letter, Janie Allan to the Scottish Secretary, 26 June 1914; The Scotsman, 27 February 1914.
8. The Scotsman, 26 February 1914; NRS, HH16/40, Dr Devon's precognition statement; Leneman (1991), p180.
9. Dundee Courier, 10 March 1914; Votes for Women, 13 March 1914.
10. The Scotsman, 11 February 1914.
11. NRS, HH16/40, Letter, Chief Constable, Leith Town Hall to Prison Commission secretary David Crombie, 26 February 1914.
12. Edinburgh Evening News, 28 February 1914.
13. Dundee Courier, 16 March 1914.
14. Emmeline Pankhurst, A Biography (2002), p253; Glasgow Herald, 10 March 1914; Leneman (1991), p184, Antonia Raeburn, The Militant Suffragettes (1973), p66.
15. The Suffragette, 20 March 1914; The Scotsman, 11 March 1914.
16. Edinburgh Evening News, 1 April 1914; The Scotsman, 8 May 1914.
17. Press & Journal, 23 May 1914; The Scotsman, 25 May 1914; Edinburgh Evening Times, 3 July 1914; Dundee Courier, 4 July 1914. The damaged portrait of King George V was not shown in public again until it was displayed in Edinburgh in 2018, to mark the centenary of the Representation of the People Act, which gave some women the vote.
18. Edinburgh Evening News, 6 July 1914; The Scotsman, 17 June 1914.
19. NRS, HH16/44, letter, John Lamb, Scottish Office, to Mr D. Crombie, secretary of Prison Commission, 19 June 1914.
20. NRS, HH16/44, Glasgow Herald article; The Suffragette, 7 August 1914.
21. NRS, HH16/44, letter, Ethel Moorhead to J. Grant, Governor HM Prison Perth, 25 June 1914.
22. NRS, HH16/44, copy letter (suppressed), Arabella to Muriel Scott, 21 July 1914; NRS, HH16/44, telegram, Muriel Scott to Dr James Devon, medical officer, Prison Commissioners, 24 June 1914.
23. Arabella Scott, My Murky Past (Frances Wheelhouse typescript).
24. NRS, HH16/44, correspondence from Dr H. Ferguson Watson, medical officer, HM Prison Perth, to D. Crombie, Secretary of the Prison Commissioners, 15 & 28 July 1914.
25. NRS, HH16/44, undated letter from Olive Walton to Governor, HM Prison Perth; Glasgow Herald, 28 July 1914.
26. Norman Watson, Dundee Suffragettes (2018), pp128-129; Daily Herald, 11 July 1914.
27. NRS, HH16/47, undated note from Maude Edwards to Prison Commissioners.
28. NRS, HH1643/6; Diane Atkinson, Rise Up Women! (2019), p505.
29. Daily Mirror, 13 July 1914.
30. The Suffragette, 7 August 1914; Edinburgh Evening News, 3 August 1914.
31. The Scotsman, 5 November 1914; Conservative & Unionist Women's Franchise Review, 1 January 1915.
32. Atkinson (2019), p37; David Morgan, Suffragists & Liberals (1975), p135.
33. Leneman (1991), p209.

RIGHT: The Scottish campaign continued to the outbreak of war in August 1914. (Courtesy of London Museum)

AFTERTHOUGHTS

*E*dinburgh is unique in the history of women's fight for the parliamentary vote. Nowhere outside London hosted National Processions with the exception of Edinburgh, which had two. Nowhere but Edinburgh had a 1000-strong non-militant society as well as law-breaking suffragettes in its own 'Votes for Women Club'. Nine women's suffrage organisations were based in the city, more than any other outside London. It was the first in Scotland to forcibly feed a hunger-striking prisoner, and an Edinburgh teacher faced this 'suffragette torture' for longer than any woman in British history.

The participatory activity described in the foregoing chapters provides compelling evidence of a practical involvement which contradicts the notion that all suffrage activity was 'imported' – or, as is often erroneously stated, that it was exclusively centred on events at Westminster. Edinburgh's women heckled politicians, held demonstrations and marches, broke the law to force arrests, smashed windows, fired letter-boxes and embarked on arson and bombings. Edith Hudson was jailed for leading a charge at Leith. Grace Cadell refused to pay government taxes. Flora Smith assaulted the Prime Minister. Arabella Scott tried to burn down a grandstand. Ethel Moorhead attacked an Edinburgh teacher. Agnes Macdonald, Lilias Mitchell, Jessie Methven and Florence McFarlane were London window-smashers. Cecilia Haig was beaten so badly that she was said to have died a suffragette 'martyr'. And, at the height of militancy, Edinburgh's citizenry awoke to the latest 'outrages' – a bomb at the Blackford Observatory, the destruction of Whitekirk church, a fire at Fettes College, a portrait of the King slashed at a city gallery – evidence of how far votes-for-women protests had come since the peaceful campaigning of the Victorian era.

For all that, it was shown that Edinburgh was more important to the development of the earlier phase of the struggle. By the mid-1800s, women involved in temperance, slavery and educational improvement saw the need for political influence. Parliamentary votes became increasingly important to the progress of such campaigns among the city's reforming societies and network of influential families. In 1867, Britain's second and Scotland's first women's suffrage society was formed in the city, and its hardworking members underpinned the momentous campaign for votes to come.

Despite great efforts, the Victorian movement brought the franchise no closer. The opposition the Liberal government mounted seems incomprehensible today, but it increasingly provoked furious and passionate protests, giving way to the widespread militancy which Edinburgh's women embraced from the beginning.

The Women's Social and Political Union's strategy was carefully stage-managed to gain the maximum impact and publicity. But escalating militancy drove women out of the WSPU as each action became more dramatic and violent than the last in the rush to attract headlines and win the propaganda war. The Pankhursts moved from fronting an organisation that enthused thousands of women in its early years to one whose autocratic barking of orders impeded the objectives on which it was founded – though a centralised WSPU was admirably resisted by Edinburgh and the organisation's three other branches in Scotland.

Meanwhile, constitutional suffragists were often at a loss over the forms of protest they should take. The Women's Freedom League was squeezed between two seemingly polarised positions: passive resistance, such as petitioning and protesting, and the disruptive tactics espoused by their sisters in the WSPU. Members of the public in Edinburgh often failed to distinguish between the two, and women from both organisations were roughly handled at meetings and demonstrations in the city's halls and green spaces. Generally, setting fire to public buildings and slashing paintings was not the WFL style and its volunteers steered away from arson and bombs. Some members, though, had less respect for plate-glass windows and, as matters transpired, the first Edinburgh suffragettes to be jailed were members of the League. The contribution of the Women's Freedom League is often overlooked in scholarly works. In charting what took place in Dundee, Glasgow and now Edinburgh, this series has tried to ensure the campaigning of its Scottish membership is no longer hidden from history. Moreover, it was shown that the League rubbed along well with the less peaceable WSPU – co-operation not evident elsewhere.

The guiding presence in Scotland of the non-militant Edinburgh National Society for Women's Suffrage propelled the evolution of the movement north of the border. Its importance to the early policy and direction of the British campaign is one of the key findings in this work. For half a century, it hosted the city's largest and most active cohort of suffragists, boasting by 1914 over 1000 members and 1500 supporters enrolled as 'friends.' As the decades unfolded, the ENSWS never strayed from constitutionalist policies. It stuck to its restrained guns and it is difficult to argue today that it was less effective for doing so, particularly when the burning of properties turned public opinion against the women's campaign. That said, headlines elsewhere boosted its profile as much as its own efforts to do so.

Men's support has also received insufficient attention from historians. The Edinburgh National Society realised from the outset that Members of Parliament, town councillors and other influential men were essential to its aims. In this respect, the city stood up to be counted – not least the working men of Leith who battled in the streets in support of their campaigning sisters.

While there is no evidence to show that Edwardian Edinburgh's working

Arabella Scott, who was forcibly fed longer than any other British suffragette, looks a picture of health in the 1950s. (Courtesy of London Museum)

205

Ethel Moorhead, who was imprisoned and forcibly fed in Edinburgh, now has a street named in her honour in Perth.

women played a significant part in the push for votes, many veteran suffragists were social activists and were aware of the domestic inequalities facing the female population – although how it was expressed sometimes appears condescending to a modern reader. Edinburgh pioneers such as Eliza Wigham and Mary Burton regarded improvements to women's everyday lives as equal in importance to the fight for political rights. The former ran a Penny Savings Bank for the poor, the latter was a friendly slum landlord.

This work also brings to prominence the names of suffragettes previously overlooked or lost to history – women such as Jessie Methven, Barbara Steel, Edith Hudson and Marion Grieve, all of whom willingly broke the law in the struggle for electoral equality. Over a dozen Edinburgh militants were jailed. It was important to record their deeds and sacrifice.

By the summer of 1914 there was growing sympathy with the women being artificially fed and condemnation of a government forced into a corner by the relentless militancy and the failure of its controversial 'Cat and Mouse' arrest and release policy. But with the WSPU careering from one increasingly desperate outrage to another, militancy also disaffected many existing and former supporters of radical tactics, notably in Scotland where several local organisers were controversially deposed by WSPU 'placewomen' from London. One-time Scottish WSPU organisers Helen Fraser and Teresa Billington Greig were among those to turn their backs on the organisation. The Edinburgh secretary Esson Maule also walked out, blaming the WSPU's "dangerous tactics." [1]

The First World War paused the suffragette revolution. But the Edinburgh women who petitioned and protested, who broke the law and went to prison, did so for a cause that was precious to them – and it is their story that fills this work.

References

1.   1. *Edinburgh Evening News, 26 August 1909.*

BIBLIOGRAPHY

Atkinson, Diane, *The Purple, White and Green: Suffragettes in London, 1906-1914*, Museum of London, 1992.

Atkinson, Diane, *Rise up Women!*, Bloomsbury, 2019.

Atkinson, Diane, *Votes for Women*, Cambridge University Press, 1988.

Baldwin, John, *Edinburgh, Lothian & Borders*, The Stationery Office, RCAHMS, 1997.

Balfour, Lady Frances, *Dr Elsie Inglis*, Hodder & Stoughton, 1920.

Bartley, Paula, *Votes for Women 1860-1928*, Hodder & Stoughton, 2001.

Breitenbach, Esther; Gordon, Eleanor, (Eds), *Out of Bounds, Women in Scottish Society 1800-1945*, Edinburgh University Press, 1992.

Brewster, Lynn M., *Suffrage in Stirling, The Struggle for Women's Votes*, Jameson Munro Trust, 2002.

Clark, Helen; Carnegie, Elizabeth, *She Was Aye Workin'; Memories of Tenement Women in Edinburgh and Glasgow*, White Cockade, 2003.

Crawford, Elizabeth, *The Women's Suffrage Movement in Britain and Ireland: A Regional Survey*, Routledge, 2006.

Crawford, Elizabeth, *The Women's Suffrage Movement: A Reference Guide 1866-1928*, Routledge, 1999.

Eustance, Claire; Ryan, Joan; Ugolini, Laura, (Eds), *A Suffrage Reader, Charting Directions in British Suffrage History*, Leicester University Press, 2000.

Ewan, Elizabeth; Innes, Sue; Reynolds, Sian, (Eds), *The Biographical Dictionary of Scottish Women*, Edinburgh University Press, 2006.

Fawcett, Millicent Garrett, *What I Remember*, T. Fisher Unwin, 1924.

Fraser, Helen, *Women and War Work*, G. Arnold Shaw, 1918.

Fulford, Roger, *Votes for Women*, Faber & Faber, 1958.

Gordon, Eleanor, *Women and the Labour Movement in Scotland, 1850-1914*, Clarendon, 1991.

Grant, James, *Old & New Edinburgh* (Vol III), Cassell, Petter, Galpin & Co, 1882.

Holton, Sandra, *Feminism and Democracy: Women's Suffrage and Reform Politics in Britain, 1900-1918*, Cambridge University Press, 2003.

Holton, Sandra, *Suffrage Days: Stories from the Women's Suffrage Movement*, Routledge, 1996.

Kelly, Ellen (Ed), *Edinburgh Women's Achievement Trail*, City of Edinburgh District Council's Women Committee, nd, c1995.

Kendler, Maureen, *Women in Britain 1850-1986*, Modern World History Evidence and Empathy, Sparticus Educational, 1987.

King, Elspeth, *The Hidden History of Glasgow's Women, The THENEW Factor*, Mainstream, 1993.

King, Elspeth, *The Scottish Women's Suffrage Movement*, People's Palace Museum, Glasgow, 1985.

Knox, William J., *Lives of Scottish Women: Women and Scottish Society, 1800-1980*, Edinburgh University Press, 2006.

Leneman, Leah, A Guid Cause, *The Women's Suffrage Movement in Scotland*, Aberdeen University Press, 1991 (also second edition, Hyperion Books, 1995).

Leneman, Leah, *The Scottish Suffragettes*, National Museum of Scotland, 2000.

Liddington, Jill; Norris, Jill, *One Hand Tied Behind Us: The Rise of the Women's Suffrage Movement*, Virago Press, 1978 and 1994.

Livingstone, Sheila, *Bonnie Fechters: Women in Scotland 1900-1951*, Scottish Library Association, 1994.

McDonald, Ian, *Vindication! A Postcard History of the Women's Movement*, McDonald-Bellow Publishing, 1989.

Mackenzie, Midge, *Shoulder to Shoulder: A Documentary*, Alfred A. Knopf, 1975.

Marlow, Joyce, *Suffragettes: The Fight for Votes for Women*, Virago Press, 2015.

Marlow, Joyce, (Ed), *Votes for Women, The Virago Book of Suffragettes*, Virago Press, 2001.

Mayhall, Laura E. Nym, *The Militant Suffrage Movement, Citizen & Resistance in Britain, 1868-1930*, Oxford University Press, 2003.

Morgan, David, *Suffragists and Liberals, The Politics of Women's Suffrage in Britain*, Blackwell, 1975.

Pankhurst, Christabel, *Unshackled, The Story of How We Won the Vote*, Hutchinson, 1959.

Pankhurst, Emmeline, *A Biography*, Routledge, London, 2002.

Pankhurst, Richard, *Sylvia Pankhurst, Artist and Crusader*, Paddington Press, 1979.

Pankhurst, Sylvia, *The Suffragette Movement*, Virago, 1977.

Peacock, John, *The Story of Edinburgh*, The History Press, 2017.

Pedersen, Sarah, *The Scottish Suffragettes and the Press*, Palgrave Macmillan, 2017.

Phillips, Melanie, *The Ascent of Women: A History of the Suffragette Movement and the ideas behind it*, Abacus, 2004.

Pugh, Martin, *The March of the Women: A Revisionist Analysis of the Campaign for Women's Suffrage, 1866-1914*, Oxford University Press, 2000.

Pugh, Martin, *The Pankhursts*, Penguin, 2001.

Raeburn, Antonia, *The Militant Suffragettes*, Michael Joseph, 1973.

Raeburn, Antonia, *The Suffragette View*, David & Charles, 1976.

Randall, Vicky, *Women & Politics: An International Perspective*, Macmillan, 1993 edition.

Richardson, Mary, *Laugh A Defiance*, Weidenfeld & Nicolson, 1953.

Smitley, Megan, *The Feminine Public Sphere, Middle-Class Women and Civic Life in Scotland, c1870-1914*, Manchester University Press, 2009.

Snellgrove, L. E., *Suffragettes and Votes for Women*, Longmans, 1966.

Tickner, Lisa, *The Spectacle of Women: Imagery of the Suffrage Campaign*, University of Chicago Press, 1988.

Tubb, Miles; McCaughie, John, *Edinburgh Memories*, The History Press, 2009.

Watson, Norman, *Dundee's Suffragettes – their remarkable struggle to win votes for women*, Dundee, 1990.

Watson, Norman, *Dundee's Suffragettes*, Percy Johnstone Publishing, 2018.

Watson, Norman, *Glasgow's Suffragettes*, Percy Johnstone Publishing, 2023.

Watson, Norman, *Suffragettes and the Post*, Dundee, 2010.

Webb, Simon, *The Suffragette Bombers; Britain's Forgotten Terrorists*, Pen and Sword, 2014.

Newspapers

Dundee Courier c1870-1914, DC Thomson & Co Ltd, Dundee.

Edinburgh Evening News c1860-1914, The British Newspaper Archive.

Edinburgh Evening Despatch, 1900-1914, Edinburgh City Libraries.

Newspapers

Forward 1906-1914, Mitchell Library, Glasgow.

The Glasgow Herald c1870-1914, Mitchell Library, Glasgow.

The Glasgow Herald Index 1906-1914, Mitchell Library, Glasgow.

The Scotsman, c1867-1914, The British Newspaper Archive.

The Suffragette 1912-1914, London Metropolitan University.

The Vote 1909-1914, The British Newspaper Archive.

Votes for Women 1909-1912, London Guildhall University.

The Weekly News (Edinburgh Edition) c1870-1914, DC Thomson & Co Ltd, Dundee.

Women's Franchise 1907-1909, The British Newspaper Archive.

Women's Suffrage Record 1903-1906, The British Newspaper Archive.

Primary sources

Agnes Macdonald Collection, Edinburgh City Libraries.

Edinburgh National Society for Women's Suffrage, annual reports 1872-1878, Cavendish Bentinck Collection, LSE, 324.6230941 NAT.

Glasgow and West of Scotland Association for Women's Suffrage, executive committee minutes and letter book, 1902-1914, Mitchell Library, Glasgow.

Janie Allan Inventory, National Library of Scotland, Acc. 4498.

Mary Gawthorpe Papers, Tamiment Library and Robert F. Wagner Labor Archive, University of New York.

Memoirs of Elizabeth Thomson, teacher, missionary, traveller and suffragette, 1847-1918, Glasgow University Archives, GB 248 UGC 053.

Scottish Office Prison Commissioners files, National Library of Scotland (Home Department series).

Suffragette Fellowship Collection, Museum of London.

Woman's Labour League correspondence, People's History Museum, WLL/1-154.

Journals and unpublished works

Crawfurd's Helen, unpublished autobiography, Max Memorial Library (Strathclyde University copy)

Cubbage, Sheila, *Memories of Isabel Carrie*, Glasgow University, 1976 (unpublished manuscript).

Flood, Catherine, *The Visual Campaign for the Vote*, Mary Evans Picture Library, undated article, pp 2-3.

Harrison, Brian, *The Act of Militancy and the Suffragettes, 1904-1914*, in *Peaceable Kingdom, Stability and Change in Modern Britain*, 1982.

Holloway Jingles, Women's Social and Political Union, Glasgow, nd, 1912.

Mercer, John, *Commercial places, public spaces: suffragette shops and the public sphere*, in *University of Sussex Journal of Contemporary History*, No. 7, 2004.

Moorhead, Ethel, *Incendiaries; work in progress*, in *This Quarter*, No 2, Paris, 1925.

Pugh, Martin, *Women's Suffrage in Britain, 1867-1928*, in *The Historical Association, General Series* 97, 1980.

Purvis, June, *The Prison Experiences of the Suffragettes* in *Edwardian Britain, Women's History Review*, Vol 4, No 1, 1995.

Rigby, Kate, *Annot Robinson, A Forgotten Suffragette*, in *Manchester Region History Review*, Vol 1, No 1, Spring 1987.

Votes for Women, The Women's Suffrage Movement in Edinburgh, Standard Grade Investigation, People's Story Museum, Edinburgh, nd, c1995.

Wheelhouse, Frances, *My Murky Past*, pre-publication typescript, notes, letters and original ephemera for proposed biography of Arabella Scott.

Suffragettes outside a temporary shop in Hawick High Street in 1909, with Edith New of Edinburgh WSPU on the right.

INDEX